# Recursion

*Recursion: Mathematics and Python* is designed to help readers develop a clear and systematic understanding of recursion as both a mathematical concept and a programming technique. Rather than presenting recursion as a collection of isolated examples, the book emphasizes recursive thinking: how complex problems can be expressed, analyzed, and solved by breaking them into simpler instances of similar structures.

The book adopts a consistent pedagogical approach throughout. Each topic begins with a mathematical or conceptual formulation that highlights the recursive structure of the problem. Readers are guided to identify parameters, base cases, and recursive relationships before translating these ideas into Python programs. Examples are chosen to identify recurring patterns across domains, including integer partitions, Tower of Hanoi, parentheses counting, binary search, quick sort, Sudoku solving, maze traversal, tree structures, and data compression. Code examples are written for clarity. Readers can follow execution flow and understand how recursive calls interact with computer memory. This book also explains how to reduce recursion time by identifying and removing redundant computation.

This book is intended for undergraduate students in computer science and computer engineering who already have basic Python programming experience and some prior exposure to recursion. It is well suited for courses in programming, discrete mathematics, data structures, or algorithms. This book can also help instructors seeking a resource that tightly integrates mathematical reasoning with executable code.

**Yung-Hsiang Lu** is a professor and University Faculty Scholar at Purdue University. He was the inaugural director of the John Martinson Engineering Entrepreneurial Center in 2020. He is a Fellow of IEEE, Distinguished Visitor of the Computer Society, Distinguished Scientist of the ACM, and Distinguished Speaker of the ACM.

**George K. Thiruvathukal** is a professor and chairperson of the Computer Science department at Loyola University Chicago and is a visiting computer scientist at Argonne National Laboratory. His research interests include high-performance computing, distributed systems, software engineering, artificial intelligence, computer vision, and the history of computing, science, and technology. Thiruvathukal received a Ph.D. from Illinois Institute of Technology.

# Recursion
## Mathematics and Python

Yung-Hsiang Lu and George K. Thiruvathukal

CRC Press
Taylor & Francis Group
Boca Raton London New York

CRC Press is an imprint of the
Taylor & Francis Group, an **informa** business

Designed cover image: Yung-Hsiang Lu and George K. Thiruvathukal

First edition published 2027
by CRC Press
2385 NW Executive Center Drive, Suite 320, Boca Raton FL 33431

and by CRC Press
4 Park Square, Milton Park, Abingdon, Oxon, OX14 4RN

*CRC Press is an imprint of Taylor & Francis Group, LLC*



ISBN: 978-1-041-14953-8 (hbk)
ISBN: 978-1-041-14955-2 (pbk)
ISBN: 978-1-003-67699-7 (ebk)

DOI: 10.1201/9781003676997

Typeset in CMR10 font
by KnowledgeWorks Global Ltd.

*Publisher's note:* This book has been prepared from camera-ready copy provided by the authors.

# *Contents*

# *List of Figures*

# List of Tables

# Preface

The concept of recursion can be found in many computer courses, including programming, discrete mathematics, data structures, algorithms, operating systems, artificial intelligence, compilers, and more. Recursion is also used in designing computer games. Despite its wide applicability, recursion is often treated superficially in many courses and books.

This book integrates recursive concepts with mathematical thinking and programming examples. The authors hope this integrated treatment of the topics can help readers better understand recursion.

This is not an introductory book. Readers are expected to already know basic Python programming and syntax.

This book is written for undergraduate students studying Computer Science or Computer Engineering. They already have a basic understanding of computer programming and possibly have seen recursion (such as Factorials or Fibonacci Numbers).

# *Source Code*

The programs in this book are available at

`https://github.com/python4recursion`.

Readers can use the source code in two ways:

1. Use Colab. The URL above has a link to the source code in Google Colab. Readers can copy and execute the code directly in Colab. This is the recommend method of using the programs in this book. Appendix C introduces Colab.
2. Clone the code. Readers can also `git clone` the repository to obtain the source code. Then, readers can execute the code on their own computers. This method is less desirable because readers may need to install the necessary packages.

# About the Authors

**Yung-Hsiang Lu** is a professor at the School of Electrical and Computer Engineering at Purdue University, West Lafayette, Indiana, U.S.A. In 2021, he was selected as a University Faculty Scholar of Purdue University. Since July 2025, he has been the director of the Purdue Engineering Honors Program. He was the inaugural director of the Purdue John Martinson Engineering Entrepreneurial Center (2020 - 2022). He is the inventor of several US patents related to computer vision and networks. He was a member of the Innovation Corps (I-Corps) of the National Science Foundation. He started the IEEE Low-Power Computer Vision Challenge in 2015. He is a Fellow of IEEE (Institute of Electrical and Electronics Engineers), Distinguished Visitor of the IEEE Computer Society, Distinguished Scientist and Distinguished Speaker of the ACM (Association for Computing Machinery). Dr. Lu received his Ph.D. degree from the Department of Electrical Engineering at Stanford University and his B.S. degree from the Department of Electrical Engineering at National Taiwan University. He is one of the authors of the book "Intermediate C Programming" (2nd) (ISBN 9781032189819 by CRC Press in 2024) and one of the editors of the book "Low-Power Computer Vision: Improve the Efficiency of Artificial Intelligence" (ISBN 9780367744700 by Chapman & Hall in 2022).

**George K. Thiruvathukal** is a professor and chairperson at the Department of Computer Science in Loyola University Chicago. He is also a visiting computer scientist at the Argonne National Laboratory in the Leadership Computing Facility. His primary research areas include high-performance computing, distributed systems, software engineering and energy-efficient computer vision. His interdisciplinary interests include computational science, data science, neuroscience, and digital humanities/platform studies. He has co-authored multiple books: Software Engineering for Science (CRC Press), Codename Revolution: The Nintendo WII Platform (MIT Press), Web Programming: Techniques for Integrating Python, Linux, Apache, and MySQL (Prentice Hall PTR), and High Performance Java Computing: Multi-Threaded and

Networked Programming (Prentice Hall PTR and Sun Microsystems Press Java Series), which was identified as a prior work in the JSR-166 Java specification for Concurrent Utilities (`java.util.concurrent`). Dr. Thiruvathukal received his Ph.D. degree from the Department of Computer Science in Illinois Institute of Technology, Illinois, U.S.A. He is one of the editors of the book "Low-Power Computer Vision: Improve the Efficiency of Artificial Intelligence" (ISBN 9780367744700, published by Chapman & Hall in 2022). He is one of authors of the book "Intermediate C Programming" (2nd) (ISBN 9781032189819 by CRC Press in 2024).

# *About the Reviewers*

Ryan Jordan graduated with a B.S. in Computer Engineering from Purdue University in 2026. He interned with Rincon Research Corporation in 2025 and previously served as an undergraduate researcher in the Artificial Intelligence for Musicians research group.

Samuel Budagher graduated with BS in Materials Science Engineering from Purdue University in 2026. Since 2023, he has been working as an intern for Sandia National Laboratories.

Pranesh Velmurugan is completing a B.S. in Computer Science and Data Science at Purdue University (expected May 2026). He interned at NASA in 2024 and Amazon Web Services in 2025.

Paolo Ziang Wang is studying Artificial Intelligence at Purdue University (B.S. expected December 2027).

Jackson Patrick Shields is a student of Computer Science and Data Science at Purdue Universit (B.S. expected May 2027).

Kayshav Bhardwaj is a student of Artificial Intelligence at Purdue University (B.S. expected in 2028).

# *Warnings*

This book is for education and entertainment purposes only. Neither the authors nor the publisher will be held liable or responsible for any actual or perceived loss or damage, caused or alleged to have been caused, directly or indirectly, by any materials in this book. Readers are encouraged to exercise caution interpreting the content of this book. Any opinions, findings, conclusions, or recommendations expressed in this book are those of the authors and do not necessarily reflect the views, positions, or policies of any organization or anyone other than the authors.

# Chapter 1

# Concepts about Recursion

Recursion is a natural way to solve many problems, and it occurs everywhere around us. This chapter gives many examples of how nature inspires recursive thinking.

## 1.1 Recursion in Nature

Recursion is natural and exists everywhere in our daily lives. For example, every person has parents and grandparents; they in turn have their own parents and grandparents. When a pattern *recurs*, we say it is an example of recursion. As another example, take two mirrors and make them face each other. An object between the two mirrors appears over and over again, smaller in each reflection. A tree's trunk is divided into branches. Each branch is further divided into smaller branches. Smaller branches are divided into twigs, eventually terminating at leaves. A leaf also contains recurring patterns: a midrib (equivalent to the trunk) splits to form veins (equivalent to the branches). All of these are natural examples of recursion.

Recursion is widely used in computing to solve complex problems. There are three essential properties of recursion:

1. *Recurring patterns.* The examples above describe some recurring patterns: for example, a person, the person's parents, the grandparents.

2. *Changes.* Recursion is more than just repetition. Recurring patterns must include changes. In a family, a child is younger than their parents. In the two mirrors, reflections become smaller. For a tree, branches become thinner. Each step of a recursive pattern has at least one change.
3. *Terminating condition (or conditions)*, also called *stop condition* or *base case*. The recurring pattern eventually stops. A family's recursion stops at the youngest member who has no children. The reflections in the facing mirrors will become smaller and eventually invisible. A tree branch will end at a leaf.

Recursion is one of nature's ways to solve many (but not all) complex problems. It is important to understand the strengths and limitations of recursion. Recursion is widely used to solve board game problems, like Chess or Go. These games have the three essential properties:

1. Recurring patterns: After moving a piece, the Chess or Go board looks very similar. Most pieces still have the same available moves.
2. Change: Each player moves one piece. Moving one piece usually affects the available moves of the other pieces and the state of the game.
3. Stop condition: When one side wins, or a draw is reached, the game ends.

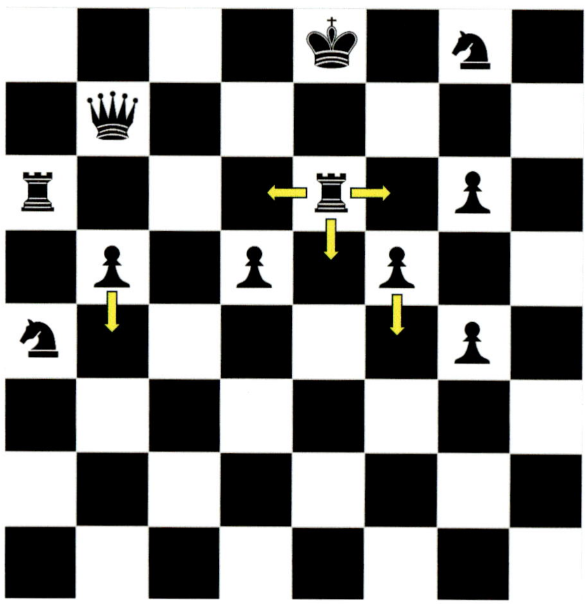

**FIGURE 1.1**: In a chess game, a player has many possible moves (marked by the arrows). After making a move (change), the chessboard is very similar (recurring pattern).

Recursion is often a good method to solve problems with many possible choices, where each choice leads to a smaller version of the same problem. In board games, players typically have several pieces they could move, and it is not always clear which move is the best. The effects of a move may only become apparent after several turns. As a result, players must evaluate each possible move and its consequences several moves ahead before selecting the best one.

Recursion can solve problems using a strategy called *divide and conquer*: Divide a complex problem into smaller problems and solve (conquer) the smaller problems. This works when the smaller problems are similar to the larger problem. To solve a problem using recursion, we can follow these three steps:

1. Identify the parameters of a problem. For computer programming, these parameters are the arguments of functions. Express the solution and the changes using the arguments.
2. Determine the simple case (or cases) where the problem becomes easy enough to solve directly without recursion.
3. Based on these relationships, we can solve the complex problems using the solutions from the simple cases. Derive the relationships between the complex case (or cases) and the simpler case (or cases). This step is usually the most difficult part of the process and requires experience. This book gives many examples to help readers understand the process.

---

## 1.2 Selecting Balls with Restrictions

There are unlimited red ($\mathbb{R}$) and blue ($\mathbb{B}$) balls in a bag. We want to select balls of these two colors under the restriction that two adjacent balls must not both be red. The order matters: The selection of $\mathbb{R}\mathbb{B}$ is different from $\mathbb{B}\mathbb{R}$: The former selects red as the first ball and blue as the second ball; the latter selects blue as the first ball and red as the second ball. How many different ways can the $n$ balls be selected?

This problem can be solved recursively because it has the three properties of recursion:

1. *Recurring patterns.* The problem can be solved by selecting one ball at a time. After selecting one ball, we only need to select $n - 1$ more balls. This new problem is similar to the original problem.
2. *Changes.* After selecting one ball, we need to select one less ball than before. Thus, the problem changes, becoming a smaller problem.
3. *Terminating condition.* After $n$ balls are selected, the problem is solved, and no more balls need to be selected.

The solution includes these three steps:

1. *Identify the parameters (i.e., arguments) of the problem:* For this problem, the number of balls, $n$, is the parameter. *Express the solution based on the argument:* Let $f(n)$ be the number of ways to select the $n$ balls. This is an important step because we have to identify what is used to specify the problem's size.

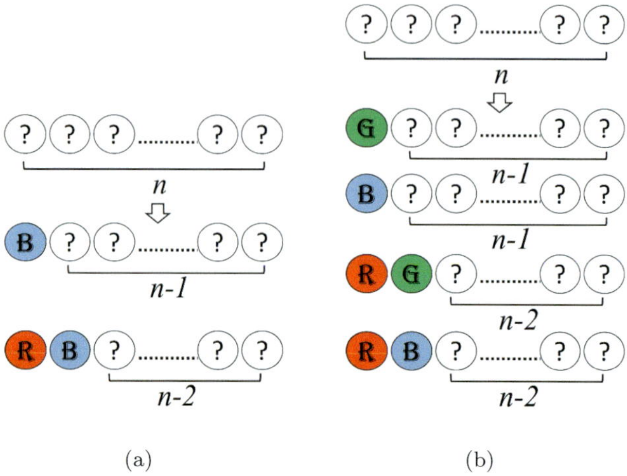


**FIGURE 1.2**: To select $n$ color balls, consider the options for the first ball. (a) Two colors: red ($\mathbb{R}$) and blue ($\mathbb{B}$). (b) Three colors: red ($\mathbb{R}$), green ($\mathbb{G}$), and blue ($\mathbb{B}$).

2. *Determine the simple cases when the problem is easy:* If only one ball is selected, there are two options: $\mathbb{R}$ or $\mathbb{B}$. Thus, $f(1)$ is 2. If two balls are selected, there are three options: $\mathbb{RB}$, $\mathbb{BR}$, and $\mathbb{BB}$. Therefore, $f(2)$ is 3.
3. *Derive the relationships between the complex cases and the simpler cases:* If there are $n$ balls ($n > 2$), the first ball can be $\mathbb{R}$ or $\mathbb{B}$. There are exactly two choices for the first ball. Figure 1.2 (a) shows the two different scenarios in the selection of the second ball. If the first ball is $\mathbb{B}$, the remaining $n-1$ balls have $f(n-1)$ options because the first blue ball does not impose any restriction on the second ball. Thus, the change is that we need to select only $n-1$ balls and the answer is $f(n-1)$. If the first ball is $\mathbb{R}$, then the second ball must be $\mathbb{B}$. After selecting blue as the second ball, the third ball can be blue or red. This is the same problem, except that we need to select only $n-2$ balls. The number of options is expressed as $f(n-2)$.

Based on this analysis, $f(n)$ can be expressed as

$$f(n) = \begin{cases} 2 & \text{when } n \text{ is 1 (simple case),} \\ 3 & \text{when } n \text{ is 2 (simple case),} \\ f(n-1) + f(n-2) & \text{when } n > 2 \text{ (recursive case).} \end{cases} \quad (1.1)$$

Why do we write $f(n) = f(n-1)+f(n-2)$ and not $f(n) = f(n-1)\times f(n-2)$?

When we have several options, how do we consider the relationships among these options? Should we add these options or multiply these options?

Let's consider an analogy. Imagine that you go to a restaurant and it offers several options for entrees: 4 beef choices, 3 chicken choices, 4 fish choices, and 5 salad choices. How many options do you have for the entree (assume that you choose only one entree)? These options are exclusive: If you choose beef, you do not choose chicken, fish, or salad. If you choose salad, you do not choose chicken, beef, or fish. The number of options is the sum of these options: $4 + 3 + 4 + 5 = 16$ options.

Now suppose you want to select a dessert after the entree. There are three options for the dessert: ice cream, strawberry cake, and apple pie. How many options do you have for this meal? Selecting an entree does not exclude the options for the dessert. Thus, there are $16 \times 3 = 48$ ways to choose an entree and a dessert. The number of options are multiplied.

Now we can explain why Equation (1.1) uses addition. When the first ball is red, it cannot be blue. If the first ball is blue, it cannot be red. These two options are exclusive. Thus, the number of options is the sum of these two cases. That is why $f(n) = f(n-1) + f(n-2)$, not $f(n) = f(n-1) \times f(n-2)$.

The problem can be extended to balls of three colors. There are unlimited red ($\mathbb{R}$), green ($\mathbb{G}$), and blue ($\mathbb{B}$) balls. Two adjacent balls cannot both be red. The order matters: $\mathbb{R}\mathbb{B}$ and $\mathbb{B}\mathbb{R}$ are different selections. How many ways can $n$ balls be selected?

When $n$ is one, there are three options:

1. $\mathbb{R}$
2. $\mathbb{G}$
3. $\mathbb{B}$.

When $n$ is two, there are eight options:

1. $\mathbb{R}\ \mathbb{G}$
2. $\mathbb{R}\ \mathbb{B}$
3. $\mathbb{G}\ \mathbb{R}$
4. $\mathbb{G}\ \mathbb{G}$
5. $\mathbb{G}\ \mathbb{B}$
6. $\mathbb{B}\ \mathbb{R}$
7. $\mathbb{B}\ \mathbb{G}$
8. $\mathbb{B}\ \mathbb{B}$.

What is the number of options for $n$ balls when $n > 2$? To solve this problem, let $f(n)$ be the answer. We already know that $f(1) = 3$ and $f(2) = 8$. When $n > 2$, consider the options for the first ball. Figure 1.2 (b) shows three scenarios:

1. If the first ball is $\mathbb{G}$, then the second ball can be any of the three colors. There is no further restriction for the remaining $n-1$ balls. Thus, there are $f(n-1)$ options for the remaining $n-1$ balls.

2. Likewise, if the first ball is $\mathbb{B}$, then the second ball can be any of the three colors. There are $f(n-1)$ options for the remaining $n-1$ balls.
3. If the first ball is $\mathbb{R}$, then there are two scenarios:
   (a) If the second ball is $\mathbb{G}$, then the third ball can be any of the three colors. There are $f(n-2)$ possible sequences for the remaining $n-2$ balls.
   (b) If the second ball is $\mathbb{B}$, then the third ball can be any of the three colors. There are $f(n-2)$ options for the remaining $n-2$ balls.

Thus, the relationships are:

$$f(n) = \begin{cases} 3 & \text{when } n \text{ is 1 (simple case)}, \\ 8 & \text{when } n \text{ is 2 (simple case)}, \\ 2f(n-1) + 2f(n-2) & \text{when } n > 2 \text{ (recursive case)}. \end{cases} \tag{1.2}$$

This is a common approach to solving recursive problems. First, we assume that we already have the answer, i.e., $f(n)$. Then, we work backward to find how the answer can be reduced into simpler forms, i.e., expressing $f(n)$ in terms of $f(n-1)$ and $f(n-2)$.

## 1.3 One-Way Streets

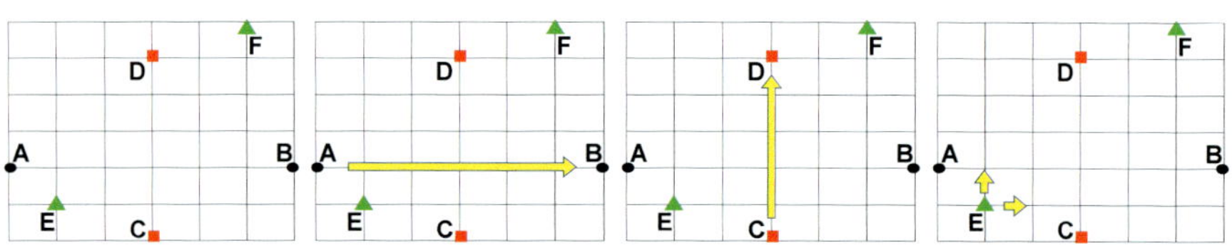


(a) (b) (c) (d)

**FIGURE 1.3**: (a) A city's streets form a grid. (b) Only one way from A to B. (c) Only one way from C to D. (d) There are some turning options when moving from E to F.

All streets in a city's downtown run either east–west or north–south forming a grid, as shown in Figure 1.3. The downtown has severe traffic congestion during rush hours, so the city government considers adopting a rule: During rush hours, cars can only move east or north. If a car needs to move south or west, it must leave the downtown, take expressways around the downtown, and reenter the downtown through the southwest corner. Assume we have the location of a car's origin and destination. How many ways can the destination be reached? This example may seem artificial, but it is actually a reasonable simplification of the one-way streets in the downtowns of many cities. This simplification is useful for analyzing traffic patterns.

Figure 1.3 marks three pairs of origins and destinations: A → B, C → D, and E → F. For the first two pairs, A → B and C → D, the driver has only one option: not to turn at all. This is shown in Figure 1.3 (b) and (c). There are more options for E → F. At E, the driver can go eastbound first or northbound first, as indicated by the two arrows in Figure 1.3 (d). The question is the number of different paths a driver can take between the origin and the destination. This question can be answered using the three steps:

1. *Identify the arguments of the problem.* Suppose E is at the intersection of $(x1, y1)$ and F is at the intersection of $(x2, y2)$. The distance between them can be expressed as $(\Delta x, \Delta y) = (x2 - x1, y2 - y1)$. *Express the solution in terms of the arguments.* Let $f(\Delta x, \Delta y)$ express the number of unique paths.
2. *Determine the simple cases when the problem is easy.* We can consider the following cases whose answers can be found easily.
   (a) $\Delta x < 0$: The destination is west of the origin, and there is no solution.
   (b) $\Delta y < 0$: Similarly, there is no solution for this case.
   (c) $\Delta x > 0$ and $\Delta y = 0$: This is the case A → B. There is precisely one solution.
   (d) $\Delta x = 0$ and $\Delta y > 0$: This is the case C → D. There is also precisely one solution.
   (e) $\Delta x = 0$ and $\Delta y = 0$: This means that the destination is at the origin. We define that there is one solution for this case.
3. *Derive the relationships between the complex cases and the simpler cases.* For the complex case when $\Delta\, x > 0$ and $\Delta\, y > 0$ (e.g., the case E → F), the driver has two options at the origin (i.e., E): The driver goes either north first or east first. If the driver heads north, then the new origin is at $(x1, y1 + 1)$. There are $f(\Delta x, \Delta y - 1)$ possible paths from this point. If the driver goes east first, then the new origin is at $(x1 + 1, y1)$. There are $f(\Delta x - 1, \Delta y)$ possible paths from this point. These are the only two possible options at position E, and they are exclusive. Therefore, when $\Delta x > 0$ and $\Delta y > 0$, the solution can expressed as $f(\Delta x, \Delta y) = f(\Delta x, \Delta y - 1) + f(\Delta x - 1, \Delta y)$.

$$f(\Delta x, \Delta y) = \begin{cases} 0 & \text{if } \Delta x < 0 \text{ or } \Delta y < 0, \\ 1 & \text{if } \Delta x = 0 \text{ and } \Delta y \geq 0, \\ 1 & \text{if } \Delta x \geq 0 \text{ and } \Delta y = 0, \\ f(\Delta x, \Delta y - 1) + f(\Delta x - 1, \Delta y) & \text{if } \Delta x > 0 \text{ and } \Delta y > 0. \end{cases} \tag{1.3}$$

In the problems about selecting colored balls, the solution has only one argument $n$. In this problem, the solution has two arguments: $\Delta x$ and $\Delta y$. As illustrated by these examples, recursion can be quite flexible, using one, two, or even more than two arguments.

---

## 1.4 The Tower of Hanoi

Several disks of different sizes are stacked on a single pole. The disks are arranged such that smaller disks are above larger disks. The problem is to move the disks from one pole (A) to another pole (B). Only one disk can be moved each time. A larger disk cannot be placed above a smaller disk. The third pole can be used for temporary storage. Figure 1.4 (a) illustrates the problem with three disks. If there are $n$ disks, how many steps are needed to move them? First, let's consider moving only one disk from A to B. This is the simplest case, and that disk can be moved directly from A to B as shown in Figure 1.4 (b). Moving two disks requires more work:

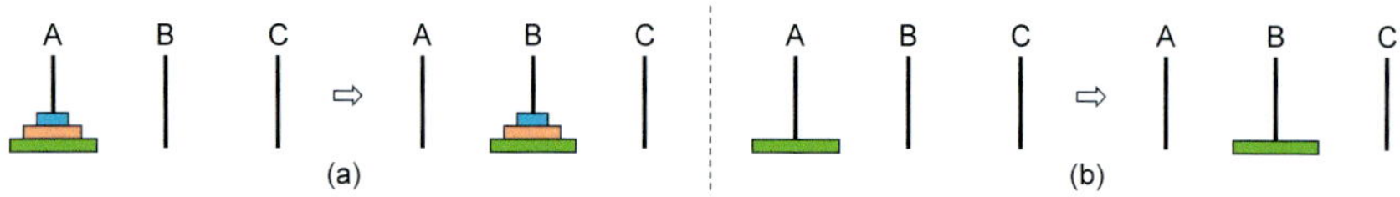


**FIGURE 1.4**: Tower of Hanoi. (a) Move three disks. (b) Moving one disk requires only one step.

1. Move the smaller disk from A to C.
2. Move the larger disk from A to B.
3. Move the smaller disk from C to B.

Moving two disks needs three steps.

This is the general strategy for moving $n$ disks: If there is only one disk (i.e.,

$n = 1$), the problem takes only one step. Otherwise, the solution is divided into three parts:

1. Move the first $n - 1$ disks from A to C. This is similar to the original problem with two differences:
   (a) This problem moves only $n - 1$ disks.
   (b) The origin is A, and the destination is C. B can be used for temporary storage.
2. Move the largest disk from A to B.
3. Move the first $n-1$ disks from C to B. This is also similar to the original problem with two differences:
   (a) This problem moves only $n - 1$ disks.
   (b) The origin is C, and the destination is B. A can be used for temporary storage.

The approach for solving this problem is described below:

1. *Identify the argument of the problem:* The number $n$ is naturally the argument for the problem. *Express the solution based on the argument:* Let $f(n)$ be the answer: how many steps are needed to move $n$ disks from A to B.
2. *Determine the simple case when the problem is easy:* If $n$ is one, only one step is sufficient; thus, $f(1)$ is 1.
3. *Derive the relationships between the complex case and the simpler case:* When $n$ is greater than one, the problem can be further divided into three parts:
   (a) Move $n-1$ disks from pole A to pole C; this requires $f(n-1)$ steps.
   (b) Move the largest disk from pole A to pole B; this requires 1 step.
   (c) Move $n-1$ disks from pole C to pole B; this requires $f(n-1)$ steps.

The following formula expresses the steps:

$$f(n) = \begin{cases} 1 & \text{if } n \text{ is } 1, \\ f(n-1) + 1 + f(n-1) = 2f(n-1) + 1 & \text{if } n \geq 2 \end{cases} \tag{1.4}$$

It is possible to find a *closed form* formula: $f(n)$ is expressed without $f(n-1)$ appearing on the right side of the = sign.

$$
\begin{aligned}
f(n) &= 2f(n-1)+1 \\
&= 2(2f(n-2)+1)+1 \\
&= 4f(n-2)+2+1 \\
&= 8f(n-3)+4+2+1 \\
&= 16f(n-4)+8+4+2+1 \\
&= 2^k f(n-k)+2^{k-1}+2^{k-2}+...+4+2+1 \\
&= 2^{n-1}f(1)+2^{n-2}+2^{n-3}+...+4+2+1, && \text{when } k=n-1 \\
&= 2^{n-1}+2^{n-2}+2^{n-3}+...+4+2+1, && \text{because } f(1)=1 \\
&= 2^n-1
\end{aligned}
\tag{1.5}
$$

---

## 1.5 Integer Partitions

A positive integer can be expressed as the sum of a sequence of positive integers. Below are some examples:

```
1 = 1       2 = 1 + 1       3 = 1 + 1 + 1       4 = 1 + 1 + 1 + 1
              = 2             = 1 + 2             = 1 + 1 + 2
                              = 2 + 1             = 1 + 2 + 1
                              = 3                 = 1 + 3
                                                  = 2 + 1 + 1
                                                  = 2 + 2
                                                  = 3 + 1
                                                  = 4
```

An *integer partition* creates such sequences of integers. For example, 5 can be broken into the sum of 1 + 2 + 2 or 2 + 3. These two partitions use different numbers and are considered distinct partitions. The order of the numbers in the partition is also important: 1 + 2 + 2 and 2 + 1 + 2 are considered different partitions because 1 appears at different positions. The number itself is also a valid partition: 4 is a valid partition of the number 4.

Consider Figure 1.5. To partition the number 4, the first number can be 1, 2, 3, or 4. When one is used, the remaining number is 3. When 1 is used as the first number, the rows are identical to partitions of 3 (marked by a light blue background). Similarly, when 2 is used as the first number, the rows are identical to partitioning 2. In general, to partition a number $n$, the first number can be 1, 2, 3, ..., $n$. This is shown in Figure 1.6.

This question is the number of different partitions for a positive integer $n$, expressed as $f(n)$. When $n$ is 1, there is only one way to partition the number.

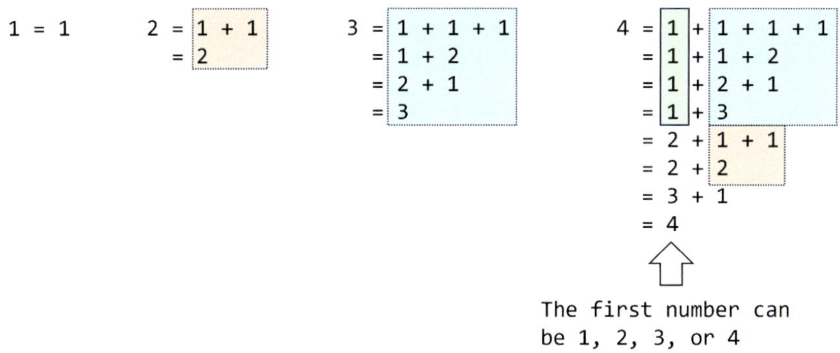


**FIGURE 1.5**: To partition number 4, the first number can be 1, 2, 3, or 4.

| First Number | Remaining Value | Number of Partitions |
|---|---|---|
| 1 | $n-1$ | $f(n-1)$ |
| 2 | $n-2$ | $f(n-2)$ |
| 3 | $n-3$ | $f(n-3)$ |
| $\vdots$ | $\vdots$ | $\vdots$ |
| $n-1$ | 1 | $f(1)$ |
| $n$ | 0 | $f(0) = 1$ |

**FIGURE 1.6**: To partition $n$, the first number can be 1, 2, ..., $n$. The remaining number is $n-1$, $n-2$, ..., 0. The value of $f(0)$ is defined as 1.

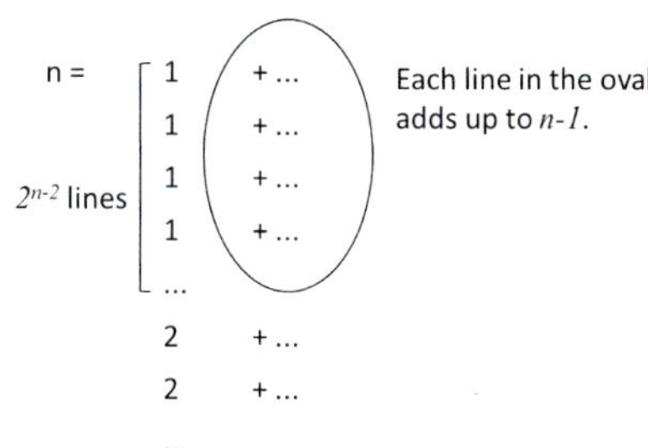


**FIGURE 1.7**: Count the occurrences of "1" when partitioning $n$.

Thus, $f(1) = 1$. When $n$ is larger than one, the solution selects the first number. This number must be an integer between 1 and $n$ inclusively. After selecting the first number, we have to partition the remaining numbers. For each of the $n$ options for the first number (1, 2, ..., $n$), we need to consider the number of options to partition the remaining number ($n-1$, $n-2$, ..., 0). The relationship can be expressed in Figure 1.6:

- If the first number is 1, then the remaining value to be partitioned is $n-1$. By definition, there are $f(n-1)$ ways to partition $n-1$.
- If the first number is 2, the remaining value to be partitioned is $n-2$. There are $f(n-2)$ ways to partition $n-2$.
- If the first number is $k$, the remaining value to be partitioned is $n-k$. There are $f(n-k)$ ways to partition $n-k$.

- If the first number is $n$, the remaining value is 0. Since $n$ itself is an acceptable partition, there is exactly one way to partition $n$ by using $n$.

The value of $f(n)$ is therefore the sum of all the different cases when the first number is 1, 2, 3, ..., $n-1$, or $n$, i.e.,

$$f(n) = f(n-1) + f(n-2) + \ldots f(1) + 1 = 1 + \sum_{i=1}^{n-1} f(i), \text{ if } n > 1 \tag{1.6}$$

The following process shows how to obtain a closed-form solution of $f(n)$.

$$\begin{array}{lllll} & f(n) & = f(n-1) & +f(n-2)+f(n-3)+...+1 \\ - & f(n-1) & = & +f(n-2)+f(n-3)+...+1 \\ \hline & f(n)-f(n-1) & = f(n-1) & \\ & f(n) & = 2f(n-1) & \end{array} \tag{1.7}$$

From Equation (1.7) and $f(1) = 1$, we conclude that there are $2^{n-1}$ ways to partition the integer $n$, i.e.,

$$f(n) = 2^{n-1}. \tag{1.8}$$

### 1.5.1 Count the Number of "1"s

The partition problem has many variations. In this variation, we count how many "1"s are used for partitioning $n$. Suppose $g(n)$ is the answer. First observe that $g(1) = 1$. When $n$ is 2, it can be partitioned as $1 + 1$ using "1" twice. Thus, $g(2) = 2$. Next, consider partitioning 3:

```
3 = 1 + 1 + 1
  = 1 + 2
  = 2 + 1
  = 3
```

The value 1 is used five times:

- 3 times in $1 + 1 + 1$
- once in $1 + 2$
- once in $2 + 1$.

The more complicated cases can be related to the simpler cases with the following reasoning. Every partition of $n$ starts with an integer between 1 and

$n$, giving us $n$ cases. Since a partition starting with $n$ does not use "1" (for $n > 1$), we only need to consider the first $n - 1$ cases. To find $g(n)$, we can add up the number of "1"s used in each case.

Consider all partitions of $n$ that start with "1". They can be formed by prepending "1" to each partition of $n - 1$. Based on Equation (1.8), there are $2^{n-2}$ partitions of $n - 1$. Hence, there are $2^{n-2}$ partitions of $n$ that start with "1". So far, we have found $2^{n-2}$ "1"s, but we are not done yet. There may be "1"s in the partitions of the remaining value, $n-1$. These "1"s are counted by $g(n - 1)$. Thus, when the first number is "1", it is used $2^{n-2} + g(n - 1)$. We do not need to worry about the value of $g(n-1)$ yet; we will solve for the closed form of $g(n)$ soon.

Next, consider the partitions of $n$ that start with "2". Unlike the previous case, the first number in the partitions is "2" and cannot be "1". Therefore, we only need to count the number of "1"s that may be used for partitioning the remaining value of $n - 2$. By definition, "1" is used $g(n - 2)$ times when partitioning $n - 2$.

In general, we can write the number of "1"s used when the first integer in the partition is $k$ as

$$q(k) = \begin{cases} 2^{n-2} + g(n-1) & \text{if } k = 1, \\ g(n-k) & \text{if } 1 < k \le n-1. \end{cases}$$

The value of $g(n)$ can be calculated as the sum of all these cases:

$$g(n) = 2^{n-2} + g(n-1) + g(n-2) + \ldots + g(1), \text{ when } n > 2 \tag{1.9}$$

We know $g(1) = 1$ because 1 is used only once when partitioning 1; also, $g(2) = 2$ because 1 is used twice in $1 + 1$. To obtain the closed form, first find the relationship between $g(n)$ and $g(n - 1)$:

$$\begin{array}{rlll} & g(n) & = 2^{n-2} + g(n-1) & + g(n-2) + g(n-3) + ... + g(1) \\ - & g(n-1) & = 2^{n-3} & + g(n-2) + g(n-3) + ... + g(1) \\ \hline & g(n) - g(n-1) & = 2^{n-3} + g(n-1) & \\ & g(n) & = 2^{n-3} + 2g(n-1) & \end{array} \tag{1.10}$$

This relationship can be expanded for $g(n - 2)$, $g(n - 3)$, ..., $g(1)$.

$$
\begin{aligned}
g(n) &= 2^{n-3} + 2g(n-1) \\
g(n-1) &= 2^{n-4} + 2g(n-2) \\
g(n-2) &= 2^{n-5} + 2g(n-3) \\
&\vdots \\
g(n-k) &= 2^{n-k-3} + 2g(n-k-1) \\
g(3) &= 2^0 + 2g(2) \qquad \text{when } k = n-3
\end{aligned}
\tag{1.11}
$$

In (1.11), the coefficient for $g(n-1)$ on the right side is two. In order to cancel $g(n-1)$, the coefficient on the left side has to increase accordingly, as shown below:

$$
\begin{array}{rll}
 & g(n) & = 2^{n-3} + 2g(n-1) \\
 & 2g(n-1) & = 2^{n-3} + 4g(n-2) \\
 & 4g(n-2) & = 2^{n-3} + 8g(n-3) \\
 & & \vdots \\
 & 2^k g(n-k) & = 2^{n-3} + 2^{k+1} g(n-k-1) \\
+ & 2^{n-3} g(3) & = 2^{n-3} + 2^{n-2} g(2) \\
\hline
 & g(n) + \sum_{i=3}^{n-1} 2^{n-i} g(i) & = (n-2)2^{n-3} + 2^{n-2} g(2) + \sum_{i=3}^{n-1} 2^{n-i} g(i) \\
 & g(n) & = (n-2)2^{n-3} + 2^{n-2} g(2) \\
 & g(n) & = (n-2)2^{n-3} + 2^{n-1} \\
 & g(n) & = (n-2)2^{n-3} + 4 \times 2^{n-3} \\
 & g(n) & = (n+2)2^{n-3} \text{ when } n > 2.
\end{array}
\tag{1.12}
$$

Table 1.1 shows the value of $g(n)$ for $1 \leq n \leq 9$.

### 1.5.2 Odd Numbers Only

We want to find the number of ways $n$ can be partitioned using only odd numbers. Consider the following examples:

```
2 = 1 + 1    3 = 1 + 1 + 1      4 = 1 + 1 + 1 + 1      5 = 1 + 1 + 1 + 1 + 1
               = 3                = 1 + 3                = 1 + 1 + 3
                                  = 3 + 1                = 1 + 3 + 1
                                                         = 3 + 1 + 1
                                                         = 5
```

From these examples, we can obtain Table 1.2. It is helpful to review how Equation (1.6) is derived. What does $f(n-1)$ mean in this equation? It means "1" is the first number. Similarly, what does $f(n-2)$ mean in this equation? It means that "2" is the first number. To restrict the partitions

**TABLE 1.1**: Numbers of "1" used in partitions.

| $n$ | 1 | 2 | 3 | 4 | 5 | 6 | 7 | 8 | 9 |
|---|---|---|---|---|---|---|---|---|---|
| $g(n)$ | 1 | 2 | 5 | 12 | 28 | 64 | 144 | 320 | 704 |

**TABLE 1.2**: Use odd numbers only.

| $n$ | 1 | 2 | 3 | 4 | 5 |
|---|---|---|---|---|---|
| partitions | 1 | 1 | 2 | 3 | 5 |

to odd numbers only, all partitions using even numbers must be discarded. Thus, $f(n-2)$, $f(n-4)$, $f(n-6)$, etc., must be excluded. Suppose $h(n)$ is the number of partitions for $n$ using odd numbers only. When $n$ is one, $h(1) = 1$ because there is one way to partition 1.

$$h(n) = h(n-1) + h(n-3) + h(n-5)... \text{ when } n > 1 \tag{1.13}$$

The last few terms will be different depending on whether $n$ itself is odd or even. If $n$ is odd, $n-1$ is even so $h(1)$ is excluded. Also, $n-3$ is an even number. The complete equation is shown below:

$$h(n) = h(n-1) + h(n-3) + h(n-5)... + h(2) + 1, \text{ when } n > 1 \text{ and } n \text{ is odd.} \tag{1.14}$$

If $n$ is even, $n-1$ is odd so $h(1)$ is included. Therefore, the complete equation is shown below:

$$h(n) = \begin{cases} 1 & \text{when } n \text{ is } 1 \\ h(n-1) + h(n-3) + h(n-5)... + h(2) + 1 & \text{when } n > 1 \text{ and } n \text{ is odd} \\ h(n-1) + h(n-3) + h(n-5)... + h(1) & \text{when } n \text{ is even} \end{cases} \tag{1.15}$$

### 1.5.3 Increasing Values

The next problem asks the number of ways to partition $n$ using increasing values or the number $n$ itself. Suppose $n$ is partitioned into the sum of $k$ numbers:

$$n = a_1 + a_2 + a_3 + ... + a_k \tag{1.16}$$

while meeting the following conditions:

1. $a_i$ $(1 \leq i \leq k)$ are positive integers
2. If $k$ is 1, using only one number $n$ itself is a valid partition.
3. If $k > 1$, $a_i < a_{i+1}$ $(1 \leq i < k)$.

Consider the first few cases using increasing numbers:

```
1 = 1         2 = 2       3 = 1 + 2       4 = 1 + 3       5 = 1 + 4
                            = 3             = 4             = 2 + 3
                                                            = 5
```

To solve this problem, two arguments are needed for the equation. We define $p(n,m)$ to be the number of ways to partition $n$, and each number must be greater than or equal to $m$. When partitioning $n$, the following explains how to use $p(n,m)$.

1. If 1 is used as the first number, then 2 is the smallest allowed number to partition $n-1$. There are $p(n-1,2)$ ways to partition $n-1$ using 2 as the smallest number.
2. If 2 is used as the first number, then 3 is the smallest allowed number to partition $n-2$. There are $p(n-2,3)$ ways to partition $n-2$ using 3 as the smallest number.
3. Obviously, $p(n,n) = 1$ because there is only one way to partition $n$ using $n$ as the smallest number.
4. If $n < m$, $p(n,m) = 0$ because it is impossible to partition an integer $n$ using a larger integer $m$.

Based on this reasoning,

$$\begin{aligned} p(n,1) &= p(n-1,2) + p(n-2,3) + ... + p(n-k,k+1) + ... + p(1,n) + 1 \\ &= 1 + \sum_{i=1}^{n-1} p(n-i,i+1) \end{aligned} \tag{1.17}$$

We can expand $p(n,m)$ in the following way:

$$\begin{aligned} p(n,m) &= p(n-m,m+1) + p(n-m-1,m+2) + ... + p(n-k,k+1) + ... \\ &= 1 + \sum_{i=m}^{\lfloor \frac{n}{2} \rfloor} p(n-i,i+1) \end{aligned} \tag{1.18}$$

Here, $\lfloor x \rfloor$ is the *floor* function: it rounds number $x$ down to the nearest integer that is less than or equal to $x$. For example, $\lfloor 3.8 \rfloor = 3$ and $\lfloor 4 \rfloor = 4$. Table 1.3 shows the number of partitions using increasing numbers.

**TABLE 1.3**: Number of partitions using increasing numbers.

| $n$ | 1 | 2 | 3 | 4 | 5 | 6 | 7 | 8 | 9 | 10 | 11 | 12 | 13 | 14 | 15 |
|---|---|---|---|---|---|---|---|---|---|---|---|---|---|---|---|
| partitions | 1 | 1 | 2 | 2 | 3 | 4 | 5 | 6 | 8 | 10 | 12 | 15 | 18 | 22 | 27 |

This problem is different from the previous ones because the recursive equations require two arguments. The fundamental recursive reasoning is the same.

### 1.5.4 Alternating Odd and Even Numbers

We want to find partitions that alternate between odd and even numbers. If an odd number is used, then the next must be an even number. If an even number is used, then the next must be an odd number. If only one number is used (i.e., the number to be partitioned itself), it is always a valid partition. The following shows the partitions of 1 to 6.

```
1 = 1                2 = 2                3 = 1 + 2
                                            = 2 + 1
                                            = 3


4 = 1 + 2 + 1        5 = 1 + 4            6 = 1 + 2 + 1 + 2
  = 4                  = 2 + 1 + 2          = 1 + 2 + 3
                       = 2 + 3              = 1 + 4 + 1
                       = 3 + 2              = 2 + 1 + 2 + 1
                       = 4 + 1              = 3 + 2 + 1
                       = 5                  = 6
```

This problem can be solved by defining two functions as follows:

1. The first function $s(n)$ is the number of ways to partition $n$ using alternating odd and even numbers, and the first number is odd.
2. The second function $t(n)$ is the number of ways to partition $n$ using alternating odd and even numbers, and the first number is even.

The number of ways to partition $n$ using alternating odd and even numbers is the sum of $s(n)$ and $t(n)$. Let's start with a few small values of $n$:

1. When $n$ is 1, there is only one way to partition 1 using an odd number. Thus, $s(1)$ is 1. It is not possible to partition 1 using an even number: $t(1)$ is 0.
2. When $n$ is 2, if the first number is 1 (an odd number), the second number is also 1. The second number is not an even number. Thus, using 1 as

the first number is invalid, and $s(2)$ is 0. We can partition 2 using an even number: 2 itself. Thus, $t(2)$ is 1.

3. When $n$ is 3, if the first number is 1 (an odd number), the second number can be 2. This is a valid partition. The number 3 can also be partitioned by using itself, 3. This is another valid partition. Thus, $s(3)$ is 2. The value 3 can also be partitioned using 2 (an even number) as the first number and 1 (an odd number) as the second number. Thus, $t(2)$ is 1.
4. When $n$ is 4, $s(4)$ is 1 because the only valid partition starting with an odd number is $1 + 2 + 1$. The only valid partition starting with an even number is 4 itself. Thus, $t(4)$ is 1.

These observations are summarized in Table 1.4.

**TABLE 1.4**: The number of solutions is the sum of $s(n)$ and $t(n)$.

| $n$ | 1 | 2 | 3 | 4 | 5 | 6 |
|---|---|---|---|---|---|---|
| $s(n)$ | 1 | 0 | 2 | 1 | 3 | 4 |
| $t(n)$ | 0 | 1 | 1 | 1 | 3 | 2 |
| sum | 1 | 1 | 3 | 2 | 6 | 6 |

To calculate $s(n)$ for a large value of $n$, the first number can be 1, 3, 5, ... and the second number must be an even number. For example, when 1 is used for the first number, then the remaining $n - 1$ must start with an even number. By definition, there are $t(n-1)$ ways to partition $n-1$ starting with an even number. When 3 is used for the first number, then there are $t(n - 3)$ ways to partition $n - 3$ starting with an even number. Based on this reasoning, $s(n)$ is defined as:

$$s(n) = t(n-1) + t(n-3) + t(n-5)... \tag{1.19}$$

By definition, $s(n)$ must not start with an even number; thus, $t(n-2)$, $t(n-4)$, ... must not be included. It is necessary to distinguish whether $n$ is odd or even while writing down the last few terms in this equation. If $n$ is an even number, then:

- $n-3$ is an odd number. This means that there are $t(n-(n-3)) = t(3)$ ways to partition $n$ with $n-3$ as the first number. For example, if $n = 10$, there are $t(3)$ ways to partition 10 with 7 as the first number. Note that $t(3) = 1$ because the only valid partition of 3 that starts with an even number is $3 = 2 + 1$.
- $n-2$ is an even number. We skip this case because $s(n)$ is only concerned with the number of ways to partition $n$ using an odd number as the first number.
- $n - 1$ is an odd number, so $t(n - (n - 1)) = t(1)$ is included in the calculation of $s(n)$.

- $n$ is an even number. We skip this case because $s(n)$ only concerns itself with partitions that begin with odd numbers.

Hence, when $n$ is an even number:

$$s(n) = t(n-1) + t(n-3) + t(n-5)... + t(3) + t(1) \tag{1.20}$$

When $n$ is an odd number:

- $n-3$ is an even number, and this case is discarded when computing $s(n)$.
- $n-2$ is an odd number, leaving 2 to be partitioned. Thus we add $t(2)$.
- $n-1$ is an even number, and this case is discarded when computing $s(n)$.
- $n$ is an odd number, and it is a valid partition for $s(n)$. This means we add 1 to the end of the equation.

When $n$ is an odd number, $s(n)$ can be written as:

$$s(n) = t(n-1) + t(n-3) + t(n-5)... + t(2) + 1 \tag{1.21}$$

Combining these two halves, we get:

$$s(n) = \begin{cases} t(n-1) + t(n-3) + t(n-5)... + t(1) & \text{when } n \text{ is even} \\ t(n-1) + t(n-3) + t(n-5)... + t(2) + 1 & \text{when } n \text{ is odd} \end{cases} \tag{1.22}$$

Using similar reasoning, $t(n)$ can be written as follows:

$$t(n) = \begin{cases} s(n-2) + s(n-4) + s(n-6)... + s(4) + s(2) + 1 & \text{when } n \text{ is even} \\ s(n-2) + s(n-4) + s(n-6)... + s(3) + s(1) & \text{when } n \text{ is odd} \end{cases} \tag{1.23}$$

A partition may start with an odd number or an even number. Thus, the total number of ways to partition $n$ using alternating odd and even numbers is the sum $s(n) + t(n)$.

## 1.6 Earliest Recursion Problem

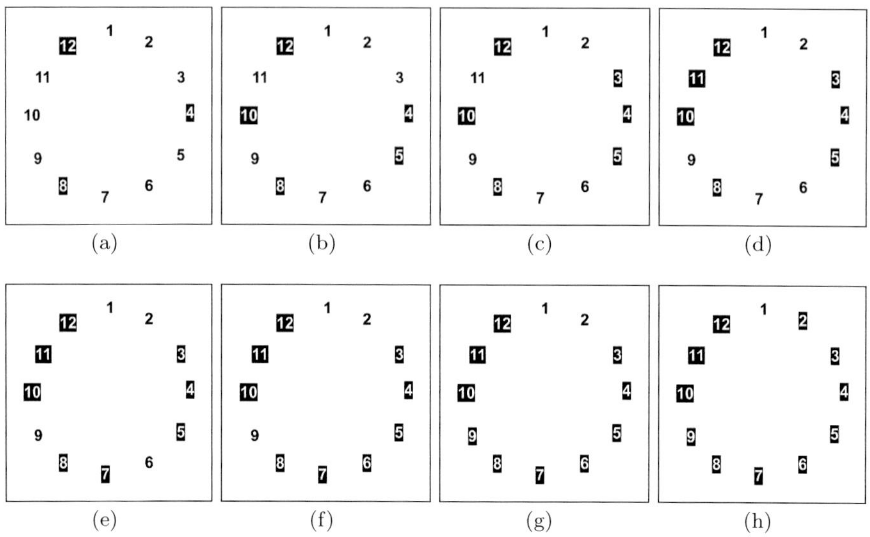


**FIGURE 1.8**: Twelve people ($n$ is 12) form a circle. Every fourth person ($k$ is 4) is removed from the group.

The earliest recursive problem is, perhaps, the *Josephus Problem* during the first century, described by Flavius Josephus about the Jewish-Roman war in the city of Yodfat. A group of $n$ people form a circle; each person is assigned a number from 1, 2, 3, ..., $n$. The group's leader chooses a positive integer $k$ ($k > 1$). Then the group counts from the person number 1 to $k$. The person who counts $k$ is removed from the group. Then, counting restarts from 1, and the process repeats until only one person is left. Which number is the last person? How can we find the answer quickly? This is called the *Josephus Problem* [1].

Consider the example shown in Figure 1.8 (a). Twelve people form a circle (i.e., $n$ is 12). Suppose $k$ is 4. Start from number 1 and count to 4. Number 4 is removed first; then numbers 8 and 12 are removed. These are shown in Figure 1.8 (a). The removed numbers are marked with a black background: 4 8, and 12. Counting restarts from 1. Since number 4 has already been removed, the fourth person is now number 5; similarly, the next person to remove is number 10. They are shown in Figure 1.8 (b). This process continues until only one person is left. In this example (when $n$ is 12 and $k$ is 4), number 1 is the last person. Table 1.5 uses another form to show the progression of the process.

**TABLE 1.5**: The black background is the fourth number and is removed. Already removed numbers are marked by -.

| | | | | | | | | | | | | |
|---|---|---|---|---|---|---|---|---|---|---|---|---|
| Number | 1 | 2 | 3 | **4** | 5 | 6 | 7 | **8** | 9 | 10 | 11 | **12** |
| Count | 1 | 2 | 3 | 4 | 1 | 2 | 3 | 4 | 1 | 2 | 3 | 4 |
| Number | 1 | 2 | 3 | - | **5** | 6 | 7 | - | 9 | **10** | 11 | - |
| Count | 1 | 2 | 3 | | 4 | 1 | 2 | | 3 | 4 | 1 | |
| Number | 1 | 2 | **3** | - | - | 6 | 7 | - | 9 | - | **11** | - |
| Count | 2 | 3 | 4 | | | 1 | 2 | | 3 | | 4 | |
| Number | 1 | 2 | - | - | - | 6 | **7** | - | 9 | - | - | - |
| Count | 1 | 2 | | | | 3 | 4 | | 1 | | | |
| Number | 1 | 2 | - | - | - | **6** | - | - | 9 | - | - | - |
| Count | 2 | 3 | | | | 4 | | | 1 | | | |
| Number | 1 | 2 | - | - | - | | - | - | **9** | - | - | - |
| Count | 2 | 3 | | | | | | | 4 | | | |
| Number | 1 | 2 | - | - | - | | - | - | - | - | - | - |
| Count | 1 | 2 | | | | | | | - | | | |
| Number | 1 | **2** | - | - | - | | - | - | - | - | - | - |
| Count | 3 | 4 | | | | | | | - | | | |
| Number | 1 | - | - | - | - | | - | - | - | - | - | - |
| Count | | | | | | | | | - | | | |

The general problem of $n$ people counting to $k$ is pretty complex. Thus, we consider a special case when $k$ is 2. We start with the smallest possible group: when $n$ is 2. Number 2 is removed, and number 1 remains. Hence, when $n = k = 2$, the last remaining person is number 1. Let $j(n)$ be the last remaining person when the total number of people starts with $n$ and $k$ is 2. When $n$ is 2, $j(n)$ is 1. Next, we double $n$ to 4. Numbers 2 and 4 are removed in the first round; numbers 1 and 3 stay. The second round starts with number 1 and number 3 is removed. Again, number 1 is the last remaining person, $j(4) = 1$. We have discovered a pattern. When $n$ is a power of 2, i.e., 2, 4, 8, 16, etc, the last remaining person is always number 1. Figure 1.9 illustrates this situation. When $k$ is 2, every other person is removed. After one round, numbers 2, 4, 6, ..., $n$ are removed. The second round starts with number 1 again, but now $n$ people remain. This process continues until only one person remains, and this person must be number 1. Based on this reasoning, we can write a general formula: $j(2^m) = 1$: When $n$ is a power of 2, i.e., $n = 2^m$ for an integer of $m$, the last remaining person is number 1.

We can generalize this reasoning and extend it to $n$ that is not a power of 2. We consider two cases: (1) When $n$ is an even number but not a power of 2 (such as 6, 10, 12) or (2) When $n$ is an odd number (such as 5 or 9). First, consider the case where $n$ is an even number. We can write $n = 2m$, where $m$

is an integer. In the first round, all even numbers (2, 4, 6, ... $2m$) are removed, and the remaining numbers are 1, 3, 5, ... $2m-1$. Figure 1.9 (a) shows the even numbers (2, 4, ..., $2m$) are removed. Figure 1.9 (b) shows that the remaining people have odd numbers (1, 3, 5, ... $2m-1$) after the first round. There are $m$ people in Figure 1.9 (c). We can reassign the $m$ numbers (1, 3, 5, ... $2m-1$) in Figure 1.9 (b) to the $m$ numbers in Figure 1.9 (c) (1, 2, 3, ..., $m$). Number $j$ in Figure 1.9 (c) corresponds to number $2j-1$ in Figure 1.9 (b). Figure 1.9 (c) is a smaller problem of $m$ people. Let $j(m)$ be the last remaining person of $m$ people. We can obtain the following equation:

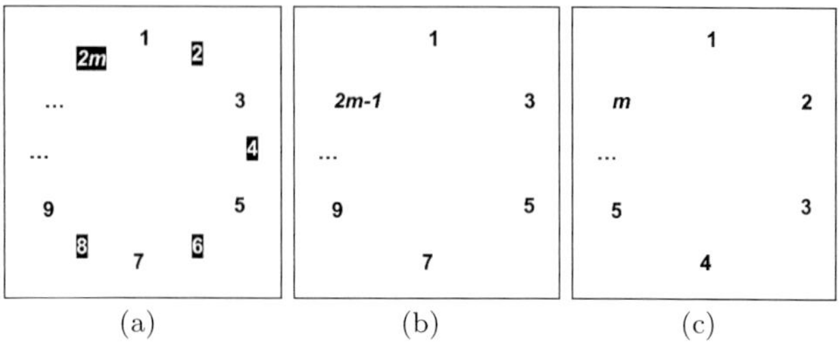


**FIGURE 1.9**: (a) If $n$ is even ($n = 2m$) and $k$ is 2, number 1 stays after the first round of removals. (b) All odd numbers stay after the first round. (c) Numbers 1, 3, 5, ... $2m-1$ can be reassigned to 1, 2, 3, ... $m$.

$$j(2m) = 2j(m) - 1. \tag{1.24}$$

Similarly, if $n$ is an odd number, we can write $n = 2m + 1$. Consider Figure 1.10. The first round removes 2, 4, 6, ..., $2m$. At the beginning of the second round, number 1 is removed. At this moment, the remaining numbers are 3, 5, 7, ..., $2m+1$, as shown in Figure 1.10 (a). There are $m$ people remaining. We can assign numbers 1, 2, 3, ... $m$ in Figure 1.10 (b) to the numbers in Figure 1.10 (a). Number $j$ in Figure 1.10 (b) is number $2j+1$ in Figure 1.10 (a). If $j(m)$ is the last remaining number in Figure 1.10 (b), this corresponds to $2j(m)+1$ when there are $2m+1$ people. Thus, we can write

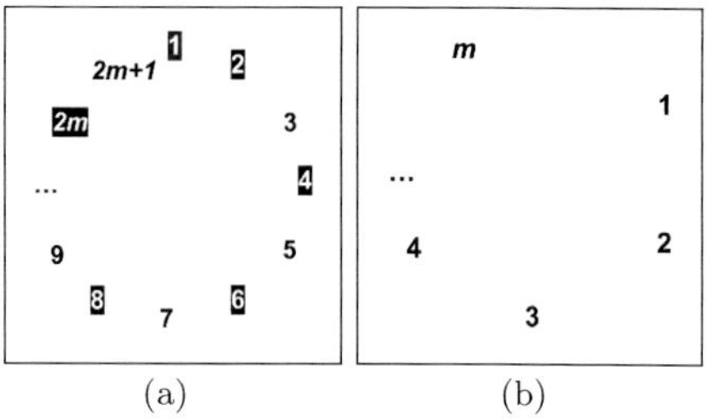


**FIGURE 1.10**: (a) If $n$ is an odd number ($n = 2m + 1$) and $k$ is 2, number 1 is eliminated at the beginning of the second round. (b) Numbers 3, 5, 7, ..., $2m+1$ can be reassigned to 1, 2, 3, ..., $m$.

$$j(2m+1) = 2j(m) + 1. \tag{1.25}$$

To summarize, the function $j(\cdot)$ is expressed by itself with a smaller number. This is another example of recursion.

---

## 1.7 Problems

### 1.7.1 Parentheses

An arithmetic expression may include one or multiple pairs of parentheses, for example

```
(3 + 5) * 4
(3 + (5 + 4) * 6) * 2
3 + (5 + 4) * (6 + 2)
(3 + (5 + 4)) * (6 + 2)
```

The parentheses must be arranged by following these rules:

1. The number of left parentheses `(` must be the same as the number of right parentheses `)`.
2. From left to right, the number of right parentheses `)` must not exceed the number of left parentheses `(` that have already been seen so far.

The following are valid arrangements of one, two, and three pairs:

```
()
(())
()()
((()))
(()())
(())()
()(())
()()()
```

The following are invalid arrangements because the number of `(` is different from the number of `)`.

```
())
()(
```

The following are invalid arrangements because more `)` appear before `(`.

```
)(
())(
))((
)()()(
```

This question asks you to determine the number of valid arrangements for 4, 5, and 6 pairs. Next, generalize the problem to consider $n$ pairs.

**Answer:**

Consider creating a function $f(n)$ as the number of valid arrangements when $n$ pairs of `(` and `)` are used. Since this problem considers `(` and `)`, $f(n)$ is further expressed by a function $g$ with two arguments: $f(n) = g(n,n)$. This new function $g$ has two arguments, and they can be different, as expressed by $n$ and $m$, i.e., $g(n,m)$. This can express the numbers of $n$ `(` and $m$ `)`. It is defined as the number of valid arrangements to use $n$ `(` and $m$ `)`, while satisfying the rules described above.

Consider arranging three pairs of `(` and `)`. The first is always `(`. Then, two `(` and three `)` are available. Thus, $f(3) = g(3,3) = g(2,3)$. The second can be `(` or `)`. These two options can be analyzed as follows:

1. If `(` is used next, one `(` and three `)` are still available. There are $g(1,3)$ arrangements.
2. Since one `(` has been used, the next can be `)`. If `)` is used, two `(` and two `)` are still available. There are $g(2,2)$ arrangements.

Thus, $f(3) = g(3,3) = g(2,3) = g(1,3) + g(2,2)$.

We need to answer the following questions:

1. What is $g(0,m)$ when $m > 0$? This is the case when no `(` is available and $m$ `)` can be used. Thus, $g(0,m) = 1$. Only $m$ `)`'s are available, and all of them must be used.
2. What is $g(n,m)$ when $n > m$? This is the case when more `(` than `)` are still available. Since `(` must be used first, it is impossible to have $n > m$: $g(n,m) = 0$ when $n > m$.
3. In general, $g(n,m) = g(n-1,m) + g(n,m-1)$. Here, $g(n-1,m)$ means using `(`, and $g(n,m-1)$ means using `)`.

Figure 1.11 shows how to calculate $f(4)$. Table 1.6 shows the values of $g(n,m)$. The elements in this table can be divided into three groups:

1. An element above the diagonal is zero: $g(n,m) = 0$ if $n > m$.
2. An element along the diagonal: $g(n,m)$ is the same as the element left, i.e., $g(n-1,m)$.
3. An element below the diagonal: $g(n,m)$ and $n < m$ is the sum of the element at left, i.e., $g(n-1,m)$ and the element above, i.e., $g(n,m-1)$.

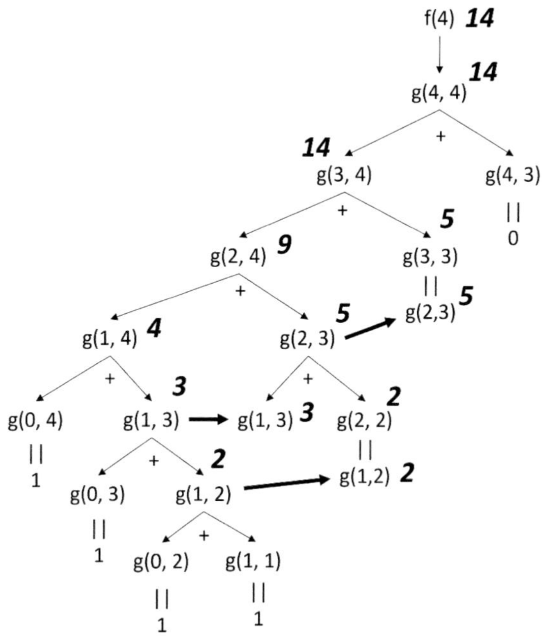


**FIGURE 1.11**: Calculate $f(4)$.

**TABLE 1.6**: Calculate $g(n, m)$ for Section 1.7.1.

| | $n$ = 0 | 1 | 2 | 3 | 4 | 5 | 6 |
|---|---|---|---|---|---|---|---|
| $m$ = 0 | - | 0 | 0 | 0 | 0 | 0 | 0 |
| 1 | 1 | 1 | 0 | 0 | 0 | 0 | 0 |
| 2 | 1 | 2 | 2 | 0 | 0 | 0 | 0 |
| 3 | 1 | 3 | 5 | 5 | 0 | 0 | 0 |
| 4 | 1 | 4 | 9 | 14 | 14 | 0 | 0 |
| 5 | 1 | 5 | 14 | 28 | 42 | 42 | 0 |
| 6 | 1 | 6 | 20 | 48 | 90 | 132 | 132 |

### 1.7.2 Ball Selection

Consider selecting balls from three possible colors: $\mathbb{R}$, $\mathbb{G}$, $\mathbb{B}$. Two adjacent balls cannot both be red or both green. Two adjacent balls can both be blue. How many options are there to select $n$ balls?

**Answer:**

When $n$ is one, there are still three options:

1. $\mathbb{R}$
2. $\mathbb{G}$
3. $\mathbb{B}$.

When $n$ is two, there are seven options.

1. $\mathbb{R}$ $\mathbb{G}$
2. $\mathbb{R}$ $\mathbb{B}$
3. $\mathbb{G}$ $\mathbb{R}$
4. $\mathbb{G}$ $\mathbb{B}$
5. $\mathbb{B}$ $\mathbb{R}$
6. $\mathbb{B}$ $\mathbb{G}$
7. $\mathbb{B}$ $\mathbb{B}$

We use a different approach to solve this problem, by using some additional functions. Each function calculates the number of possible sequences when selecting $n$ balls.

- $r(n)$: the first ball is $\mathbb{R}$.
- $g(n)$: the first ball is $\mathbb{G}$.
- $b(n)$: the first ball is $\mathbb{B}$.
- $f(n)$: the first ball can be any of the three colors. Apparently, $f(n) = r(n) + g(n) + b(n)$.

How is $r(n)$ calculated when $n$ is greater than 2? By definition, $r(n)$ denotes the number of possible sequences of $n$ balls when the first one is $\mathbb{R}$. For the remaining $n - 1$ balls, the first of the $n-1$ balls (the second among the $n$ balls) can be either $\mathbb{G}$ or $\mathbb{B}$. If the first of the $n - 1$ balls (the second among the $n$ balls) is $\mathbb{G}$, there are $g(n - 1)$ options. Similarly, when the first of the $n - 1$ balls (the second among the $n$ balls) is $\mathbb{B}$, there are $b(n - 1)$ options. Thus, $r(n) = g(n - 1) + b(n - 1)$. Because the same restrictions apply to both red and green balls, we can use the same reasoning to write $g(n) = r(n - 1) + b(n - 1)$.

**TABLE 1.7**: Number of options when $n$ is 1 to 6.

| n | 1 | 2 | 3 | 4 | 5 | 6 |
|---|---|---|---|---|---|---|
| r(n) | 1 | 2 | 5 | 12 | 29 | 70 |
| g(n) | 1 | 2 | 5 | 12 | 29 | 70 |
| b(n) | 1 | 3 | 7 | 17 | 41 | 99 |
| f(n) | 3 | 7 | 17 | 41 | 99 | 239 |

How many options are there when selecting $n$ balls and the first ball is $\mathbb{B}$? There is no restriction on the second ball in the sequence. The second ball can be red, green, or blue; thus, we can write $b(n) = g(n-1)+b(n-1)+r(n-1)$. This is equal to $f(n - 1)$ because it means selecting $n - 1$ balls and the first ball can be $\mathbb{G}$, $\mathbb{B}$, or $\mathbb{R}$. There are $f(n - 1)$ possible sequences of length $n - 1$ balls so $b(n) = f(n - 1)$. The complete solution is shown below:

$$
\begin{aligned}
r(n) &= g(n-1) + b(n-1) \\
g(n) &= r(n-1) + b(n-1) \\
b(n) &= f(n-1) \\
f(n) &= r(n) + g(n) + b(n)
\end{aligned}
\tag{1.26}
$$

Table 1.7 shows the values of these functions for $n$ equal to 1 to 6.

### 1.7.3 Partition Using Odd and Even Numbers

Section 1.5.1 explains how to find the number of partitions using odd numbers only. The answer is expressed as $h(n)$. A similar procedure can be used to find the number of partitions using only even numbers. Let's call it $u(n)$. Section 1.5.4 defines $s(n)$ and $t(n)$. Is $s(n) + t(n)$ equal to $h(n) + u(n)$? Please explain your answer.

**Answer:**

No. $s(n) + t(n) \neq h(n) + u(n)$.

When $n$ is 2

- $h(2) = 1$: There is one way to partition 2 using only odd numbers: $1 + 1$
- $u(2) = 1$: There is one way to partition 2 using only even numbers: 2
- $s(2) = 0$: There is no way to partition 2 using an odd number first and an even number second.
- $t(2) = 1$: There is one way to partition 2 using an even number first: 2

Thus, $h(2) + u(2) = 2$ and $s(2) + t(2) = 1$. They are different.

### 1.7.4 Tower of Hanoi: Movements of the Smallest Disk

Consider the problem of the Tower of Hanoi. There are three poles and six disks. How many times is the smallest disk moved?

**Answer:**

32 times.

- The largest disk is moved only once.
- The second largest disk is moved twice.
- The third largest disk is moved four times.

If there are $n$ disks, the smallest disk is moved $2^{n-1}$ times. In this problem, $n$ is 6. Thus, the smallest disk is moved $2^{6-1} = 2^5 = 32$ times.

### 1.7.5 Tower of Hanoi: Four Poles

Consider the problem of the Tower of Hanoi. There are four poles and six disks. How many times are these disks moved?

**Answer:**

21 times.

Consider that all disks are originally at pole A and the destination is pole B. Poles C and D can be used for temporary storage of disks.

```
    # right: how many ) have been used
    ind = left + right
    outstr = '' # empty string
    if (left == total):
        # use up all (
        # remaining are all )
        for i in range(0, ind):
            outstr = outstr + parentheses[i]
        for i in range(right, total):
            outstr = outstr + ')'
        results.append(outstr)
        return
    # next one can always be (
    parentheses[ind] = '('
    helper(parentheses, total, left + 1, right, results)
    # ) can be used only if more ( have been used than )
    if (left > right):
        parentheses[ind] = ')'
        helper(parentheses, total, left, right + 1, results)
def generate(n):
    results = []
    parentheses = ['0'] * (2 * n)
    helper(parentheses, n, 0, 0, results)
    return results
import random
def testgenerate():
    n = random.randint(3,9)
    results = generate(n)
    for res in results:
      print(res)
    print(f'n = {n}, {len(results)} results')
testgenerate()
```

The program's output for 3 pairs:

```
((()))
(()())
(())()
()(())
()()()
n = 3, 5 results
```

## 2.6 Shuffle Cards

When you spend time with friends, playing a card game sounds exciting. A deck of cards has four suits in two colors:

1. Red Diamond ♢
2. Red Heart ♡
3. Black Spade ♠
4. Black Club ♣

Each suit has 13 cards, marked as A, 2, 3, ...9, 10, J, Q, K. There are $13 \times 4 = 52$ cards total. Many card games require that players do not know which card will come next. Before playing any of these games, the cards need to be shuffled. The purpose of shuffling cards is to make the sequence of cards difficult to predict. If a deck of cards is perfectly shuffled, the first card can be any of the 52 cards. Thus, there is $\frac{1}{52}$ chance of guessing the first card correctly. After revealing the first card, 51 cards are left. The chance of guessing the second card correctly is $\frac{1}{51}$. After revealing 51 cards, only one card is left, and all players know which card is left.

*Riffle shuffling* is a widely used method for shuffling. The method has two steps:

1. Divide a deck of cards into two groups: the upper group and the lower group. They are called the left deck and the right deck (held by the left hand and the right hand). Each group has at least one card. The two groups may have different numbers of cards. This is one reason why the shuffling results are hard to predict. Figure 2.1 shows three ways to divide 8 cards.
2. Interleave the cards. Typically, the cards are released by the thumbs of the two hands. It is possible (in fact, likely) that the two thumbs are not perfectly coordinated and more than one card from one hand is released at once. The order of cards in the left hand does not change: If one card is above another in the left hand, the former is still above the latter after interleaving the cards from the right hand. Similarly, the order of the cards in the right hand does not change.

Figure 2.2 shows three ways to interleave the two decks of cards. The cards in the left deck are marked with a black background. Please notice that the order of the cards in the left deck is unchanged; the order of the cards in the right deck is also unchanged. Card A is always above card 2. Card 2 is always above card 3.

```
['A', '4', '2', '3']
['4', 'A', '2', '3']
n = 4, number of results = 14
```

Earlier, we mentioned that some orders of cards do not appear after shuffling once. If the original cards are A, 2, 3, shuffling once will not produce the order of 3, 2, A. We want to calculate the number of results using Riffle shuffling for $n$ cards. Suppose the left hand has $k$ cards and the right hand has $n - k$ cards ($1 \leq k \leq n - 1$, to ensure that each hand has at least one card). There are

$$\frac{n!}{k!(n-k)!} \tag{2.1}$$

ways to interleave the $n$ cards while maintaining the orders of the $k$ cards in the left hand and the $n-k$ cards in the right hand. How do we get this result? The numerator $n!$ is obtained by selecting the $n$ cards in order. This is called the *permutation* problem. There are $k!$ ways to order the $k$ cards in one hand. Since the order of the cards in each hand must be preserved, the result must be divided by $k!$ to eliminate the possibility of ordering the $k$ cards in one hand. Similarly, we need to eliminate the possibility of ordering $n - k$ cards in the other hand. Thus, the result should also be divided by $(n - k)!$. This is the *combination* problem. The left deck has at least one card, thus, $k \geq 1$. The right deck has at least one card, thus, $k \leq n - 1$. The number of possible results is

$$\sum_{k=1}^{n-1} \frac{n!}{k!(n-k)!}. \tag{2.2}$$

Consider the expansion of the binomial of the $n$-th order:

$$(x+y)^n = \sum_{k=0}^{n} \frac{n!}{k!(n-k)!} x^k y^{n-k}. \tag{2.3}$$

By setting $x = y = 1$, we can obtain

$$2^n = \sum_{k=0}^{n} \frac{n!}{k!(n-k)!}. \tag{2.4}$$

Equation (2.2) does not have the first term (when $k$ is 0) and the last term (when $k$ is $n$). Thus, Equation (2.2) is

$$2^n - 2 = \sum_{k=1}^{n-1} \frac{n!}{k!(n-k)!}. \tag{2.5}$$

Please notice that this double-counts the order of A, 2, 3 when only three cards are used.

To arrange 4 cards, there are $4! = 24$ possible ways. Riffle Shuffling produces the original order 2, 3, 4, 5 three times. Even if we count this order three times, Riffle Shuffling can produce only $2^4 - 2 = 14$ results. Many possible results are missing if the cards are shuffled only once. Table 2.1 shows that as $n$ becomes larger, $2^n - 2$ becomes a smaller portion of the $n!$ possible results.

**TABLE 2.1**: As $n$ becomes larger, Riffle Shuffling can produce smaller portions of the possible orders.

| $n$ | 2 | 3 | 4 | 5 | 6 | 7 | 8 |
|---|---|---|---|---|---|---|---|
| $2^n - 2$ | 2 | 6 | 14 | 30 | 62 | 126 | 254 |
| $n!$ | 2 | 6 | 24 | 120 | 720 | 5040 | 40320 |
| $\frac{2^n-2}{n!}$ | 100% | 100% | 58.3% | 25% | 8.6% | 2.5% | 0.63% |

We can increase the number of possible results by shuffling the cards again. We extend the program so that the cards can be shuffled more than once. This program is similar to the previous, with a few changes.

1. The `shuffle` function takes two arguments: the number of cards and the number of rounds.
2. The `divide` function also takes two arguments. The first is the array of cards to be divided. The second argument is the number of rounds to shuffle. If the second argument is zero, no more division or interleaving is needed, and the cards are saved (lines 24-26).
3. In the `interleave` function, if one deck is empty (lines 5 or 10), the remaining cards are used. Instead of printing the result, the `interleave` function sends the result to `divide` for the next round.
4. In this program, `divide` calls `interleave` (line 32); `interleave` calls `interleave` (lines 18 and 22); `interleave` also calls `divide` (lines 8 and 13). As shown in this example, the recursive function may call itself indirectly.
5. The program uses `set` to eliminate duplicates (line 48) and calculates unique results.

```
1  # Section 2.6: shuffle2.py
2  # shuffle multiple times
3  def interleave(combined, leftgroup, rightgroup, r, results):
4      newgroup = list(combined)
5      if (leftgroup == []):
6          for i in range(0, len(rightgroup)):
7              newgroup.append(rightgroup[i])
8          divide(newgroup, r - 1, results)
```

```
        return
    if (rightgroup == []):
        for i in range(0, len(leftgroup)):
            newgroup.append(leftgroup[i])
        divide(newgroup, r - 1, results)
        return
    newgroup = list(combined)
    newgroup.append(leftgroup[0])
    llen = len(leftgroup)
    interleave(newgroup, leftgroup[1:llen + 1], rightgroup, r, results)
    newgroup = list(combined)
    newgroup.append(rightgroup[0])
    rlen = len(rightgroup)
    interleave(newgroup, leftgroup, rightgroup[1:rlen + 1], r, results)
def divide(array, r, results):
    if (r == 0): # round is zero, no more shuffling
        results.append (array)
        return
    k = len(array)
    for i in range (1, k):
        leftgroup = array[0:i]
        rightgroup = array[i: k + 1]
        combined = []
        interleave(combined, leftgroup, rightgroup, r, results)
def shuffle(k, r):
    array = ['A']
    results = list()
    for i in range (2, k + 1):
        array.append(str(i))
    divide(array, r, results)
    return results
import random
def testshuffle2():
    n = random.randint(3, 7) # number of cards
    r = random.randint(1, 5) # number of rounds
    results = shuffle(n, r)
    for res in results:
        print (res)
    print(f'n = {n}, r = {r}: number of results = {len(results)}')
```

```
    print(f'unique results = {len(set(tuple(res) for res in
    ↪ results))}')
testshuffle2()
```

This is the last two lines of the output when `n` is 7 and `r` is 2:

```
n = 7, r = 2: number of results = 15876
unique results = 3728
```

The number of output is $(2^7 - 2)^2 = 126^2 = 15876$. Please note that there are only 3728 unique results. For seven cards, the number of permutation is $7! = 5040$ different results. In other words, shuffling seven cards twice does not produce all possible orders.

---

## 2.7 Binary Search

The previous sections introduced many recursive programs for solving the problems described in the previous chapter. This section introduces a new problem: We want to find a value (called a *key*) in a sorted array and return its index. If this array does not contain this value, then $-1$ is returned because $-1$ is an invalid index for any array. It is natural to ask why this array is already sorted. Sorting an array takes time. If this array is searched only once, it is not worth spending time sorting the elements. If this array may be searched many times, sorting can pay off.

The function for binary search has two arguments:

1. An array of numbers sorted in ascending order. It is possible that some elements have the same value. If repetitions occur, this function will find the index of one of these elements.
2. The value to search for (i.e., the key).

Since the array is already sorted, it is possible to quickly discard many elements (approximately half in each step) by comparing the key with the element at the center of the array. There are three possible outcomes of this comparison:

1. If the two values are the same, the key has been found, and the index of this element is reported.
2. If the key is smaller than that element, we do not need to search the upper part of the array.
3. If the key is larger than that element, we do not need to search the lower part of the array.

The second or the third step will shrink the size of the array to be considered.

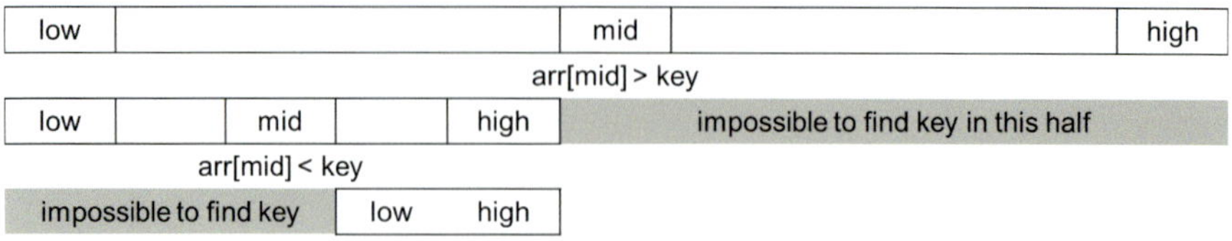


**FIGURE 2.3**: Binary search compares the value of the key with the element at the center of the array. If the key is smaller, we can ignore all elements in the upper half (i.e., the right half) of the array.

Thus, the amount of data will become smaller in each step. These steps continue until one of two conditions is met: (1) The key is found, or (2) no data is left, and it is impossible to find a match. Figure 2.3 is a graphical view of the steps. In each step, the binary search reduces the number of elements to search by half (and one additional element in the middle).

```
# Section 2.7: binarysearch.py
import random
def helper(arr, low, high, key):
  if (low > high): # empty array
      return -1
  mid = int((low + high) / 2)
  if (arr[mid] == key): # found
      return mid
  if (arr[mid] > key): # ignore the upper half
      return helper(arr, low, mid - 1, key)
  return helper(arr, mid + 1, high, key)
def binarySearch(arr, key):
  return helper(arr, 0, len(arr) - 1, key)
if __name__ == "__main__":
    length = 15
    arr = []
    for ind in range(0, length):
        arr.append(random.randint(1, 5 * length))
    arr.sort() # binary search needs a sorted array
    print(arr)
    val = random.randint(1, 5 * length)
    print(f'search {val}')
    print(f'index = {binarySearch(arr, val)}')
```

In this program, `binarySearch` has only two arguments: the array and the key. The recursive function requires two additional arguments to specify the range of the array to search (called `low` and `high` as the range of the indexes to be considered). This program uses a helper function for the additional arguments. Please pay attention to how the range changes in recursive calls: The range must shrink in each call. This ensures that the recursive calls eventually reach a stop condition (line 4 or 7). The first stop condition occurs when no more elements are left to search. Please notice that this condition is `low > high`, not `low >= high`. If `low` equals `high`, there is still one element to search. Line 6 uses integer division because `ind` needs to be an integer. Line 7 compares the key with the array element with the index `mid`. If they match, the key has been found. Line 10 uses `mid - 1` for the new `high` index. Using `mid - 1` ensures that the range shrinks. The element `arr[mid]` has already been checked at line 7; it is not necessary to consider this element again. When `low` is the same as `high`, `ind` is also the same. If line 10 were to use `mid` instead of `mid - 1`, then the next recursive call would still have `low` and `high` unchanged, and the recursion would not end. Similarly, in line 11, the low index must be `mid + 1`, not `mid`. The following shows two executions of the program. The first search fails: The number is not in the array, and the program returns $-1$.

```
[5, 6, 14, 16, 17, 18, 22, 35, 37, 42, 42, 49, 50, 60, 73]
search 48
index = -1
```

The second search succeeds, and the program returns a valid index.

```
[6, 23, 24, 25, 31, 34, 35, 37, 42, 44, 47, 60, 64, 64, 71]
search 42
index = 8
```

Binary search is very efficient: Half of the elements can be discarded by a single comparison at line 10 or 11. This makes binary search's execution time grow slowly (logarithmically) as the size of the array increases. If the size of the sorted array doubles, the search function needs to perform only one additional comparison. If the array has $n$ elements, binary search takes approximately $\log(n)$ time. We can think of the efficiency in this way. The comparisons in lines 7 and 9 take approximately one nanosecond in a modern computer. In other words, in one nanosecond, we can divide a sorted array into two halves. We can double the size of the array for every additional nanosecond. One second has $10^9$ nanoseconds and can process an array as large as $2^{10^9} = 2^{1,000,000,000}$ elements. Scientists estimate that this universe has approximately $10^{80}$ atoms, or $2^{266}$ atoms. This is a tiny fraction of $2^{1,000,000,000}$. Of course, it is not possible to have an array of $2^{1,000,000,000}$ elements because we run out of atoms. When this book was written, the fastest supercomputer in the world had 512GB of memory per compute node. This is approximately $2^{39}$ bytes. The entire system has thousands of compute nodes, and the total amount of memory is about 5PB, approximately $2^{52}$ bytes. If data is scattered among multiple computers, comparing two integers may take much longer than one nanosecond.

---

## 2.8 Quick Sort

Binary search needs sorted arrays. How can we sort arrays? We need sorting algorithms. Quick sort is a widely used sorting algorithm. Quick sort is faster than many other sorting algorithms (such as selection sort or insertion sort) because it uses *transitivity*: If $x > y$ and $y > z$, then $x > z$. It is not necessary to compare $x$ with $z$. The algorithm first selects one element from the array as a reference, called the *pivot*. It can be any element in the array. Some implementations use the first or last element; some implementations use a randomly selected element. After selecting the pivot, the algorithm divides the array into three parts:

1. elements smaller than the pivot,
2. elements equal to the pivot,
3. elements greater than the pivot.

Based on transitivity, the values in the first part are always smaller than the values in the third part. Comparing the first part with the third part is not needed. Part 1 may be empty if the pivot is the smallest element in the array. Similarly, part 3 may be empty if the pivot is the largest element in the array. If all elements have the same value as the pivot, then parts 1 and 3 are empty.

The sorting algorithm then recursively sorts the first and the third parts. The program stops when all elements have been sorted. This occurs when each part has only one element or no element. Here are the steps to divide the array into three parts:

1. Determine the value of the pivot. Suppose the first element is used. Arrange the elements horizontally with ascending indexes.
2. Go through the elements using two indexes called `low` and `high`. The initial value of `low` is one higher than the index of the pivot. The initial value of `high` is the largest index of the range being considered. An example is shown below. Suppose the original array has 12 elements: `19 7 12 23 8 31 6 42 28 16 51 33`. We select the first element, 19, as the pivot. The pivot's index is 0; `low` is 1; `high` is 11.

| **index** | 0 | 1 | 2 | 3 | 4 | 5 | 6 | 7 | 8 | 9 | 10 | 11 |
|---|---|---|---|---|---|---|---|---|---|---|---|---|
| **value** | 19 | 7 | 12 | 23 | 8 | 31 | 6 | 42 | 28 | 16 | 51 | 33 |
| **variable** | pivot | low | | | | | | | | | | high |

3. From the left side, if an element is smaller than the pivot, `low` increments. If an element is greater than the pivot, stop changing `low`. Using the example shown above, 7 is smaller than 19, `low` increments to index 2.

| **index** | 0 | 1 | 2 | 3 | 4 | 5 | 6 | 7 | 8 | 9 | 10 | 11 |
|---|---|---|---|---|---|---|---|---|---|---|---|---|
| **value** | 19 | 7 | 12 | 23 | 8 | 31 | 6 | 42 | 28 | 16 | 51 | 33 |
| **variable** | pivot | | low | | | | | | | | | high |

The next value, 12, is also smaller than the pivot 19, and `low` increments again to index 3. The next value is 23, and it is greater than 19. Thus, `low` stops incrementing.

| **index** | 0 | 1 | 2 | 3 | 4 | 5 | 6 | 7 | 8 | 9 | 10 | 11 |
|---|---|---|---|---|---|---|---|---|---|---|---|---|
| **value** | 19 | 7 | 12 | 23 | 8 | 31 | 6 | 42 | 28 | 16 | 51 | 33 |
| **variable** | pivot | | | low | | | | | | | | high |

4. From the right side, if an element is greater than the pivot, `high` decrements. If an element is smaller than the pivot, stop changing `high`. In this example, the element at `high` is 33, and it is greater than the pivot. Thus, `high` decrements by one.

| **index** | 0 | 1 | 2 | 3 | 4 | 5 | 6 | 7 | 8 | 9 | 10 | 11 |
|---|---|---|---|---|---|---|---|---|---|---|---|---|
| **value** | 19 | 7 | 12 | 23 | 8 | 31 | 6 | 42 | 28 | 16 | 51 | 33 |
| **variable** | pivot | | | low | | | | | | | high | |

Now, the element at `high` is 51, and it is greater than the pivot. Thus, `high` decrements by one again.

| **index** | 0 | 1 | 2 | 3 | 4 | 5 | 6 | 7 | 8 | 9 | 10 | 11 |
|---|---|---|---|---|---|---|---|---|---|---|---|---|
| **value** | 19 | 7 | 12 | 23 | 8 | 31 | 6 | 42 | 28 | 16 | 51 | 33 |
| **variable** | pivot | | | low | | | | | | high | | |

5. At this moment, the value whose index is `low` is greater than the pivot. The value whose index is `high` is smaller than the pivot. We swap these two values.

| **index** | 0 | 1 | 2 | 3 | 4 | 5 | 6 | 7 | 8 | 9 | 10 | 11 |
|---|---|---|---|---|---|---|---|---|---|---|---|---|
| **value** | 19 | 7 | 12 | 16 | 8 | 31 | 6 | 42 | 28 | 23 | 51 | 33 |
| **variable** | pivot | | | low | | | | | | high | | |

6. Continue steps 2 to 5 until `low` is greater than `high`. The value at `low` is 16, and `low` increments.

| index | 0 | 1 | 2 | 3 | 4 | 5 | 6 | 7 | 8 | 9 | 10 | 11 |
|---|---|---|---|---|---|---|---|---|---|---|---|---|
| value | 19 | 7 | 12 | 16 | 8 | 31 | 6 | 42 | 28 | 23 | 51 | 33 |
| variable | pivot | | | | low | | | | | high | | |

Because 8 is smaller than 19, `low` increments again.

| index | 0 | 1 | 2 | 3 | 4 | 5 | 6 | 7 | 8 | 9 | 10 | 11 |
|---|---|---|---|---|---|---|---|---|---|---|---|---|
| value | 19 | 7 | 12 | 16 | 8 | 31 | 6 | 42 | 28 | 23 | 51 | 33 |
| variable | pivot | | | | | low | | | | high | | |

Because 31 is greater than 19, `low` stops here. Since 23 is greater than the pivot, `high` decrements.

| index | 0 | 1 | 2 | 3 | 4 | 5 | 6 | 7 | 8 | 9 | 10 | 11 |
|---|---|---|---|---|---|---|---|---|---|---|---|---|
| value | 19 | 7 | 12 | 16 | 8 | 31 | 6 | 42 | 28 | 23 | 51 | 33 |
| variable | pivot | | | | | low | | | high | | | |

The index `high` decrements twice more, and the value at `high` is 6.

| index | 0 | 1 | 2 | 3 | 4 | 5 | 6 | 7 | 8 | 9 | 10 | 11 |
|---|---|---|---|---|---|---|---|---|---|---|---|---|
| value | 19 | 7 | 12 | 16 | 8 | 31 | 6 | 42 | 28 | 23 | 51 | 33 |
| variable | pivot | | | | | low | | high | | | | |

| index | 0 | 1 | 2 | 3 | 4 | 5 | 6 | 7 | 8 | 9 | 10 | 11 |
|---|---|---|---|---|---|---|---|---|---|---|---|---|
| value | 19 | 7 | 12 | 16 | 8 | 31 | 6 | 42 | 28 | 23 | 51 | 33 |
| variable | pivot | | | | | low | high | | | | | |

The values at `low` and `high` are swapped.

| index | 0 | 1 | 2 | 3 | 4 | 5 | 6 | 7 | 8 | 9 | 10 | 11 |
|---|---|---|---|---|---|---|---|---|---|---|---|---|
| value | 19 | 7 | 12 | 16 | 8 | 6 | 31 | 42 | 28 | 23 | 51 | 33 |
| variable | pivot | | | | | low | high | | | | | |

Increment `low` and decrement `high` again.

| index | 0 | 1 | 2 | 3 | 4 | 5 | 6 | 7 | 8 | 9 | 10 | 11 |
|---|---|---|---|---|---|---|---|---|---|---|---|---|
| value | 19 | 7 | 12 | 16 | 8 | 6 | 31 | 42 | 28 | 23 | 51 | 33 |
| variable | pivot | | | | | high | low | | | | | |

At this moment, `low` is greater than `high`. That means the entire array has been examined. Check whether the value at `high` is smaller than the pivot. If so, swap the two values so that the pivot is placed between the first and the third parts.

| **index** | 0 | 1 | 2 | 3 | 4 | 5 | 6 | 7 | 8 | 9 | 10 | 11 |
|---|---|---|---|---|---|---|---|---|---|---|---|---|
| **value** | 6 | 7 | 12 | 16 | 8 | 19 | 31 | 42 | 28 | 23 | 51 | 33 |
| **variable** | pivot | | | | | high | low | | | | | |

The algorithm next sorts the first part using the same procedure.

| **index** | 0 | 1 | 2 | 3 | 4 |
|---|---|---|---|---|---|
| **value** | 6 | 7 | 12 | 16 | 8 |
| **variable** | pivot | low | | | high |

The algorithm also sorts the third part using the same procedure.

| **index** | 6 | 7 | 8 | 9 | 10 | 11 |
|---|---|---|---|---|---|---|
| **value** | 31 | 42 | 28 | 23 | 51 | 33 |
| **variable** | pivot | low | | | | high |

Please notice that the pivot (value 19) is already at the correct position and does not need to be sorted.

A sample implementation of quick sort is shown below. The function `quickSort` takes only one argument: the array to be sorted. The recursive function needs three arguments: the array and the range of indexes to be sorted (expressed as `low` and `high`). Thus, a helper function is created. This helper function divides the array elements into three parts and recursively sorts the first and the third parts.

```
# Section 2.8: quicksort.py
import random
def helper(arr, first, last):
    if (first >= last):  # zero or one element, already sorted
        return
    pivot = arr[first]
    low = first + 1
    high = last
    while (low < high): # move low and high indexes
        while ((low < last) and (arr[low] <= pivot)): # notice
         ↪  <=
```

```
11             low = low + 1
12         while ((first < high) and (arr[high] > pivot)): # notice >
13             high = high - 1
14         if (low < high):
15             arr[low], arr[high] = arr[high], arr[low] # swap
16     if (pivot > arr[high]):
17         arr[first], arr[high] = arr[high], arr[first] # swap
18     helper(arr, first, high - 1) # sort the first part
19     helper(arr, low, last) # sort the third part
20 def quickSort(arr):
21     helper(arr,0, len(arr) - 1)
22     return arr
23 def checkOrder(arr):
24     for ind in range(0, len(arr) - 1):
25         if (arr[ind] > arr[ind + 1]):
26             print('Error')
27 if __name__ == "__main__":
28     length = 100
29     arr = []
30     for ind in range(0, length):
31         arr.append(random.randint(1, 3 * length))
32     quickSort(arr)
33     checkOrder(arr)
```

This program may appear straightforward. A closer look, however, reveals that some common mistakes can easily occur. The helper function's second and third arguments specify the range of indexes that are being sorted. This function assumes `last` is a valid index, so `quickSort` must use `len(arr) - 1` at line 21. If this line uses `len(arr)`, then the program may access an invalid memory location because `len(arr)` is not a valid index. Next, consider line 10, which uses `arr[low] <= pivot`. If it is rewritten as `arr[low] < pivot`, problems occur when some of the array's elements have the same value as the pivot. When this occurs, and line 10 has no `=` in the condition, `low` does not increment. If `arr[high]` is smaller than the pivot, then `high` does not decrement. As a result, neither `low` nor `high` changes, and the recursive call does not end because `low < high` is always true.

If the original array is already sorted, then the first element is always the smallest, and the first part is empty. As a result, the algorithm does not take advantage of transitivity. Some implementations of quick sort randomly select one array element for the pivot, instead of the first. Using a randomly selected element for the pivot reduces the chance that the pivot is always the smallest element.

## 2.9 List Contents in Directories

Directories (also called folders) in file systems are inherently recursive. A directory may contain files and directories. Each directory may contain additional files and directories. In Linux, the `tree` command lists the contents of directories in a tree-like format. The following is an excerpt of the output of `tree --charset=ascii` of the directories used by this book. Here `--charset=ascii` is used so that the outputs use only ASCII (American Standard Code for Information Interchange). Without `--charset=ascii`, `tree`'s output uses Unicode and may not be printable.

```
|-- book cover
|   `-- book cover.ipynb
|-- CH02 Recursive Programs
|   |-- 2-10-1-factorial.ipynb
|   |-- 2-10-2-fibonacci.ipynb
|   |-- 2-1-balls.ipynb
|   |-- 2-2-oneway.ipynb
|   |-- 2-3-hanoi.ipynb
...
16 directories, 122 files
```

The following Python program prints directories and files in a format similar to the `tree` command:

```python
# Section 2.9: directory.py
# list files and directories in a tree-like format
import os
def tree(dir_path, fhd, prefix = "", file_count=0, dir_count=0):
    entries = sorted(os.listdir(dir_path), key=str.casefold)
    entries_count = len(entries)
    for index, entry in enumerate(entries):
        full_path = os.path.join(dir_path, entry)
        if (index == entries_count - 1):
            connector = "`-- "
        else:
            connector = "|-- "
        if os.path.isdir(full_path):
            fhd.write(prefix + connector + entry + '\n')
            dir_count += 1
            if (index == entries_count - 1):
                extension = "    "
```

```
18             else:
19                 extension = "|   "
20             file_count, dir_count = tree(full_path, fhd, prefix
               ↪  + extension, file_count, dir_count)
21         else:
22             fhd.write(prefix + connector + entry + '\n')
23             file_count += 1
24     return file_count, dir_count
25 !git clone https://github.com/python4recursion/bookcode.git
26 base_path = 'bookcode/'
27 myoutput_file = os.path.join(base_path, 'mytree_output.txt')
28 fhd = open(myoutput_file, 'w')
29 file_count, dir_count = tree(base_path, fhd)
30 fhd.write(f'\n{dir_count} directories, {file_count} files\n')
```

This program uses Python's `os` module to list the content in a directory (line 5). A directory may have files or directories. Line 5 uses `sorted` to sort the content. If this is the last content in a directory, the `connector` is `‘--` (lines 9 - 10). If this is not the last, the `connector` is `|--` (lines 11 - 12). If this content is a directory (line 13), the program visits the directory using a recursive call (line 20).

---

## 2.10 Recursive Problems Without Recursive Programs

Some problems can be solved recursively even though the problems are not defined recursively. For example, search and sorting are not defined recursively, but they can be solved recursively using binary search and quick sort. Meanwhile, some problems are defined recursively, but they do not need to be solved by recursive programs. In fact, in some cases, non-recursive solutions may be preferred because they can be more efficient. Appendix A explains that function calls need to push and pop frames in stack memory. These activities take time. It is important to understand how recursion impacts execution time. Appendix B explains the concept of *tail recursion* and how to convert tail recursion to `while`.

Many introductory books use *factorial* and *Fibonacci Numbers* as examples of recursion. These problems are defined recursively. However, their solutions do not need to use recursion. Straightforward recursive implementations may be inefficient. As a result, readers are often confused as to why recursion is needed at all. This section explains why factorials and Fibonacci numbers are not good examples for recursive programs. Let's start with factorials.

### 2.10.1 Factorials

Factorials are defined as

$$f(n) = \begin{cases} 1 & \text{if } n = 1, \\ n \times f(n-1) & \text{if } n > 1. \end{cases} \tag{2.6}$$

The following is a simple implementation of factorials.

```
# Section 2.10.1: factorial1.py
import sys
def f1(n):
  if (n == 1):
    return 1
  return n * f1(n - 1)
```

Equation (2.6) can be rewritten as

$$f(n) = n \times (n-1) \times (n-2) ... \times 1 \text{ if } n > 1. \tag{2.7}$$

Factorials are not good examples to explain recursion because recursion is not needed to calculate factorials. The following is an implementation without recursion:

```
def f2(n):
  if (n == 1):
    return 1
  product = 1
  for x in range(2, n + 1):
    product *= x
  return product
```

There is no true reason why factorials must be implemented using recursion. Even though Equation (2.6) is recursive, it is possible to implement the solution without recursion. Some introductory books use factorials as the first example of recursion. Unfortunately, these books may unintentionally give readers the impression that recursion is unnecessary. The following program uses `timeit` to measure the execution time in seconds (running each function 10000 times) and also calculates the ratios.

```
import timeit
for n in range(41, 51):
  if (f1(n) != f2(n)):
    print(f'f1({n}) = {f1(n)}, f2({n}) = {f2(n)}')
  t1 = timeit.timeit(lambda: f1(n), number = 10000)
```

```
    t2 = timeit.timeit(lambda: f2(n), number = 10000)
    print(f'n = {n}, t1= {t1:.6e}, t2 = {t2:.6e}, ratio = {t1/t2:.4}')
```

This is the program's output:

```
n = 41, t1= 4.055400e-02, t2 = 3.127151e-02, ratio = 1.297
n = 42, t1= 4.198190e-02, t2 = 2.701503e-02, ratio = 1.554
n = 43, t1= 4.254361e-02, t2 = 2.759581e-02, ratio = 1.542
n = 44, t1= 4.300595e-02, t2 = 3.223995e-02, ratio = 1.334
n = 45, t1= 4.418152e-02, t2 = 3.082441e-02, ratio = 1.433
n = 46, t1= 4.497132e-02, t2 = 2.937980e-02, ratio = 1.531
n = 47, t1= 4.611847e-02, t2 = 3.289959e-02, ratio = 1.402
n = 48, t1= 4.635357e-02, t2 = 2.741286e-02, ratio = 1.691
n = 49, t1= 4.604656e-02, t2 = 2.977703e-02, ratio = 1.546
n = 50, t1= 4.675175e-02, t2 = 3.282295e-02, ratio = 1.424
```

As can be seen from this comparison, the execution time of `f1` is about 29.7% - 69.1% longer than the execution time of `f2`. In other words, the recursive implementation is slower.

### 2.10.2 Fibonacci Numbers

Calculating Fibonacci numbers is another popular example used in introductory books teaching recursion. The numbers are defined as follows:

$$f(n) = \begin{cases} 1 & \text{if } n \text{ is 1 or 2} \\ f(n-1) + f(n-2) & \text{if } n > 2. \end{cases} \tag{2.8}$$

This formula is similar to the ball selection problem in Section 1.2, but the base conditions are different. The difference is the starting values of $f(1)$ and $f(2)$. Below is a straightforward implementation of the definition:

```
# Section 2.10.2: fibonacci.py
def fib1(n):
    if (n < 1): # invalid
        return 0
    if ((n == 1) or (n == 2)):
        return 1
    return (fib1(n-1) + fib1(n-2))
```

This is a "top-down" approach. It computes $f(n)$ by using the values of $f(n-1)$ and $f(n-2)$. If $n$ is greater than 2, then the function computes $f(n-1)$ by using the values of $f(n-2)$ and $f(n-3)$. This process continues until $n$ is either 1 or 2.

It is possible to calculate Fibonacci numbers without recursion as shown here.

```
8  def fib2(n):
9      if (n < 1): # invalid
10         return 0
11     if ((n == 1) or (n == 2)):
12         return 1
13     a = 1
14     b = 1
15     for i in range(3, n + 1):
16         a, b = b, a + b
17     return b
```

This program does not use recursion, even though the definition of $f(n)$ is recursive. This program calculates $f(n)$ "bottom-up". Instead of calculating $f(n) = f(n-1) + f(n-2)$, this method stores the values of $f(1)$ and $f(2)$ in `a` and `b` respectively. Then, the function computes $f(3)$ by using the sum of `a` and `b`. We can reuse the variables: For the next iteration, the value in `b` is stored in `a`; the value of `a` + `b` is stored in `b` (line 16). At this point `b` stores $f(3)$ and `a` stores $f(2)$. From $f(2)$ and $f(3)$, we can calculate $f(4)$. This process repeats until we get $f(n)$.

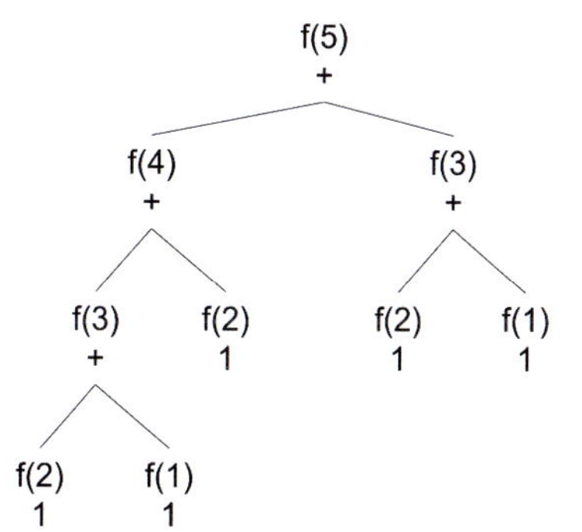

**FIGURE 2.4**: *Call graph* of $f(5)$.

Why do we bother to consider the bottom-up approach? Isn't the recursive function good enough? It certainly looks simple since it is a direct translation from the mathematical definition. The problem is that the recursive function does a lot of unnecessary work, making it rather slow. Figure 2.4 illustrates the sequence of computation. To compute $f(5)$, it is necessary to compute $f(4)$ and $f(3)$. To compute $f(4)$, it is necessary to compute $f(3)$ and $f(2)$. Computing $f(3)$ requires the sum of $f(2)$ and $f(1)$. Figure 2.4 shows that $f(3) = f(2) + f(1)$ is computed twice. Is computing $f(3) = f(2) + f(1)$ twice a problem? Let's compute $f(n)$ when $n$ is large. By definition,

$$f(n) = f(n-1) + f(n-2). \tag{2.9}$$

We can apply this definition to compute $f(n-1)$ using $f(n-2)$ and $f(n-3)$:

$$f(n-1) = f(n-2) + f(n-3). \tag{2.10}$$

Thus, we can express $f(n)$ using $f(n-2)$ and $f(n-3)$:

$$\begin{aligned} f(n) &= f(n-1) & & & + \ & f(n-2) \\ &= f(n-2) & + \ & f(n-3) & + \ & f(n-2) \\ &= 2f(n-2) & + \ & f(n-3). & & \end{aligned} \tag{2.11}$$

This equation indicates that in order to compute $f(n)$, we need to compute $f(n-2)$ twice (the coefficient is 2). This is a waste of time because we should calculate $f(n-2)$ only once and remember its value, without computing it again the second time. If $n$ is large, $n-2$ is not a base condition. Thus, we have to compute $f(n-2)$ using $f(n-3)$ and $f(n-4)$.

$$f(n-2) = f(n-3) + f(n-4). \tag{2.12}$$

Replacing $f(n-2)$ in Equation (2.11), we can obtain

$$\begin{aligned} f(n) &= 2f(n-2) & + \ & f(n-3) \\ &= 2f(n-3) + 2f(n-4) & + \ & f(n-3) \\ &= 3f(n-3) & + \ & 2f(n-4). \end{aligned} \tag{2.13}$$

The coefficient 3 in front of $f(n-3)$ means we need to compute $f(n-3)$ three times in order to compute $f(n)$. The following equations show that the coefficients become larger and larger as the arguments approach the base conditions.

$$\begin{aligned} f(n) &= f(n-1) & + \ & f(n-2) & & \\ &= 2f(n-2) & + \ & f(n-3) & & \\ &= 2(f(n-3) & + \ & f(n-4)) & + \ & f(n-3) \\ &= 3f(n-3) & + \ & 2f(n-4) & & \\ &= 3(f(n-4) & + \ & f(n-5)) & + \ & 2f(n-4) \\ &= 5f(n-4) & + \ & 3f(n-5) & & \\ &= 5(f(n-5) & + \ & f(n-6)) & + \ & 3f(n-5) \\ &= 8f(n-5) & + \ & 5f(n-6) & & \\ &= 8(f(n-6) & + \ & f(n-7)) & + \ & 5f(n-6) \\ &= 13f(n-6) & + \ & 8f(n-7). & & \end{aligned} \tag{2.14}$$

This type of redundant computation becomes a serious problem if $n$ is large: Table 2.2 lists the coefficients for computing $f(n)$. Let $c_{n,k}$ be the coefficient of $f(n-k)$. Using the recursive form, we need to compute $f(n-k)$ as many as $c_{n,k}$ times. As you can see $c_{n,k}$ becomes larger as $k$ becomes larger (i.e., $n-k$ becomes smaller). The coefficient of $f(n-k)$ is actually $f(k+1)$. Table 2.2 and Figure 2.4 both express similar concepts. If we count the occurrences of $f(2)$ in Figure 2.4, we find that it is called three times. The recursive method for calculating Fibonacci numbers is slow because it computes the same values over and over again.

Does this mean that recursion is slow? Why should we even bother to learn recursion? The problem is not recursion, but this example. In this example, recursion is used incorrectly. Recursion can be fast in some efficient algorithms explained earlier (such as binary search in Sections 2.7 and quick sort in 2.8).

**TABLE 2.2**: Coefficients for computing $f(n-k)$.

| function | coefficient |
|---|---|
| $f(n-1)$ | $1 = f(2)$ |
| $f(n-2)$ | $2 = f(3)$ |
| $f(n-3)$ | $3 = f(4)$ |
| $f(n-4)$ | $5 = f(5)$ |
| $f(n-5)$ | $8 = f(6)$ |
| $f(n-6)$ | $13 = f(7)$ |

Recursion is a useful tool, but like any tool, it should be applied appropriately. You wouldn't use a knife to hit a nail, nor a hammer to cut paper. Neither tool is inherently better. Their usefulness depends on the task you are trying to complete. Let's consider another scenario: You have a bike, and you have a car. Which one is better? If a bike is always better, why do you need a car? If a car is always better, why do you need a bike? To decide which is better, you need to ask, "Where do I want to go?" If you want to visit a friend living half a kilometer away, a bike can be more convenient than a car. If your destination is one hundred kilometers away, a car is faster than a bike. You need to select the right tool for the problem.

Many books use Fibonacci numbers to explain recursion but do not explain that this particular top-down method is slower than the bottom-up method. As a result, some readers mistakenly generalize and think recursion is always slow. The truth is that recursion is a good method for solving some problems, not all problems. Recursion is slow if it is not properly used.

Python has a way to reduce unnecessary computation by remembering (i.e., *caching*) a function's value if this function has already been called earlier using the same argument. In computers, *caching* means storing frequently used information in faster memory. The following program uses `@cache` from Python's `functools`.

```
from functools import cache
@cache
def fib3(n):
  if (n < 1): # invalid
```

```
    return 0
  if ((n == 1) or (n == 2)):
    return 1
  else:
    return (fib3(n - 1) + fib3(n - 2))
```

The program uses `timeit` to measure the execution time. The following program compares the execution time of the three implementations of Fibonacci numbers:

```
import time
def execution_time(func, range):
  times = {}
  for n in range:
    start_time = time.time() # Record the start time
    val = func(n)
    end_time = time.time() # Record the end time
    times[n] = end_time - start_time
  return times
if __name__ == "__main__":
  r = range(10, 41)
  time1 = execution_time(fib1, r)
  time2 = execution_time(fib2, r)
  time3 = execution_time(fib3, r)
  for k in time1:
    print(f'n={k}: t1/t2 = {time1[k] / time2[k]:.6e}, t2/t3 =
    ↪ {time2[k] / time3[k]:.6e}')
```

This is the program's output. As you can see, `fib2` is much faster than `fib1` because `fib2` has no redundant computation; `fib3` is even faster than `fib2` because `fib3` uses cache to remember the values of earlier called functions.

```
n=24: t1/t2 = 7.981000e+03, t2/t3 = 4.000000e+00
n=25: t1/t2 = 1.104883e+04, t2/t3 = 3.000000e+00
n=26: t1/t2 = 2.050225e+04, t2/t3 = 2.000000e+00
n=27: t1/t2 = 2.797020e+04, t2/t3 = 5.000000e+00
n=28: t1/t2 = 3.584250e+04, t2/t3 = 3.000000e+00
n=29: t1/t2 = 7.149020e+04, t2/t3 = 1.666667e+00
n=30: t1/t2 = 9.414633e+04, t2/t3 = 3.000000e+00
n=31: t1/t2 = 2.499530e+05, t2/t3 = 2.500000e+00
n=32: t1/t2 = 4.630705e+05, t2/t3 = 3.000000e+00
n=33: t1/t2 = 9.012210e+05, t2/t3 = 2.500000e+00
n=34: t1/t2 = 1.228496e+06, t2/t3 = 3.000000e+00
n=35: t1/t2 = 1.278247e+06, t2/t3 = 1.666667e+00
n=36: t1/t2 = 1.479278e+06, t2/t3 = 3.500000e+00
```

```
n=37: t1/t2 = 2.793747e+06, t2/t3 = 6.000000e+00
n=38: t1/t2 = 4.555079e+06, t2/t3 = 3.500000e+00
n=39: t1/t2 = 8.129839e+06, t2/t3 = 3.000000e+00
n=40: t1/t2 = 1.097218e+07, t2/t3 = 3.500000e+00
```

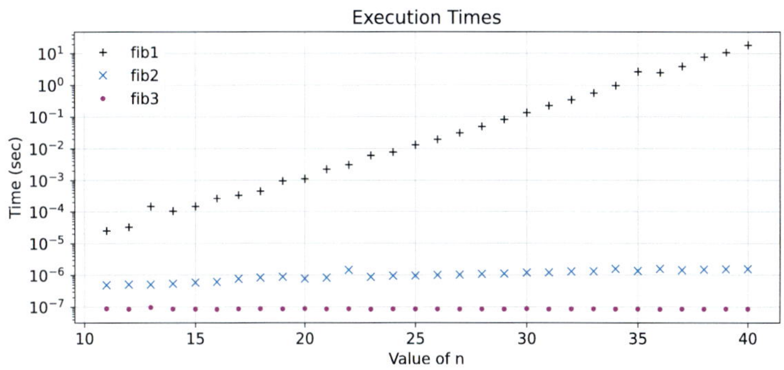


**FIGURE 2.5**: Execution time of the three implementations. The execution time of `fib1` grows exponentially.

The following program can draw the execution time as the argument changes:

```
import matplotlib.pyplot as plt
k_values = list(time1.keys())
plt.figure(figsize=(10, 4))
plt.plot(k_values, list(time1.values()), 'k+', label='fib1')
plt.plot(k_values, list(time2.values()), 'x',  label='fib2')
plt.plot(k_values, list(time3.values()), 'm.', label='fib3')
plt.xlabel('Value of n')
plt.ylabel('Time (sec)')
plt.title('Execution Times')
plt.yscale('log') # set the y-axis to a logarithmic scale
plt.grid(True)
plt.legend() # display the legend
plt.show()
```

Figure 2.5 is the program's output. Please notice the y-axis is on a log scale. The execution time of the recursive implementation (`fib1`) grows quickly. The execution times of the other two implementations remain almost unchanged. The figure shows that `fib2` takes longer than `fib3`. The execution times of `fib2` and `fib3` are very small and can fluctuate slightly. Using `@cache` makes `fib3` even faster than `fib2` because `fib3` remembers the previous calculated values: `fib3(1)`, `fib3(2)`, ..., `fib3(n−1)`. To calculate `fib3(n)`, `fib3` needs only one addition `fib3(n−1) + fib3(n−2)`. In contrast, `fib2` needs to calculate `fib2(3)`, `fib2(4)`,..., `fib2(n−1)` every time.

It is possible to calculate Fibonacci numbers even faster than `fib2` or `fib3`. Let's go back to the Fibonacci numbers. Equation (2.14) suggests the following:

$$f(n) = f(x+1)f(n-x) + f(x)f(n-x-1) \tag{2.15}$$

Suppose $n$ is an even number. Then there exists an integer $m$ such that $n = 2m$. Set $x$ equal to $m$. The equation can be rewritten as

$$\begin{aligned} f(2m) &= f(m+1)f(2m-m) + f(m)f(2m-m-1) \\ &= f(m+1)f(m) + f(m)f(m-1) \\ &= f(m)(f(m+1) + f(m-1)) \\ &= f(m)(f(m+1) + f(m+1) - f(m)) \\ &= f(m)(2f(m+1) - f(m)). \end{aligned} \tag{2.16}$$

This means that $f(2m)$ can be calculated by using $f(m+1)$ and $f(m)$ without going through $f(2m-1)$, $f(2m-2)$, $f(2m-3)$, and so on. This recursive method can calculate the Fibonacci numbers much faster. Similarly, suppose $n$ is an odd number: $n = 2m+1$ and set $x$ to $m$, Equation (2.15) can be rewritten as

$$\begin{aligned} f(2m+1) &= f(m+1)f(2m+1-m) + f(m)f(2m+1-m-1) \\ &= f(m+1)f(m+1) + f(m)f(m) \\ &= f(m+1)^2 + f(m)^2. \end{aligned} \tag{2.17}$$

Consider Equations (2.16) and 2.17). The argument $2m$ or $2m+1$ can be reduced by half to $m+1$ or $m$. This can calculate Fibonacci numbers in logarithmic time:

```python
def fib4helper(n): # log time implementation
    if (n <= 1):
        return (1, 1)
    else:
        a, b = fib4helper(n // 2)
        # If n = 2m or 2m + 1, n // 2 is m.
        # a is f(m), b is f(m+1)
        c = a * (2 * b - a) # f(2m)
        d = a * a + b * b   # f(2m + 1)
        if (n % 2) == 0:
```

```
66            return (c, d) # f(2m), f(2m + 1)
67        else:
68            return (d, c + d) # f(2m + 1), f(2m + 2)
69 def fib4(n):
70   return fib4helper(n)[0]
```

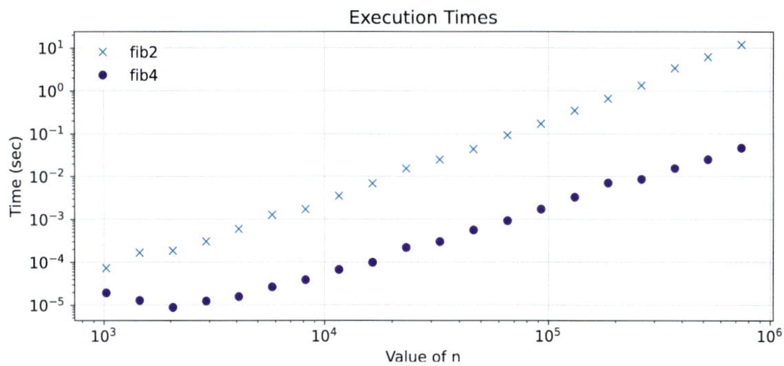


**FIGURE 2.6**: When $n$ is very large, `fib4` is faster than `fib2`.

Line 60 uses Python's integer division `//`. If `n` is an even number, `n = 2m`, then `n // 2` is `m`. If `n` is an odd number, `n = 2m + 1`, then `n // 2` is also `m`. The values of `a` and `b` are `f(m)` and `f(m+1)` respectively. From Equations (2.16) and (2.17), `c` and `d` are `f(2m)` and `f(2m + 1)`. Figure 2.6 compares the execution times of `fib2` and `fib4`. As the figure shows, when `n` is very large, `fib4` is faster than `fib2`. When `n` is small (not shown in the figure), `fib2` is faster because `fib4` needs many operations, including addition, multiplication, and subtraction. Please notice that both the x-axis and the y-axis use log scales. When $n$ is large, the Fibonacci numbers are extremely large and need many digits. Fortunately, Python has *arbitrary precision* for integers and can use as many digits as needed.

Appendix B explains another way to accelerate the computation of recursion by removing *tail recursion*. With this understanding about when recursion is slow and how to make recursion faster, the rest of this book will focus on functionalities and clarity of explanation. Some of the implementations may be inefficient. Readers are encouraged to discover when efficiency can be improved by eliminating redundant computation.

## 2.11 Problems

### 2.11.1 Fibonacci Numbers: Count Number of Calls

Using the definition of Fibonacci numbers in (2.8), write a program that counts how many times the function $f$ is called when $n$ is between 2 and 9.

**Answer:**

```
# Section 2.11.1: countfib.py
# count the number of times the fib function is called
def fib(n, counts):
    counts[n] += 1
    if (n < 1): # invalid
        return 0
    if (n == 1):
        return 1
    if (n == 2):
        return 1
    return (fib(n-1, counts) + fib(n-2, counts))
if __name__ == "__main__":
    size = 9
    for n in range(2, size + 1):
        counts = [0 for ind in range(n + 1)]
        fib(n, counts)
        print(f'fib({n}), counts={counts}')
```

This is the program's output:

```
fib(2), counts=[0, 0, 1]
fib(3), counts=[0, 1, 1, 1]
fib(4), counts=[0, 1, 2, 1, 1]
fib(5), counts=[0, 2, 3, 2, 1, 1]
fib(6), counts=[0, 3, 5, 3, 2, 1, 1]
fib(7), counts=[0, 5, 8, 5, 3, 2, 1, 1]
fib(8), counts=[0, 8, 13, 8, 5, 3, 2, 1, 1]
fib(9), counts=[0, 13, 21, 13, 8, 5, 3, 2, 1, 1]
```

This shows that $f(0)$ is never called because the base conditions are $f(1)$ and $f(2)$. If we check the output vertically, $f(1)$ is called 1, 1, 2, 3, 5, 8, 13 times. This is actually the Fibonacci numbers, as explained on Page 59.

### 2.11.2 Balls of Three Colors

Write a program to generate Table 1.7.

**Answer:**

The following program can print the table:

```python
# Section 2.11.2: threecolorballs.py
# print the number of options for selecting balls of three colors
import sys
def r(n): # number of options to select n balls, first is red
  if (n <= 1):
    return 1
  return (b(n-1) + g(n-1))
def g(n): # number of options to select n balls, first is green
  if (n <= 1):
    return 1
  return (r(n-1) + b(n-1))
def b(n): # number of options to select n balls, first is blue
  if (n <= 1):
    return 1
  return (r(n-1) + g(n-1) + b(n-1))
def f(n): # number of options to select n balls
  return (r(n) + g(n) + b(n))
def print_options(label, func, num):
  print(f'{label}(n)', end=' | ')
  for n in range(1, num + 1):
    print(f'{func(n):5}', end=' ')
  print('')
def three_colors_balls(num):
  print('    ', end=' | ')
  for n in range(1, num + 1):
    print(f'{n:5}', end=' ')
  print('')
  print('-' * 50)
  print_options('r', r, num)
  print_options('g', g, num)
  print_options('b', b, num)
  print_options('f', f, num)
three_colors_balls(6)
```

This is the program's output when the input argument is 6:

```
      |     1     2     3     4     5     6
-------------------------------------------------
r(n)  |     1     2     5    12    29    70
g(n)  |     1     2     5    12    29    70
b(n)  |     1     3     7    17    41    99
f(n)  |     3     7    17    41    99   239
```

### 2.11.3 Count the Parentheses

Write a Python program to generate Table 1.6.

**Answer:**

The following program can print the table:

```python
# Section 2.11.3: parenthesestable.py
def g(n, m):
  if (n > m):
    return 0
  if ((n == 0) and (m != 0)):
    return 1
  if ((n == 0) and (m == 0)):
    return 0
  return g(n - 1, m) + g(n, m - 1)
import random
def countparentheses():
  n = random.randint(1,8) + 1
  # print(f'g({n},{m}) = {g(n,m)}')
  print(' ',end=' | ')
  for r in range(1, n):
    print(f'{r:5}', end=' ')
  print('')
  print('-' * 7 * n)
  for m in range(1, n):
    print(m, end=' | ')
    for r in range(1, n):
      print(f'{g(r,m):5}', end=' ')
    print('')
countparentheses()
```

This is the program's output when the input argument is 6:

```
  |     0     1     2     3     4     5     6
-------------------------------------------------
0 |     0     0     0     0     0     0     0
```

```
1 |      1     1     0     0     0     0     0
2 |      1     2     2     0     0     0     0
3 |      1     3     5     5     0     0     0
4 |      1     4     9    14    14     0     0
5 |      1     5    14    28    42    42     0
6 |      1     6    20    48    90   132   132
```

### 2.11.4 Fibonacci Numbers

Prove Equation (2.15) is true.

**Answer:**

The equation is true when $x$ is 1, 2, 3, up to $n-2$ (because $n-x-1$ must be greater than zero). We can use *mathematical induction* to prove that the equation is true in general. Suppose the equation is true for $n$ is 1, 2, ..., up to $k$. What happens when $n$ is $k+1$?

$$\begin{aligned} f(k+1) &= f(k) + f(k-1) \\ &= f(x+1)f(k-x) + f(x)f(k-x-1) + \\ &\quad f(x+1)f(k-1-x) + f(x)f(k-1-x-1) \\ &= f(x+1)(f(k-x) + f(k-1-x)) + \\ &\quad f(x)(f(k-x-1) + f(k-1-x-1)) \\ &= f(x+1)f(k+1-x) + f(x)f(k+1-x-1) \end{aligned} \tag{2.18}$$

Equation (2.15) is still valid when $n$ is $k+1$. Thus, the equation is valid for any integer $n > 2$.

### 2.11.5 Integer Partition

Consider the program on Page 33. The original line is

```
for val in range(1, num + 1):
```

If it is replaced by

```
for val in range(1, num): # remove + 1
```

How are the outputs changed?

**Answer:**

The program produces no output because the condition at line 8 is never satisfied.

---

Modify the program on Page 33 so that it prints alternate odd and even numbers.

**Answer:**

```
# Section 2.11.5: partitionoddeven.py
from datetime import datetime
class Counter:
    def __init__(self):
        self.value = 0
    def increment(self):
        self.value += 1
def partition1(num, usedint, ind, count, results):
    # generate only valid partitions
    count.increment()
    if (num == 0): # stop condition
        results.append(usedint[0:ind])
        return
    for val in range(1, num + 1):
        valid = False
        if (ind == 0):
            valid = True
        elif ((usedint[ind - 1] % 2) != (val % 2)):
            valid = True
        if (valid == True):
            usedint[ind] = val
            partition1(num - val, usedint, ind + 1, count,
             ↪ results)
def partition2(num, usedint, ind, count, results):
    # generate all partitions, print only valid partitions
    count.increment()
    if (num == 0):
        valid = True
        for i in range(1, ind):
            if ((usedint[i - 1] % 2) == (usedint[i] % 2)):
                valid = False
        if (valid == True):
            results.append(usedint[0:ind])
        return
    for val in range(1, num + 1):
        usedint[ind] = val
        partition2(num - val, usedint, ind + 1, count, results)
def measuretime(num, func, message):
    usedint = [0] * num # initialize to 0
    count = Counter()
    results = []
    start_time = datetime.now()
```

```
42      func(num, usedint, 0, count, results)
43      end_time = datetime.now()
44      print(message)
45      if (num < 9):
46        print(results)
47      print(f'len = {len(results)}')
48      print(f'count: {count.value}')
49      print(f'time: {end_time - start_time}')
50  def partition(num):
51      measuretime(num, partition1, '--- partition 1 ---')
52      measuretime(num, partition2, '--- partition 2 ---')
53  if __name__ == "__main__":
54      n = 7
55      partition(n)
```

Please pay special attention to lines 14 - 20. A number can be used if one of two conditions is satisfied:

1. This is the first number (line 16).
2. This is not the first number, and its parity is different from the previous number (line 18). An integer's parity indicates whether it is an odd number or an even number.

This is the program's output when partitioning 7:

```
--- partition 1 ---
[[1, 2, 1, 2, 1], [1, 6], [2, 1, 4], [2, 3, 2], [2, 5], [3, 4],
↪  [4, 1, 2], [4, 3], [5, 2], [6, 1], [7]]
len = 11
count: 31
time: 0:00:00.000045
--- partition 2 ---
[[1, 2, 1, 2, 1], [1, 6], [2, 1, 4], [2, 3, 2], [2, 5], [3, 4],
↪  [4, 1, 2], [4, 3], [5, 2], [6, 1], [7]]
len = 11
count: 128
time: 0:00:00.000442
```

This is the program's output when partitioning 25:

```
--- partition 1 ---
len = 13785
count: 41942
time: 0:00:00.024696
--- partition 2 ---
len = 13785
```

```
count: 33554432
time: 0:00:34.399300
```

As can be seen, the first method is much faster (shorter execution time) because it generates only valid partitions. In contrast, the second method generates all possible partitions and prints only the valid partitions. The second method generates many invalid partitions unnecessarily.

---

Section 1.5.3 explains a method to calculate the number of partitions using increasing values. Table 1.3 shows the numbers for partitioning 1 to 15.

This problem asks you to write a program that partitions 20 using increasing values. The program uses two different methods:

1. Generate only valid partitions: Check the previous value and use a larger value.
2. Generate all partitions and print only valid partitions.

Compare the execution time of these two methods.

**Answer:**

The following program compares these two methods.

```python
# Section 2.11.5: partitionincreasing.py
# partition a number using increasing numbers
from datetime import datetime
class Counter:
    def __init__(self):
        self.value = 0
    def increment(self):
        self.value += 1
def partition1(num, usedint, ind, minval, count, results):
    # generate only valid partitions
    count.increment()
    if (num == 0): # stop condition
        results.append(usedint[0:ind])
        return
    for val in range(minval, num + 1):
        valid = False
        if (ind == 0):
            valid = True
        elif (usedint[ind - 1] < val):
            valid = True
        if (valid == True):
            usedint[ind] = val
```

```
            partition1(num - val, usedint, ind + 1, val + 1, count, results)
def partition2(num, usedint, ind, minval, count, results):
    # generate all partitions, print only valid partitions
    count.increment()
    if (num == 0):
        valid = True
        for i in range(1, ind):
            if (usedint[i - 1] >= usedint[i]):
                valid = False
        if (valid == True):
            results.append(usedint[0:ind])
        return
    for val in range(1, num + 1):
        usedint[ind] = val
        partition2(num - val, usedint, ind + 1, minval, count, results)
def measuretime(num, func, message):
    usedint = [0] * num # initialize to 0
    count = Counter()
    results = []
    start_time = datetime.now()
    func(num, usedint, 0, 1, count, results)
    end_time = datetime.now()
    print(message)
    if (num < 10):
        print(results)
    print(f'count: {count.value}')
    print(f'time: {end_time - start_time}')
def partition(num):
    measuretime(num, partition1, '--- partition 1 ---')
    measuretime(num, partition2, '--- partition 2 ---')
if __name__ == "__main__":
    n = 9
    partition(n)
```

This is the program's output when `n` is 9:

```
--- partition 1 ---
[[1, 2, 6], [1, 3, 5], [1, 8], [2, 3, 4], [2, 7], [3, 6], [4, 5], [9]]
count: 33
time: 0:00:00.000025
--- partition 2 ---
```

```
[[1, 2, 6], [1, 3, 5], [1, 8], [2, 3, 4], [2, 7], [3, 6], [4,
    5], [9]]
count: 512
time: 0:00:00.000245
```

This is the program's output when `n` is 25:

```
--- partition 1 ---
count: 904
time: 0:00:00.000488
--- partition 2 ---
count: 33554432
time: 0:00:21.380244
```

As we can see, the second method takes much longer than the first method. The second method is called many more times than the first method. The first method is more efficient because it generates only valid partitions (controlled by line 21). In contrast, the second method generates all possible partitions and discards invalid partitions only before printing (line 32). The two functions do not print the partitions (lines 13 and 33). Instead, they append the results to the lists called `results`. Both `partition1` and `partition2` are recursive, but their execution time varies significantly: `partition2` takes much longer time. The differences between these two functions may be subtle. This is another example illustrating the importance of using recursion carefully.

### 2.11.6 Shuffle Cards

Table 2.1 shows that shuffling only once does not produce all possible orders. Will shuffling twice produce all possible orders of 8 cards? For 52 cards, how many times should the cards be shuffled?

**Answer:**

If we shuffle $n$ cards twice, we can obtain $(2^n - 2)^2$ results (some results are counted multiple times). Table 2.3 shows the number of unique orders after shuffling twice. As you can see, shuffling twice greatly increased the number of possible results, but many are still missing.

**TABLE 2.3**: Number of unique orders after shuffling twice.

| $n$ | 2 | 3 | 4 | 5 | 6 | 7 | 8 |
|---|---|---|---|---|---|---|---|
| $(2^n - 2)^2$ | 4 | 36 | 196 | 900 | 3844 | 15876 | 64516 |
| unique orders | 2 | 6 | 24 | 119 | 662 | 3728 | 20160 |
| $n!$ | 2 | 6 | 24 | 120 | 720 | 5040 | 40320 |
| ratio | 100% | 100% | 100% | 99.2% | 91.9% | 74.0% | 50% |

These numbers are obtained by the following command in Linux:

```
python3 shuffle2.py 8 2 | sort | uniq | wc
```

The output of the `shuffle2.py` program is sent to the `sort` program using Linux *pipe*. In Linux, adding `|` between two programs means the first program's output is sent to the second program's input. The `sort` program arranges the cards so that the same orders appear together. We use pipe again and send the sorted result to the `uniq` command. This command removes duplicates. The next command `wc` produces three numbers:

1. the number of lines,
2. the number of words,
3. the number of bytes.

The first shows the unique orders after shuffling 8 cards twice.

For a deck of 52 cards, how many times should the deck be shuffled? We are going to use $2^n - 2$ to estimate the number of results, even though it counts some orders multiple times. The question can be formulated as finding $m$ such that

$$(2^n - 2)^m > n!. \tag{2.19}$$

When $n$ is 52, $2^n - 2$ is approximately $4.5 \times 10^{15}$, and $n!$ is approximately $8.1 \times 10^{67}$. To calculate $m$, take the logarithm on both sides:

$$m \times \log(2^{52} - 2) > \log(52!) \Rightarrow m > \frac{\log(52!)}{\log(2^{52} - 2)}. \tag{2.20}$$

The value of $\log(52!)$ is approximately 67.9; the value of $\log(2^{52} - 2)$ is approximately 15.7. The ratio is approximately 4.33. Thus, $m > 4.33$. We need to shuffle five times. Please note that this estimation counts some orders multiple times. Also, this estimation considers the cases when one hand may have very few cards (as few as only one card). In reality, the two hands will likely have nearly the same number of cards. As a result, the actual number of results will be lower than this estimation. Some careful analyses suggest that 52 cards should be shuffled at least 7 times.

### 2.11.7 Tower of Hanoi with 4 Poles

Expand Section 2.3 and consider four poles. How many movements are needed if there are six disks?

**Answer:**

The following program prints the movements of disks:

```
# Section 2.11.7: hanoi4.py (4 poles)
class Counter:
  def __init__(self):
    self.count = 0
  def increment(self, num = 1):
    self.count += num
  def get(self):
    return self.count
def move4(disk, src, dest, additional1, additional2, cnt):
  if (disk <= 0):
    print('Invalid argument')
    return
  if (disk == 1):
    cnt.increment()
    print('move disk 1 from ' + src + ' to ' + dest)
    return
  if (disk == 2):
    cnt.increment(3)
    print('move disk 1 from ' + src + ' to ' + additional1)
    print('move disk 2 from ' + src + ' to ' + dest)
    print('move disk 1 from ' + additional1 + ' to ' + dest)
    return
  move4(disk - 2, src, additional1, additional2, dest, cnt)
  cnt.increment(3)
  print('move disk ' + str(disk - 1) +  ' from ' + src + ' to ' + additional2)
  print('move disk ' + str(disk) +  ' from ' + src + ' to ' + dest)
  print('move disk ' + str(disk - 1) +  ' from ' + additional2 + ' to ' + dest)
  move4(disk - 2, additional1, dest, src, additional2, cnt)
def testhanoi4():
    counters = {}
    for num in range(2, 7):
      cnt = Counter()
      print(f'\nnum = {num}')
      move4(num, 'A', 'B', 'C', 'D', cnt)
      counters[num] = cnt.get()
    print('\ncounters:')
    for num in counters:
      print(f'num = {num}, counter = {counters[num]}')
testhanoi4()
```

This is the output when moving 5 disks:

```
move disk 1 from A to D
move disk 2 from A to B
move disk 3 from A to C
move disk 2 from B to C
move disk 1 from D to C
move disk 4 from A to D
move disk 5 from A to B
move disk 4 from D to B
move disk 1 from C to A
move disk 2 from C to D
move disk 3 from C to B
move disk 2 from D to B
move disk 1 from A to B
```

# Chapter 3

# Sudoku

This chapter explains how to solve Sudoku problems. Figure 3.1 shows an example of a Sudoku puzzle and its solution. Each number has a specific color.

## 3.1 Depth-First Search

Recursion is frequently used for solving many board games (such as Go or Chess). In these games, the effects of a single decision are not immediately obvious. Instead, the impact depends on both prior and future decisions. As a result, a player must think several decisions ahead. A player may consider a sequence of decisions and discover that the first decision is undesirable. Then, this player considers another sequence of decisions.

Figure 3.2 (a) shows a *decision graph.* At the top, a game player has three options marked A, B, and C. The arrows indicate the possible subsequent options. In this graph, if the player chooses A, two options, D and E, become available. If the player chooses B, the next option is only F. Some different options may share the same next options. Option J is available if the player chooses D or E. Some options will lose the game. This graph shows that options I, H, and O will lose (marked by crosses). Option J leads to winning the game (expressed by a check mark). Option N leads to more options, and the game continues.

When the player encounters the options A, B, and C, the player does not know which one is good and which one is bad. The player has to consider the options after choosing one of them. Suppose this player chooses A first. Then, the player faces two options, D and E. The player chooses D. Now, the player has two more options: I and J. Choosing I will lose the game. Thus, I is a bad option. From D, the player may choose J and win the game. The player decides to choose the sequence A, D, and J. Please notice that this player has not considered options B or C. When the player discovers that I is a bad option, the player goes back one step and considers the other option from D,

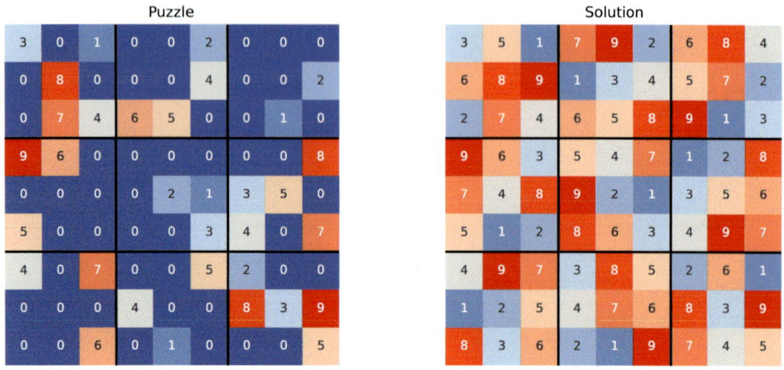


(a) (b)

**FIGURE 3.1**: (a) A Sudoku puzzle and (b) the solution.

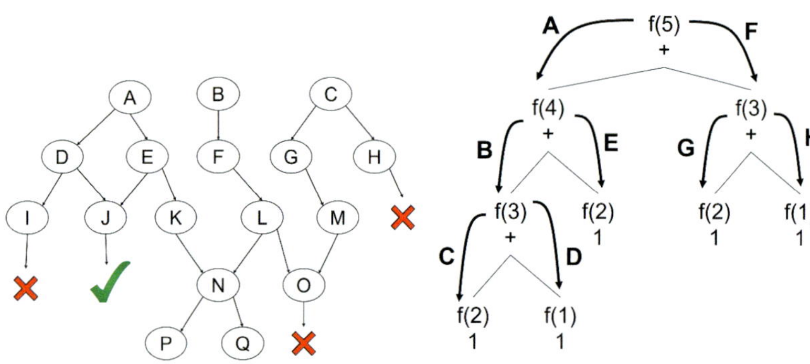


(a) (b)

**FIGURE 3.2**: (a) A decision graph. (b) Execution order of Figure 2.4 if Python cache is not used. Python cache was explained in Section 2.10.2.

while keeping the first decision of choosing A. This is called the *depth-first search* strategy. The player chooses one option and goes as far as possible. If an option is undesirable (I loses the game), the player returns to the most recent decision (D) and takes another option (J). This is called *backtrack*.

Suppose the player starts with option C instead. After selecting C, the player may choose G or H. If the player chooses H, the player loses. Thus, H is a bad choice. The player considers the only other option, G. From G, the player must choose M and then O. This sequence of options loses the game. After

| | | | | | | | | |
|---|---|---|---|---|---|---|---|---|
| 1 | 8 | 3 | 2 | 7 | 6 | 5 | 4 | 9 |
| 5 | 2 | 7 | 4 | 9 | 8 | 3 | 1 | 6 |
| 6 | 4 | 9 | 1 | 3 | 5 | 7 | 2 | 8 |
| 7 | 9 | 1 | 5 | 6 | 2 | 8 | 3 | 4 |
| 2 | 3 | 8 | 7 | 4 | 9 | 6 | 5 | 1 |
| 4 | 5 | 6 | 3 | 8 | 1 | 2 | 9 | 7 |
| 8 | 1 | 2 | 9 | 5 | 7 | 4 | 6 | 3 |
| 9 | 6 | 4 | 8 | 2 | 3 | 1 | 7 | 5 |
| 3 | 7 | 5 | 6 | 1 | 4 | 9 | 8 | 2 |

(a)

| | | | | | | | | |
|---|---|---|---|---|---|---|---|---|
| 1 | 8 | 3 | 2 | 7 | 6 | 5 | 4 | 9 |
| 5 | 2 | 7 | 4 | 9 | 8 | 3 | 1 | 6 |
| 6 | 4 | 9 | 1 | 3 | 5 | 7 | 2 | 8 |
| 7 | 9 | 1 | 5 | 6 | 2 | 8 | 3 | 4 |
| 2 | 3 | 8 | 7 | 4 | 9 | 6 | 5 | 1 |
| 4 | 5 | 6 | 3 | 8 | 1 | 2 | 9 | 7 |
| 8 | 1 | 2 | 9 | 5 | 7 | 4 | 6 | 3 |
| 9 | 6 | 4 | 8 | 2 | 3 | 1 | 7 | 5 |
| 3 | 7 | 5 | 6 | 1 | 4 | 9 | 8 | 2 |

(b)

| | | | | | | | | |
|---|---|---|---|---|---|---|---|---|
| 1 | 8 | 3 | 2 | 7 | 6 | 5 | 4 | 9 |
| 5 | 2 | 7 | 4 | 9 | 8 | 3 | 1 | 6 |
| 6 | 4 | 9 | 1 | 3 | 5 | 7 | 2 | 8 |
| 7 | 9 | 1 | 5 | 6 | 2 | 8 | 3 | 4 |
| 2 | 3 | 8 | 7 | 4 | 9 | 6 | 5 | 1 |
| 4 | 5 | 6 | 3 | 8 | 1 | 2 | 9 | 7 |
| 8 | 1 | 2 | 9 | 5 | 7 | 4 | 6 | 3 |
| 9 | 6 | 4 | 8 | 2 | 3 | 1 | 7 | 5 |
| 3 | 7 | 5 | 6 | 1 | 4 | 9 | 8 | 2 |

(c)

**FIGURE 3.3**: An example of Sudoku [2].

considering all options after C is chosen, the player concludes that C is a bad option and considers B or A.

Recursion is a way to implement depth-first searching with backtracking. Consider the integer partition on Page 34. The program chooses 1 as the first number and prints all possible partitions starting with 1. Then, the program considers 2 as the first number and prints all possible partitions starting with 2.

Next, consider the recursive method to compute Fibonacci numbers. Figure 3.2 (b) shows the execution order of Figure 2.4. To compute $f(5)$, the program first computes $f(4)$, marked by A. To compute $f(4)$, the program computes $f(3)$, marked by B. To compute $f(3)$, the program computes $f(2)$, marked by C. As Figure 3.2 (b) shows, the program finishes the left side of the call graph before it starts the right side of the graph. This is another example of depth-first: The program takes the left side of the call graph and goes as far (deep) as possible, before computing the right side (backtrack).

---

## 3.2 Sudoku Game

Sudoku is a single-player number game with a board of $9 \times 9$ (81) cells of numbers. Each cell is assigned a number between 1 and 9 (inclusive). Figure 3.3 (a) shows an example of a solution to a Sudoku puzzle. A Sudoku solution must satisfy three rules. Each number between 1 and 9 must appear exactly once in the 9 cells of

1. Each column, as shown in Figure 3.3 (a)
2. Each row, as shown in Figure 3.3 (b)

| | | | | | | | | |
|---|---|---|---|---|---|---|---|---|
| 1 | 8 | 3 | 2 | 7 | 6 | 5 | 4 | 9 |
| 5 | 2 | 7 | 4 | 9 | 8 | 3 | 1 | 6 |
| 6 | 4 | 9 | 1 | 3 | 5 | 7 | 2 | 8 |
| 7 | 9 | 1 | 5 | 6 | 2 | 8 | 3 | 4 |
| 2 | 3 | 8 | 7 | 4 | 9 | 6 | 5 | 1 |
| 4 | 5 | 6 | 3 | 8 | 1 | 2 | 9 | 7 |
| 8 | 1 | 2 | 9 | 5 | 7 | 4 | 6 | 3 |
| 9 | 6 | 4 | 8 | 2 | 3 | 1 | 7 | 5 |
| 3 | 7 | 5 | 6 | 1 | 4 | 9 | 8 | 2 |

(a)

| | A | B | C | D | E | F | G | H | I |
|---|---|---|---|---|---|---|---|---|---|
| 1 | 1 | | 3 | | | | 5 | 4 | 9 |
| 2 | 5 | | | 4 | 9 | 8 | 3 | | 6 |
| 3 | | | | 1 | | | | | 8 |
| 4 | | 9 | 1 | | 6 | | | 3 | 4 |
| 5 | 2 | | | 7 | | 9 | | | 1 |
| 6 | 4 | 5 | | | 8 | | 2 | 9 | |
| 7 | 8 | | | | | 7 | | | |
| 8 | 9 | | 4 | 8 | 2 | 3 | | | 5 |
| 9 | 3 | 7 | 5 | | | | 9 | | 2 |

(b)

| | A | B | C | D | E | F | G | H | I |
|---|---|---|---|---|---|---|---|---|---|
| 1 | 1 | | 3 | | | | 5 | 4 | 9 |
| 2 | 5 | **2** | **7** | 4 | 9 | 8 | 3 | **1** | 6 |
| 3 | **6** | | | 1 | | | | | 8 |
| 4 | **7** | 9 | 1 | | 6 | | | 3 | 4 |
| 5 | 2 | | | 7 | | 9 | | | 1 |
| 6 | 4 | 5 | | | 8 | | 2 | 9 | |
| 7 | 8 | | | | | 7 | | | |
| 8 | 9 | | 4 | 8 | 2 | 3 | | | 5 |
| 9 | 3 | 7 | 5 | | | | 9 | | 2 |

(c)

**FIGURE 3.4**: (a) The 81 cells are divided into nine $3 \times 3$ blocks. (b) A Sudoku puzzle has some unfilled cells. (c) Row 2, column A is filled. Row 3, column c is unfilled.

3. Each $3 \times 3$ block as shown in Figure 3.3 (c). The 81 cells are divided into nine $3 \times 3$ blocks, as shown in Figure 3.4 (a).

September 9th is International Sudoku Day because this day is written as 9/9. A Sudoku puzzle has some of the cells empty, and the problem is to fill these cells. Figure 3.4 (b) shows a Sudoku puzzle. Figure 3.4 (b) marks the rows as 1, 2, 3, ..., 9 and the columns as A, B, C, ..., I. We will refer to a cell by its (row, column). For example, (1, C) has value 3 and (9, B) has value 7. To play this game, let's first consider column A. Seven of the nine cells have already been filled, and the two missing numbers are 6 and 7 at (3, A) and (4, A). Row 4 already has 6 (at column E). Thus, cell (3, A) must be 6, and cell (4, A) must be 7. These two newly filled cells are marked in boldface in Figure 3.4 (c).

Next, let's consider row 2. Three numbers are missing in this row: 1, 2, and 7 for cells (2, B), (2, C), and (2, H). Block (1, A) - (3, C) already has 1 at (1, A). Thus, 1 cannot be used for (2, B) or (2, C). Cell (2, H) must be 1. Cell (2, B) must not use 7 because (9, B) already has 7. Thus, (2, B) must be 2 and (2, C) must be 7. The partially filled puzzle is shown in Figure 3.4 (c).

Next, let's consider the block (1, G) - (3, I). Numbers 2 and 7 are missing. Column G already has 2 in cell (6, G). Thus, number 2 must be used in column H, and column G has only one choice: 7. Cells (6, I) and (7, I) need to be filled with numbers 3 and 7. Row 7 already has 7, so number 7 must be used for (6, I), and number 3 is used for (7, I). This partial result is shown in Figure 3.5 (a). Three numbers, 5, 6, and 8, are missing in the block (4, G) - (6, I). The unfilled cells are (4, G), (5, G), and (5, H). Column G already has 5 at (1, G), and 5 must be used in (5, H). Row 4 already has a number 6 at (4, E), and 6 must be used in (5, G). The only unfilled cell is 8, and it must be used at (4,

| | A | B | C | D | E | F | G | H | I |
|---|---|---|---|---|---|---|---|---|---|
| 1 | 1 | | 3 | | | | 5 | 4 | 9 |
| 2 | 5 | 2 | 7 | 4 | 9 | 8 | 3 | 1 | 6 |
| 3 | 6 | | | 1 | | | **7** | **2** | 8 |
| 4 | 7 | 9 | 1 | | 6 | | | 3 | 4 |
| 5 | 2 | | | 7 | | 9 | | | 1 |
| 6 | 4 | 5 | | | 8 | | 2 | 9 | **7** |
| 7 | 8 | | | | | 7 | | | **3** |
| 8 | 9 | | 4 | 8 | 2 | 3 | | | 5 |
| 9 | 3 | 7 | 5 | | | | 9 | | 2 |

(a)

| | A | B | C | D | E | F | G | H | I |
|---|---|---|---|---|---|---|---|---|---|
| 1 | 1 | | 3 | | | | 5 | 4 | 9 |
| 2 | 5 | 2 | 7 | 4 | 9 | 8 | 3 | 1 | 6 |
| 3 | 6 | | | 1 | | | 7 | 2 | 8 |
| 4 | 7 | 9 | 1 | | 6 | | **8** | 3 | 4 |
| 5 | 2 | | | 7 | | 9 | **6** | **5** | 1 |
| 6 | 4 | 5 | | | 8 | | 2 | 9 | 7 |
| 7 | 8 | | | | | 7 | **4** | | 3 |
| 8 | 9 | | 4 | 8 | 2 | 3 | **1** | | 5 |
| 9 | 3 | 7 | 5 | | | | 9 | | 2 |

(b)

| | A | B | C | D | E | F | G | H | I |
|---|---|---|---|---|---|---|---|---|---|
| 1 | 1 | | 3 | | | | 5 | 4 | 9 |
| 2 | 5 | 2 | 7 | 4 | 9 | 8 | 3 | 1 | 6 |
| 3 | 6 | | | 1 | | | 7 | 2 | 8 |
| 4 | 7 | 9 | 1 | | 6 | | 8 | 3 | 4 |
| 5 | 2 | | | 7 | | 9 | 6 | 5 | 1 |
| 6 | 4 | 5 | | | 8 | | 2 | 9 | 7 |
| 7 | 8 | | | | | 7 | 4 | **6** | 3 |
| 8 | 9 | **6** | 4 | 8 | 2 | 3 | 1 | **7** | 5 |
| 9 | 3 | 7 | 5 | | | | 9 | **8** | 2 |

(c)

**FIGURE 3.5**: More cells are filled.

G). Column G has only two unfilled cells now: (7, G) and (8, G). The unused numbers are 1 and 4. Row 8 already has 4 at (8, C), so 4 must be used at (7, G). The remaining number 1 is used at (8, G). The partially filled puzzle is shown Figure 3.5 (b). Row 8 has two missing numbers: 6 and 7 for (8, B) and (8, H). Column B already has 7 at (9, B), so (8, H) must be 7, and (8, B) must be 6. Column H has two missing numbers: 6 and 8 for (7, H) and (9, H). Number 8 appears at (7, A), so (9, H) must be 8; (7, H) must be 6. The result is shown in Figure 3.5 (c).

---

## 3.3 Implementation

If you are a Sudoku lover, you would be delighted to know that a million Sudoku puzzles are available for download at `https://www.kaggle.com/datasets/bryanpark/sudoku`. Our solution will use the same data format as `kaggle`. In this collection of Sudoku puzzles, each line has 164 letters. Table 3.1 shows the format of a single line.

| | | | | |
|---|---|---|---|---|
| puzzle (81 numbers) | , (comma) | solution (81 numbers) | line break (\n) | |

**TABLE 3.1**: Format of a line in the `kaggle` Sudoku puzzles. In the puzzle, unfilled cells are marked as zeros. The numbers are arranged by rows (i.e., row 1 followed by row 2, etc.).

This program creates a class called `Sudoku`.

```
# CH03: sudoku.py
```

```
import random
class Sudoku:
    def __init__(self, filename, dim = 1, debug = False):
        self.filename = filename
        self.dim = dim
        self.debug = debug
        self.cells = [[0 for c in range(9)] for r in range(9)]
        self.filled = 0
        # a list of numbers 1, 2, ..., 9
        allow = [val for val in range(1, 10)]
        # each cell has a list of allowed values
        self.allow = [[allow.copy() for c in range(9)] for r in
        ↪  range(9)]
```

The Sudoku class has the following attributes:

- `filename`: The name of a file that stores Sudoku puzzles and answers in the same format as the `kaggle` puzzles.
- `dim`: The dimension of the output. In the `kaggle` puzzles, each puzzle and its solution are stored in the same line. This one-dimensional format is easier for computer storage. This format is difficult for human understanding because Sudoku is a two-dimensional game. The attribute controls whether the output is for computers (one dimension) or humans (two dimensions).
- `debug`: If it is `True`, debugging information is printed.
- `cells`: This is a two-dimensional $9 \times 9$ array storing the values of the cells.
- `filled`: How many cells have been filled? The value is initialized to 0. If it is 81, the puzzle is solved.
- `allow`: For each cell, what values are still allowed? At the beginning, each cell can allow all nine numbers: 1, 2, 3, ..., 9. If a cell's value is given by the puzzle, only this given number is allowed. Then, this number is removed from the allowed values of all cells of the same row, the same column, and the same $3 \times 3$ block.

The `read` function opens the input file, reads all lines, and finds the number of lines in the input file.

```
    def read(self, filename):
        fhd = open(filename, 'r')
        alllines = fhd.readlines()
        numlines = len(alllines)
```

The first line (index zero) specifies the format, and every line below it contains a puzzle. Thus, the starting value of `randint` is one, not zero. The function randomly selects one of the puzzles.

```
19          # skip the first line because the first line stores
20          # the format: quizzes,solutions
21          whichline = random.randint(1, numlines - 1)  # select
            ↪  one puzzle
22          if (self.debug):
23              print('whichline:', whichline)
```

After selecting one line, the function reads the puzzle (line 25, the first 81 characters) and the solution (line 28, the $83^{rd}$ through $163^{rd}$ characters). Please be careful about the indices used in Python. The index of an array starts at zero. Also, when using `[a:b]` as the range of elements in an array, the element at index `a` is included, and the element at index `b` is excluded. The puzzle is the first 81 characters: using `[0, 81]` includes the first 81 characters. The solution starts at the $83^{th}$ character, whose index is 82.

```
24          # the first 81 characters are the quiz
25          line = alllines[whichline][0:81]
26          # the 81th characters is a comma
27          # the next 81 characters are the solution
28          self.solution = alllines[whichline][82:163]
```

The program prints the correct solution if `self.debug` is `True`.

```
29          if (self.debug):
30              print(f'solution = {self.solution}')
31              print(f'line = {line}')
```

After reading the puzzle, the function fills the cells. If the value is zero, this cell is not filled, and the cell should be skipped. Line 40 calls the `removedUsed` function to remove the number of all cells of the same row, the same column, and the same $3 \times 3$ block.

```
32          index = 0
33          for row in range(9):
34              for col in range(9):
35                  val = int(line[index])
36                  index += 1
37                  if (val != 0):  # 0 means unfilled
38                      self.cells[row][col] = val
39                      self.filled += 1
40                      self.removeUsed(row, col, val)
```

Lines 41-44 print debugging information: the puzzle and which values are allowed in each cell.

```
41          if (self.debug):
42              self.printCells()
```

```
43             print('***********')
44             print('Allowed')
45             self.printAllow()
```

The removedUsed function is called when a cell's value is certain. This can happen in two scenarios: First, the value is given from the puzzle. Second, the cell has only one value allowed because the other values have been used in the same row, the same column, or the same block. This function first assigns this value to self.allow at line 48. Then, the function removes the value from the cell's row (lines 50 to 52), the same column (lines 54 to 56), and the same block (lines 58 to 63).

```
46     def removeUsed(self, row, col, val):
47         # cell[row][col] is val
48         self.allow[row][col] = [val]  # will be removed later
49         # remove val from the same row
50         for c in range(9):
51             if (val in self.allow[row][c]):
52                 self.allow[row][c].remove(val)
53         # remove val from the same column
54         for r in range(9):
55             if (val in self.allow[r][col]):
56                 self.allow[r][col].remove(val)
57         # remove val from the same 3x3 square
58         rowstart = int(row / 3) * 3
59         colstart = int(col / 3) * 3
60         for r in range(rowstart, rowstart + 3):
61             for c in range(colstart, colstart + 3):
62                 if (val in self.allow[r][c]):
63                     self.allow[r][c].remove(val)
```

The fillValue function looks for a cell that has only one allowed value (line 68). This value is assigned to the cell (line 70); then the program calls removeUsed.

```
64     def fillValue(self):
65         # if a cell has only one allowed value, fill it
66         for row in range(9):
67             for col in range(9):
68                 if (len(self.allow[row][col]) == 1):
69                     val = self.allow[row][col][0]
70                     self.cells[row][col] = val
71                     self.filled += 1
72                     self.removeUsed(row, col, val)
```

The `solve` function calls the `nonrecursive` function that uses the three rules (on Page 79) repeatedly to fill as many cells as possible. If the three rules cannot fill all 81 cells (line 96), `solve` calls the recursive solution (line 97). If all 81 cells are filled, the function checks whether the solution is correct (line 98). The function prints the cells' values at line 99.

```
94      def solve(self):
95          self.nonrecursive()
96          if (self.filled != 81):
97              self.recursiveSolve()
98          self.checkSolution()
99          self.printCells()
```

The `nonrecursive` function calls `fillValue` repeatedly until no more cells can be filled. This is checked at line 80: When the number of filled cells does not change, the function stops.

```
73      def nonrecursive(self):
74          progress = True
75          # fill in the cells that have only one allowed value
76          # stop when no more cells can be filled
77          while (progress):
78              filled = self.filled
79              self.fillValue()
80              if (filled == self.filled):
81                  progress = False
```

The `checkSolution` function converts the cells' values from two dimensions stored in `self.cells` to one dimension for comparison (line 87). Line 88 compares whether the solution matches the solution read from the file.

```
82      def checkSolution(self):
83          # create a one-dimensional string
84          onedimsion = ''
85          for row in range(9):
86              for col in range(9):
87                  onedimsion += str(self.cells[row][col])
88          if (onedimsion == self.solution):
89              print('Correct')
90          else:
91              print('Incorrect')
92              print(f'onedimension = {onedimsion}')
93              print(f'self.solution = {self.solution}')
```

## 3.4 Recursive Solution

For easy Sudoku games, the unique values in the unfilled cells can be determined by repetitively checking the three rules on page 79. These rules can determine the values of individual cells. More difficult Sudoku games need to consider the values in several cells together before deciding whether these values are valid. Figure 3.6 shows an example. Some cells have several options, and a player needs to guess the values in some cells first. After more and more cells are filled, the player can determine whether the earlier guesses are correct. If the guesses are correct so far, the player fills in more cells. If the guesses are wrong and lead to violating one or multiple rules, the player has to change the guessed values. This guess-then-correct method is an example of the depth-first search and backtrack method explained at the beginning of this chapter.

First, we can apply the three rules to fill as many cells as possible:

- Cell (8, I)'s value is 4.
- Cell (7, I)'s value is 1.
- Cell (9, I)'s value is 3.

| | A | B | C | D | E | F | G | H | I |
|---|---|---|---|---|---|---|---|---|---|
| 1 | | | 6 | | | | | | 9 |
| 2 | | | 4 | 7 | 1 | 3 | | | |
| 3 | | 2 | | | 6 | | 7 | 1 | |
| 4 | | | 3 | 6 | | | | 8 | 7 |
| 5 | 7 | | | | | | | | 6 |
| 6 | 8 | 6 | | | | 4 | 3 | | |
| 7 | | 3 | 7 | | 8 | | | 2 | |
| 8 | | | | 3 | 2 | 1 | 5 | | |
| 9 | 2 | | | | | | 8 | | |

**FIGURE 3.6**: A more difficult Sudoku puzzle.

Next, consider cell (1, A). The values 2, 4, and 6 are already used in the same block. The first row uses 9 in (1, I) and cannot be used again in (1, A). Column A uses 7 and 8, and they cannot be used in (1, A), either. The three remaining options are 1, 3, and 5. At this moment, we do not have enough information to decide which of the three is the correct answer. We guess it is 1. Figure 3.7 (a) shows the current state; the gray background of (1, A) indicates that this is a guess.

Now cell (1, B) has options 5, 7, and 8. We consider 5 for (1, B) as shown in Figure 3.7 (b). The next unfilled cell is (1, D), and the options are 2, 4, and 8. It is temporarily set to 2. This process continues for (1, E) and (1, F). The current state is shown in Figure 3.7 (c). At this point, cell (1, G) has no solution because row 1 has already used 1, 2, 4, 5, 6, 8, and 9, and column G already has 3, 7, and 8. To find a solution for (1, G), we go back (i.e., *backtrack*) and check the most recently filled cell (1, F). If (1, D) is 2 and (1, E) is 4, 8 is the only solution for (1, F). We need to go back to (1, E). If (1, D) is 2, then (1, E) must be 4. Thus, we need to go back to change (1, D).

| | A | B | C | D | E | F | G | H | I |
|---|---|---|---|---|---|---|---|---|---|
| 1 | **1** | | 6 | | | | | | 9 |
| 2 | | | 4 | 7 | 1 | 3 | | | |
| 3 | | 2 | | | 6 | | 7 | 1 | |
| 4 | | | 3 | 6 | | | | 8 | 7 |
| 5 | 7 | | | | | | | | 6 |
| 6 | 8 | 6 | | | | 4 | 3 | | |
| 7 | | 3 | 7 | | 8 | | | 2 | 1 |
| 8 | | | | 3 | 2 | 1 | 5 | | 4 |
| 9 | 2 | | | | | | 8 | | 3 |

(a)

| | A | B | C | D | E | F | G | H | I |
|---|---|---|---|---|---|---|---|---|---|
| 1 | **1** | **5** | 6 | | | | | | 9 |
| 2 | | | 4 | 7 | 1 | 3 | | | |
| 3 | | 2 | | | 6 | | 7 | 1 | |
| 4 | | | 3 | 6 | | | | 8 | 7 |
| 5 | 7 | | | | | | | | 6 |
| 6 | 8 | 6 | | | | 4 | 3 | | |
| 7 | | 3 | 7 | | 8 | | | 2 | 1 |
| 8 | | | | 3 | 2 | 1 | 5 | | 4 |
| 9 | 2 | | | | | | 8 | | 3 |

(b)

| | A | B | C | D | E | F | G | H | I |
|---|---|---|---|---|---|---|---|---|---|
| 1 | **1** | **5** | 6 | **2** | **4** | **8** | | | 9 |
| 2 | | | 4 | 7 | 1 | 3 | | | |
| 3 | | 2 | | | 6 | | 7 | 1 | |
| 4 | | | 3 | 6 | | | | 8 | 7 |
| 5 | 7 | | | | | | | | 6 |
| 6 | 8 | 6 | | | | 4 | 3 | | |
| 7 | | 3 | 7 | | 8 | | | 2 | 1 |
| 8 | | | | 3 | 2 | 1 | 5 | | 4 |
| 9 | 2 | | | | | | 8 | | 3 |

(c)

**FIGURE 3.7**: (a) Cell (1, A) is temporarily marked as 1. (b) Cell (1, B) is temporarily marked as 5. (c) Cell (1, D) is temporarily marked as 2. The gray background of a cell indicates that the value is a guess.

Figure 3.8 (a) shows the decision process. For (1, A), there are three options: 1, 3, and 5. If we choose 1 for (1, A), there are three options for (1, B): 5, 7, and 8. If we choose 5 for (1, B), there are three options for (1, D): 2, 4, and 8. It does not matter which is chosen for (1, D), there is no solution for (1, G). Thus, we have to consider changing the value for (1, B) or even (1, A). This process continues until a solution is found (assuming the puzzle is valid). This is an example of the depth-first search with a backtracking strategy.

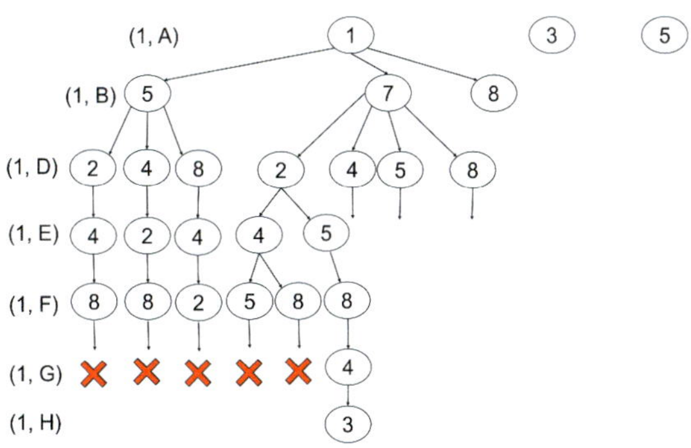


(a)

| | A | B | C | D | E | F | G | H | I |
|---|---|---|---|---|---|---|---|---|---|
| 1 | 1 | 7 | 6 | 2 | 5 | 8 | 4 | 3 | 9 |
| 2 | 9 | 8 | 4 | 7 | 1 | 3 | 6 | 5 | 2 |
| 3 | 3 | 2 | 5 | 4 | 6 | 9 | 7 | 1 | 8 |
| 4 | 5 | 4 | 3 | 6 | 9 | 2 | 1 | 8 | 7 |
| 5 | 7 | 1 | 9 | 8 | 3 | 5 | 2 | 4 | 6 |
| 6 | 8 | 6 | 2 | 1 | 7 | 4 | 3 | 9 | 5 |
| 7 | 4 | 3 | 7 | 5 | 8 | 6 | 9 | 2 | 1 |
| 8 | 6 | 9 | 8 | 3 | 2 | 1 | 5 | 7 | 4 |
| 9 | 2 | 5 | 1 | 9 | 4 | 7 | 8 | 6 | 3 |

(b)

**FIGURE 3.8**: (a) Decision process for solving Figure 3.7. (b) Answers for Figure 3.6.

## 3.5 Implement the Recursive Solution

Line 134 calls the `recursiveFill` function, and it calls the `fillHelper` function with two arguments `row` and `col`. The reason is that we need to keep track of the position of the cell under consideration. The recursive solution starts from the upper left corner, cell (1, A), of the puzzle, where the row and the column are both zero.

```
138     def recursiveFill(self):
139         if (self.debug):
140             print('Recursive Method')
141         self.fillHelper(0, 0) # upper left corner
```

The `fillHelper` function finds an unfilled cell (the value is zero). If it is not possible to find an unfilled cell, all cells have been filled, and the `fillHelper` function returns `True` (line 153). This unfilled cell should have multiple options, checked in lines 154 - 156. These options are recorded in `self.allow` and updated when the non-recursive solution calls `removeUsed`. Lines 157 - 162 implement a depth-first search with backtracking. The function selects one of the allowed values (line 157) and checks whether this value violates any rule. If this value does not violate any rule, the function assigns this value to the cell (line 159) and fills the other cells (line 160). Please notice that this is a recursive call. The function returns `True` at line 153 when all cells are successfully filled. If the function returns `False`, the rules are violated, and the function assigns 0 back to this cell. The function reaches line 164 if no allowed value can satisfy the rules. Returning `False` means the function backtracks.

```
142     def fillHelper(self, row, col):
143         foundcell = False  # find an unfilled cell
144         findrow = row
145         findcol = col
146         while ((foundcell == False) and (findrow < 9) and
          ↪ (findcol < 9)):
147             if (self.cells[findrow][findcol] == 0):  # not
              ↪ assigned
148                 foundcell = True
149             else:
150                 [findrow, findcol] = self.moveNext(findrow,
                  ↪ findcol)
151         if (foundcell == False):
152             self.filled = 81
```

```
153                 return True
154             if (len(self.allow[findrow][findcol]) <= 1):
155                 print('allow error')
156                 return False
157             for val in self.allow[findrow][findcol]:
158                 if (self.isValid(findrow, findcol, val) == True):
159                     self.cells[findrow][findcol] = val
160                     if (self.fillHelper(findrow, findcol) == True):
161                         return True
162                     # earlier guess wrong, reset
163                     self.cells[findrow][findcol] = 0
164             return False
```

The `moveNext` function goes to the next column of the same row. If this is the last column, the function moves to the first column of the next row.

```
182         def moveNext(self, row, col):
183             col += 1
184             if (col == 9):
185                 row += 1
186                 col = 0
187             return [row, col]
```

The `isValid` function checks whether assigning the value to the cell violates any rule.

```
165         def isValid(self, row, col, val):
166             for c in range(9):
167                 if (c != col):
168                     if (self.cells[row][c] == val): # already used
169                         return False
170             for r in range(9):
171                 if (r != row):
172                     if (self.cells[r][col] == val):
173                         return False
174             rowstart = int(row/3) * 3
175             colstart = int(col/3) * 3
176             for r in range(rowstart, rowstart + 3):
177                 for c in range(colstart, colstart + 3):
178                     if ((r != row) or (c != col)):
179                         if (self.cells[r][c] == val):
180                             return False
181             return True
```

Sudoku is an example where recursion can be used because the cells have multiple options, and line 157 checks each of the allowed values. Sudoku has recurring patterns because each cell has to follow the same rules. The changes occur because the cells are filled gradually. The stop condition is met when all cells are filled.

---

## 3.6 Graphical Representation

Figure 3.1 is produced using `seaborn.heatmap`. The following function draws Sudoku.

```
import matplotlib.pyplot as plt
import seaborn as sns
def draw_sudoku(sdk, title = 'Solution'):
  plt.figure(figsize=(5, 5))
  ax = sns.heatmap(sdk.cells, annot= True, cmap='coolwarm', cbar=False, xticklabels=False, yticklabels=False, vmin = -1, vmax = 9)
  # Add lines to delineate 3x3 blocks
  for i in range(1, 3):
      ax.axhline(3 * i, color='black', linewidth=2)
      ax.axvline(3 * i, color='black', linewidth=2)
  plt.title(title)
  plt.show()
```

---

## 3.7 Design Decisions

This section explains the thought process behind the implementation decisions. Understanding these design decisions helps readers evaluate the solution's approach.

When writing the solution for Sudoku, an important question is how to keep track of the state of progress. At a minimum, the program must track the numbers stored in the 81 cells. Thus, the only needed attribute is a $9 \times 9$ array of numbers, called `cells`. It is also possible to create another $9 \times 9$ array of `True/False` to indicate whether a cell's value has been determined. The presented solution does not use the second array; instead, the solution uses zero to indicate that a cell's value has not been assigned. Since a valid solution can use only numbers between 1 and 9, it is easy to choose an invalid value (any number other than 1 to 9) to indicate that a cell has not been assigned a value. Using another array would require the program to update both arrays when assigning a value to a cell. These two attributes are related, and keeping them consistent is important. Since it is possible to use one array (value zero or 1 to 9) to generate the other array of `False` or `True`, it is not necessary to create the second array of `False` or `True`. Please notice that saving memory is *not* a factor for consideration because an array of 81 `False` or `True` needs a tiny amount of memory in any modern computer (usually has multiple GB of memory).

If the $9 \times 9$ array is the only needed data for tracking progress, it is not even necessary to create the class `Sudoku`. The reference solution creates the `Sudoku` class because it has additional attributes: `self.filled` and `self.allow`. Both of them can be derived from `self.cells`. Why does the `Sudoku` class have these two attributes? The values of these two attributes change as more cells are filled. If `Sudoku` does not have these two attributes, their values need to be calculated many times, and such calculations can slow down the program unnecessarily. A more important reason is that these two attributes can be used to keep track of the program's progress. If `self.filled` is 81, all cells are filled, and the program can stop. The lists stored in `self.allow` can be used to determine which values are available for each cell. These two attributes can simplify the program, even though they can be derived from `self.cells`. The attributes `self.filled` and `self.allow` can help show the program's progress and make debugging easier.

The `Sudoku` class has two $9 \times 9$ arrays for `self.cells` and `self.allow`. Each element of `self.cells` is an integer between 0 and 9 (0 means unassigned). Each element of `self.allow` is a list of numbers between 1 and 9. Is it better to create another class called `Cell` and make the `Sudoku` class contain $9 \times 9$ `Cell` objects, as shown below?

```
class Cell:
    def __init__(self):
        self.value = 0
        self.allow = [val for val in range(1, 10)]
class Sudodu:
    def __init__(self):
        self.cells = [[Cell() for c in range(9)] for r in
        ↪  range(9)]
```

Why does the sample solution not use this `Cell` class? Each `Cell` object has only two attributes, and there are few advantages of creating the `Cell` class. The list of allowed values depends on the values stored in the other cells of the same row, same column, and same block. Thus, the list of allowed numbers depends on multiple cells and should be an attribute of `Sudoku`, not `Cell`. If a `Cell` object has only one attribute for storing an integer, there is no need to create the `Cell` class.

When are the attributes of `Sudoku` updated? The `read` function must update `self.cells` to reflect the initial state. The other attributes are used for the solution. They can also be updated in the `read` function, as shown in the program. This program updates `self.filled` and `self.allow` in the `read` function for several reasons. First, updating these two attributes requires visiting every cell. The `read` function already visits every cell. Second, updating `self.filled` and `self.allow` in `read` reflects the initial state of the puzzle, and these two attributes are consistent with `self.cells`.

The attribute `self.allow` is updated by the non-recursive solution. It is read but not updated in the recursive solution. As explained earlier, `self.filled` and `self.allow` can be derived from `self.cells`. When `self.cells` is updated in `fillHelper` (lines 159 and 163), we should update `self.filled` and `self.allow` for consistency. However, `self.allow` is used to control which values are considered (line 157). If `self.allow` is updated while it is also used to control the program, confusion (of the computer and of the readers) arises. Thus, `fillHelper` does not update `self.allow`.

Do you think these design decisions are reasonable?

---

## 3.8 Problems

### 3.8.1 Sudoku with 17 Filled Cells

Does this puzzle have a unique solution?

```
000000010
400000000
020000000
000050407
008000300
001090000
300400200
050100000
000806000
```

**Answer:**

Yes, this is the solution:

```
693784512
```

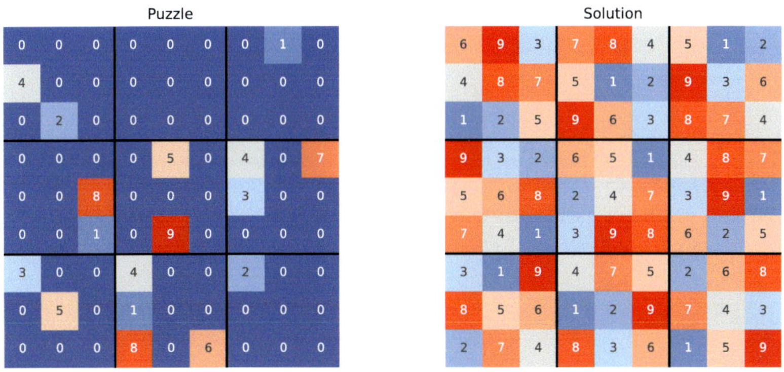


(a) (b)

**FIGURE 3.9**: (a) A difficult Sudoku puzzle. (b) Solution.

```
487512936
125963874
932651487
568247391
741398625
319475268
856129743
274836159
```

A technologyreview.com posting in 2012 mentions that if 16 or fewer cells are filled, the puzzle does not have a unique solution.

### 3.8.2 Check the Solution

Write a program to determine whether a file contains a valid Sudoku solution.

**Answer:**

```python
# Section 3.8.2: check.py
# check whether a 9x9 matrix of numbers is a solution of Sudoku
import sys
def check9cells(cells):
    if (len(cells) != 9):
        return False
    sorted = cells.copy() # do not modify the original
    sorted.sort()
```

```
    for i in range(0, 9):
        if (int(sorted[i]) != (i + 1)):
            print('invalid: ' + str(cells))
            return False
    return True
def check(filename):
    fhd = open(filename, 'r')
    lines = fhd.readlines();
    if (len(lines) != 9):
        return False
    cells = dict()
    for r in range(0, len(lines)):
        # remove '\n' at the end
        cells[r] = [int for int in (lines[r]).rstrip()]
    # check rows
    for r in range(0, 9):
        if (check9cells(cells[r]) == False):
            return False
    # check column
    for c in range(0, 9):
        column = []
        for r in range(0, 9):
            column.append(cells[r][c])
        if (check9cells(column) == False):
            return False
    for br in range(0, 7, 3):
        for bc in range(0, 7, 3):
            block = []
            for r in range(0, 3):
                for c in range(0, 3):
                    block.append(cells[br + r][bc + c])
            if (check9cells(block) == False):
                return False
    return True
if __name__ == "__main__":
    if (len(sys.argv) != 2):
        sys.exit('Need an input file')
    # names of input and output files
    if (check(sys.argv[1]) == False):
        print('Invalid Sudoku')
    else:
        print('Valid Sudoku')
```

This program reads each row, column, and block. The program sorts the numbers and checks whether each of the nine numbers appears exactly once.

### 3.8.3 Rotate Sudoku

If a valid Sudoku is rotated 90 degrees, is it still a valid Sudoku solution? Rotation is defined below:

Suppose a cell's position can be expressed by row $i$ and column $j$; $1 \leq i, j \leq 9$. Rotation means this cell becomes cell or row $j$ and column $9 - i$.

**Answer:**

Yes, it is still a valid Sudoku solution after rotation.

# Chapter 4

## Find the Exit of a Maze

This chapter develops a computer program that finds a way to get out of a maze. This is another example of *depth-first search* with *backtrack*.

### 4.1 Find the Exit

A maze is described by a file containing the following characters:

- `b`: brick.
- `␣`: (space) corridor.
- `E`: exit, i.e., the destination.
- `s`: starting location.

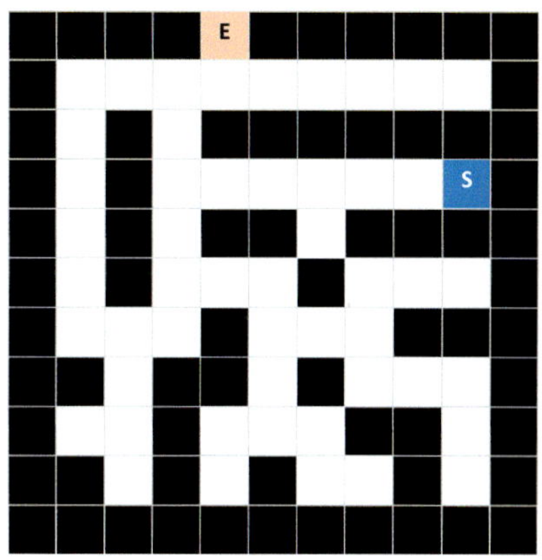


**FIGURE 4.1**: Input. Black: brick. E: Exit. S: Starting point. White: Corridor.

The maze is divided into grids of cells. Each cell is represented by a coordinate: (row, column). Row indices increase downward vertically, and column indices increase rightward horizontally. The top left corner is $(0, 0)$. After moving right one step, the coordinate becomes (0, 1). From (0, 1), moving down one step reaches the coordinate (1, 1). Figure 4.2 shows the coordinates.

Suppose the maze is dark and you can see only one cell in front of you. You do not know if a corridor is a dead end until you reach the end. If you discover that a corridor is a dead end, you must move backward to the last intersection and choose a different route. Imagine that it is possible to leave marks in the cells. The following is the first part of a strategy to find the exit.

| | column 0 | column 1 | column 2 | column 3 |
|---|---|---|---|---|
| row 0 | (0, 0) | (0, 1) | (0, 2) | (0, 3) |
| row 1 | (1, 0) | (1, 1) | (1, 2) | (1, 3) |
| row 2 | (2, 0) | (2, 1) | (2, 2) | (2, 3) |
| row 3 | (3, 0) | (3, 1) | (3, 2) | (3, 3) |

(a)

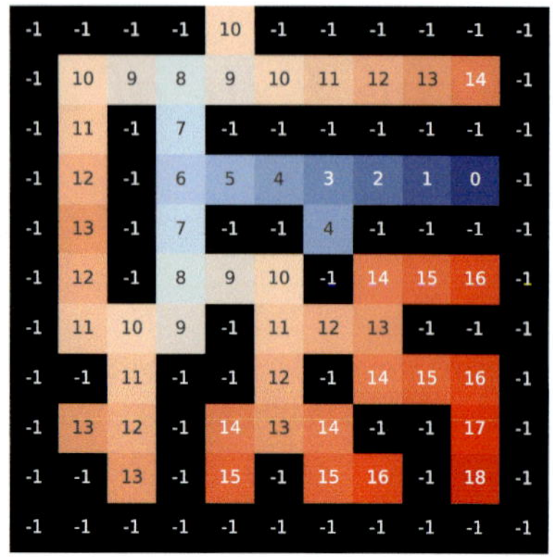


(b)

**FIGURE 4.2**: (a) Coordinates of maze cells. (b) Distance from the starting point; bricks are marked as $-1$.

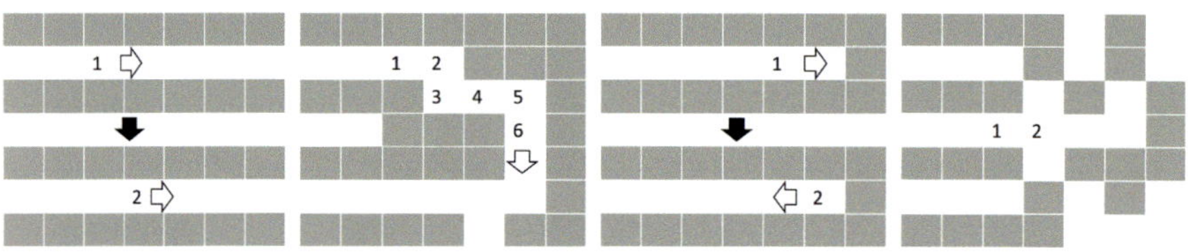


**FIGURE 4.3**: Strategy to find the exit.

1. Inside a corridor, go as far as possible, as shown in Figure 4.3 (a).
2. If the bricks force a turn, turn and keep moving forward, as shown in Figure 4.3 (b).
3. If a corridor reaches a dead end, turn around and move backward along the same corridor, as shown in Figure 4.3 (c).
4. If an intersection is encountered, choose one direction and follow rules No. 1 and No. 2 above. If a dead end is encountered, follow rule No. 3 to return to the intersection and choose another direction.

Next, we consider the strategy to handle intersections. An intersection is a cell with multiple neighbor cells to choose from, as shown at cell 2 in Figure 4.3 (d). At this cell, it is possible to go right, up, or down.

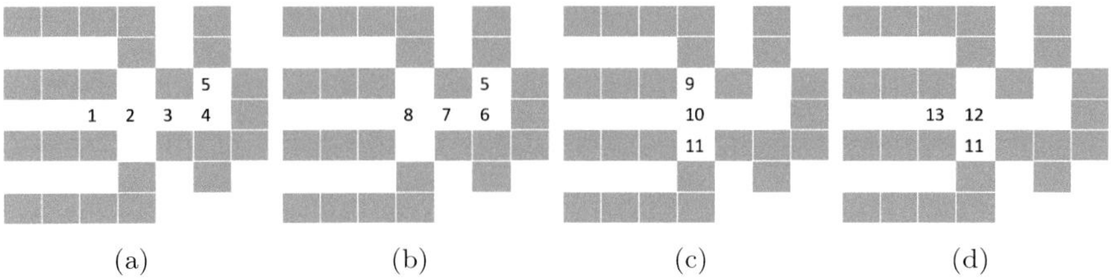


**FIGURE 4.4**: Strategy at an intersection.

Figure 4.4 shows the strategy to handle intersections. Suppose our first choice is to go right and move to cell 3. Rule No. 1 keeps moving forward if it is possible. Thus, the next step moves to cell 4 and then 5, as shown in Figure 4.4 (a) At cell 5, a dead end is detected. By Rule No.3, we move backward to cell 8 (earlier it was cell 2), shown in Figure 4.4(b). By Rule No. 4, we choose a different direction. Suppose we choose to go up and move to cell 9. Another dead end is discovered. Thus, we move down to cell 10 (it was cell 8 earlier). We can keep moving down and enter cell 11, shown in Figure 4.4 (c). At the moment, we have concluded that we have to move backward. We move to cell 12 (earlier it was cell 10) and cell 13 (earlier it was cell 1). This strategy is another example of *depth-first search* with *backtracking*. When several options are available, this solution chooses one option and moves as far as possible (depth-first). If this option turns out to be a dead end, the solution goes back to an intersection (backtrack) and chooses another option.

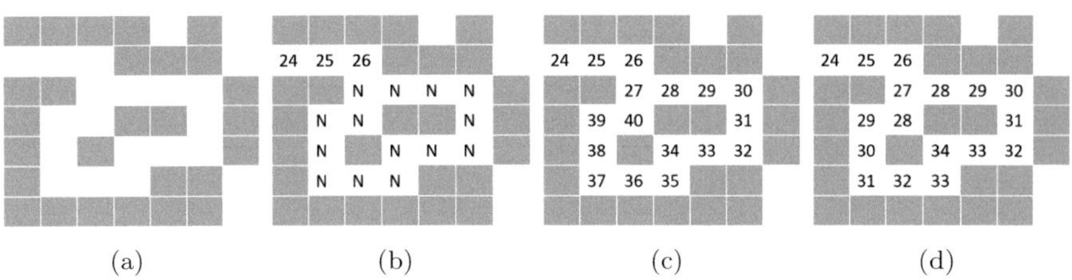


**FIGURE 4.5**: Handle multiple paths.

What happens if there are multiple paths between two cells? Figure 4.5 (a) shows an example. Since we are allowed to mark the visited cells, we can mark the distance from the starting point as zero. When we move to the next cell, it is marked as one, then two, then three. Consider the situation when we come to these cells from the upper left with the distances marked 24, 25, and 26. If a cell has not been visited, it has no mark, and we use "N" to indicate the unvisited cells, as shown in Figure 4.5 (b). As we move forward, we mark the cells by increasing numbers, until we reach cell 40, shown in Figure 4.5 (c).

If we move forward, we will mark the next cell as 41. However, this cell was earlier marked 27. That means this cell was visited before, and the distance to the starting point is shorter (only 27). Thus, we should not move forward anymore. Instead, we should treat this situation like reaching a dead end and go back to the previous intersection. Cell 27 must be an intersection: That is why it can be reached through two paths. From cell 27, we can choose another option: Going down this time, marking the cells as 28, 29, ... as shown in Figure 4.5 (d). Continue going forward until cell 34. If we go any further, we will mark the next cell as 35, but it was already marked 33. Thus, we should not go any further. Then, the solution backtracks to the previous intersection.

---

## 4.2 Implement the Strategy

The solution creates a class called `Maze`. The attributes are

- `numrow`: This is the number of rows (counted vertically, i.e., height) of the maze from the top brick to the bottom brick.
- `numcol`: This is the number of columns (counted horizontally, i.e., width) of the maze. It is the length of the longest line.
- `startrow` and `startcol`: This is the coordinate of the starting point. We assume there is only one starting point.
- `exitrow` and `exitcol`: This is the coordinate of the exit. We assume there is only one exit.
- `lines`: These are the lines from a maze file.
- `distance`: Each cell has a distance from the starting point. The values are initialized to the product of the maze's height and width. This initial value is greater than any possible distance from the starting point. If a cell is a brick, the distance is $-1$ because distances are always positive. A negative value means that it is not possible to enter a brick.

The program defines four directions using a class called `Direction` using the `Enum` class as the base class. The program specifies four constants: `NORTH`, `EAST`, `SOUTH`, and `WEST`.

```
from enum import Enum
class Direction(Enum):
    NORTH = 0
    EAST  = 1
    SOUTH = 2
    WEST  = 3
```

The `Maze` class reads from the file using the `readlines` function in Python.

```
class Maze:
    def __init__(self, filename):
        self.path = {}
        self.readMaze(filename)
    def readMaze(self, filename):
        # read maze from a file
        fhd = open(filename, 'r')
        self.lines = fhd.readlines()
        fhd.close()
        self.numrow = len(self.lines)
        # length of the longest line
        self.numcol = len(max(self.lines, key=len))
        self.mazesize = self.numrow * self.numcol
        # create a 2-D matrix keeping the distance
        # the distance is initialized to mazesize
        # because mazesize is larger than any possible
        # distance from the starting point
        self.distances = [[self.mazesize for i in range(0, self.numcol)]
                          for j in range(0, self.numrow)]
```

After reading the input, the program finds the starting point and the exit.

```
        # find the exit and the starting point
        for r in range(0, self.numrow):
            cs = self.lines[r].find('s') # cell of starting point
            if (cs != -1):
                self.startrow = r
                self.startcol = cs
                self.distances[r][cs] = 0
            ce = self.lines[r].find('E') # cell of exit
            if (ce != -1):
                self.exitrow = r
                self.exitcol = ce
            # go through the columns, assign -1 to the cells of bricks
            for c in range(0, len(self.lines[r])):
                if (self.lines[r][c] == 'b'):
                    self.distances[r][c] = -1
            # if the maze is not rectangular, assign -1 to the ending elements
```

```
43             for c in range(len(self.lines[r]), self.numcol):
44                 self.distances[r][c] = -1
```

The `solve` function calls the `move` function from the starting location, with a distance of zero.

```
93     def solve(self):
94         self.move(self.startrow, self.startcol, 0)
```

The `move` function starts by checking whether the program enters a brick. If the cell is the exit, it is not necessary to visit any more cells. Thus, the `move` function returns.

```
71     def move(self, row, col, distance):
72         self.distances[row][col] = distance
73         self.path[(row, col)] = distance
74         if (distance == -1):
75             print ("ERROR, enter a brick")
76             return
77         if (self.lines[row][col] == 'E'): # reach the exit
78             return
```

The function intends to enter the neighbor cells in the order of east-west-north-south. Before entering a cell, the function checks whether a neighbor cell's distance is larger than the current cell's distance plus one. If it is, then entering this neighbor cell can shorten the neighbor's distance from the starting point. This is a recursive function.

```
79         # move to a cell only if doing so can shorten the
               ↪ distance
80         dist = self.getDistance(row, col, Direction.EAST)
81         # moving to a neighbor
82         if (dist > (distance + 1)):
83             self.move(row, col + 1, distance + 1)
84         dist = self.getDistance(row, col, Direction.WEST)
85         if (dist > (distance + 1)):
86             self.move(row, col - 1, distance + 1)
87         dist = self.getDistance(row, col, Direction.NORTH)
88         if (dist > (distance + 1)):
89             self.move(row - 1, col, distance + 1)
90         dist = self.getDistance(row, col, Direction.SOUTH)
91         if (dist > (distance + 1)):
92             self.move(row + 1, col, distance + 1)
```

The `move` function calls the `getDistance` function. The function provides information on whether entering a cell is valid or not. If this cell is outside the maze (lines 47 - 62), the function returns $-1$. If this cell is a brick (lines 64 - 65), the function returns $-1$. If this cell is the starting point (lines 66 - 67), the function returns 0. If none of the above conditions match, the function returns the current distance of the cell from the starting point.

```
    def getDistance(self, row, col, dir):
        # return -1 for invalid move or a brick
        if (dir == Direction.NORTH):
            row = row - 1
        if (row < 0):
            return -1
        if (dir == Direction.SOUTH):
            row = row + 1
        if (row >= self.numrow):
            return -1
        if (dir == Direction.WEST):
            col = col - 1
        if (col < 0):
            return -1
        if (dir == Direction.EAST):
            col = col + 1
        if (col >= len(self.lines[row])):
            return -1
        # row and col are valid
        if (self.lines[row][col] == 'b'):
            return -1 # cannot enter a brick
        if (self.lines[row][col] == 's'):
            self.distances[row][col] = 0
            return 0 # distance of the starting point is zero
        # return the current distance from the starting point
        return self.distances[row][col]
```

---

## 4.3 Graphical Representation using a Heat Map

The following function uses a *heatmap* to color the cells. The bricks are colored black. If a cell's distance to the starting point is smaller, the cell is colored blue. If the distance is longer, the cell is colored red.

```
import matplotlib.pyplot as plt
import seaborn as sns
import ipywidgets as widgets
import numpy as np
from matplotlib.colors import ListedColormap
```

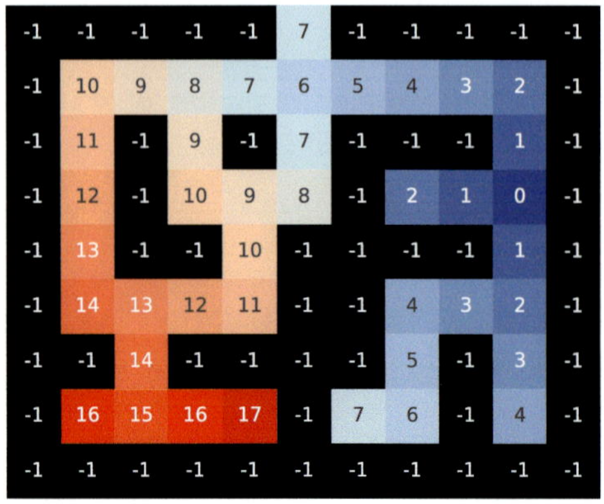


(a)

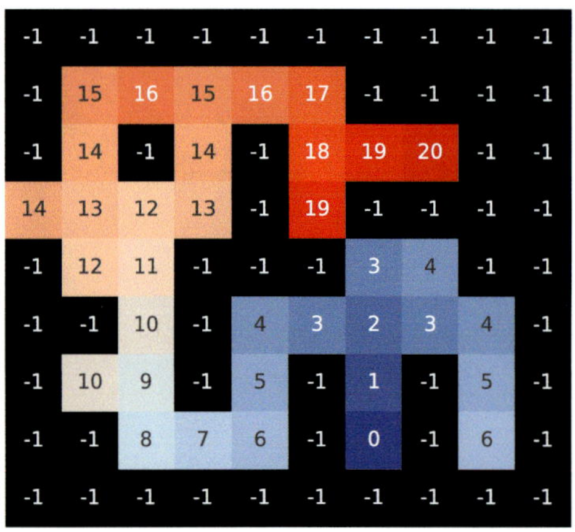


(b)

**FIGURE 4.6**: Heatmaps show the distances from the starting points. Bricks and unreachable cells are marked with −1.

```
def draw_heatmap(maz):
  # Create a custom colormap
  # Use black for -1, and 'coolwarm' for other values
  colors = plt.cm.coolwarm(np.linspace(0, 1, 256))
```

```
colors[0] = [0, 0, 0, 1]  # Set the the color of -1 to black
# the first three numbers correspond to RGB (red, green, and blue)
# the values should between 0 and 1
custom_cmap = ListedColormap(colors)
plt.figure(figsize=(maz.numcol/2, maz.numrow/2))
sns.heatmap(maz.distances, annot= True, cmap=custom_cmap, cbar=False, vmin = -1, vmax = maz.longest, xticklabels=False, yticklabels=False)
plt.title('Heatmap of Maze Distances')
plt.xlabel('Column')
plt.ylabel('Row')
plt.show()
```

---

## 4.4 Problems

### 4.4.1 Brick Color

Change `draw_heatmap` so that bricks are light gray.

**Answer:**

The colors use RGB (red, green, blue), and each value is between 0 and 1.

Replace

```
colors[0] = [0, 0, 0, 1]
```

by

```
colors[0] = [0.95, 0.95, 0.95, 1]
```

can make bricks light gray. Here are some other color options:

```
colors[0] = [1, 0, 0, 1] // red bricks
colors[0] = [0, 1, 0, 1] // green bricks
colors[0] = [0, 0, 1, 1] // blue bricks
```

### 4.4.2 Mark of Bricks

Explain why assigning $-1$ can prevent entering a cell filled by a brick? Can any other negative value serve the same purpose (prevent entering a brick)? Can zero also serve the same purpose?

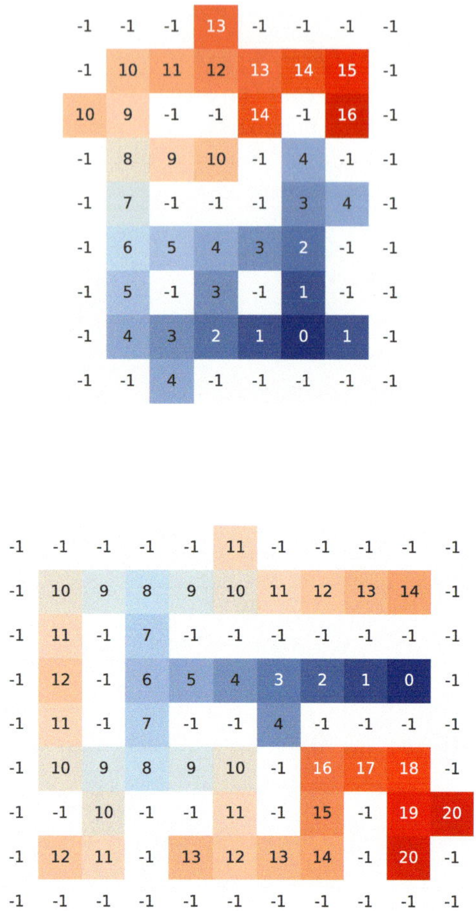


**FIGURE 4.7**: Replace black bricks with light gray.

**Answer:**

The shortest distance from the starting cell is zero. If a cell has a negative value, entering this cell cannot make the distance shorter. Thus, a negative value can prevent entering this cell. Any negative value (including floating-point value) can serve the same purpose.

Zero cannot be used because zero is used to mark the starting location.

### 4.4.3 Order of Directions

The `move` function checks whether it is possible to go to the east neighbor first. If it checks the east neighbor last (after west, north, and south), will the output be different?

**Answer:**

The order of visited cells will be different, but the shortest distance of each cell will remain unchanged.

# Chapter 5

## Go Game

Go is a popular board game, and it was considered one of the most difficult challenges for computers, until AlphaGo defeated two of the best human players: Lee Sedol in 2016 and Ke Jie in 2017. AlphaGo is a computer program designed by DeepMind (owned by Google) to play the Go game. Go has simple rules, but the number of possible options is extremely large. It is impossible to give a comprehensive explanation of computer solutions for Go games in a single chapter. Instead, this chapter uses recursion to solve one important problem in Go games— calculating liberties.

### 5.1 Rules

Go has several important properties:

- *Go Board*: A Go board is composed of squares. A standard board has 18 $\times$ 18 squares created by 19 $\times$ 19 lines. Figure 5.1 (a) shows a miniature Go board with 5 $\times$ 5 squares (6 $\times$ 6 lines).
- *Two Players*. Go is a two-player game: The two players take turns. The result of a Go game can be one winner (and one loser) or a tie.
- *Board Configurations*: A board configuration is given by the positions of the black and white stones at any given time. We will use numbers 1, 2, ... to indicate the rows (horizontal lines) and letters A, B, ... to indicate the columns (vertical lines). Figure 5.1 (b) shows a black stone occupying the position (3, C), and a white stone occupying the position (4, D).
- *Black and White Stones*: The two players hold black and white stones. The stones are placed at the intersections of the lines, as shown in Figure 5.1 (b). The player holding black stones will place the first stone. A player can place a stone only at an intersection that is not currently occupied by any stone. After a stone is placed at an intersection, it cannot be moved to any other intersection. Each player has more than enough stones (usually $361 \div 2 = 180$). Usually, a winner can be decided

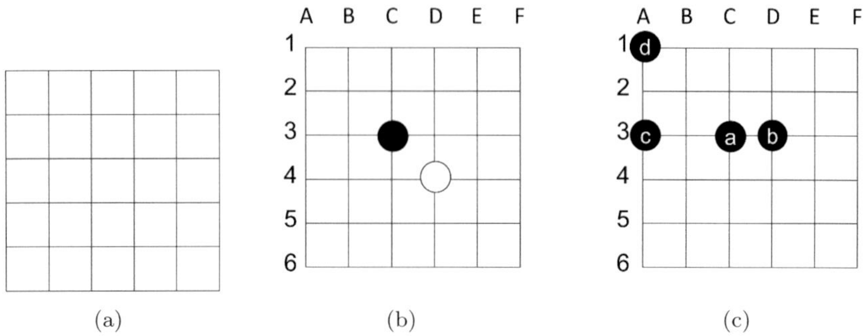


**FIGURE 5.1**: (a) A Go board is composed of squares. (b) The stones are placed at the intersections. (c) These stones have different numbers of liberties.

before using up all the stones. In rare situations when a winner cannot be decided before a player runs out of stones, more stones can be added so that the game can continue.

- *Take Turns.* The two players take turns making their decisions. A player may pass the turn and allow the other player to place two stones consecutively. If both players pass consecutively, the game ends, and the winner is decided.
- *Certainty.* Go does not involve any component of luck or uncertainty, such as tossing a die. If two players repeat the same steps, they will reach the same outcome (i.e., who wins the game or ties).
- *No Memory.* The two players can make decisions based on the information presented on the board. There is no need to remember what actions have been taken earlier, except for the "No Repetition" rule described below.
- *No Repetition.* Go games do not allow players to reproduce the same board configuration earlier in the game. The purpose of this rule is to prevent players from repeating the same configuration and thus making no progress toward deciding the winner. This is called the *ko rule.* The ko rule has two different versions: The first version prohibits placing a stone that will reproduce the previous configuration. This version allows placing multiple stones to reproduce a configuration that has been seen before, as long as the same configuration does not appear immediately. The second version is more restrictive: it does not allow reproducing any configuration that has been seen throughout the game. This rule does not contradict the "No Memory"' rule. The No Memory rule says players do not have to remember the *sequence* of actions. They need to remember only the configurations of the board.

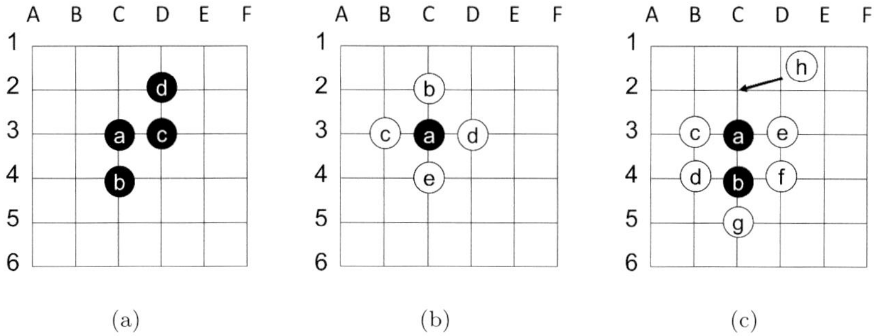


**FIGURE 5.2**: (a) A chain of stones. (b) Stone `a` has zero liberties, so this stone is captured by the opponent. (c) If a chain has zero liberties, all stones are captured. In this example, the white stone `h` makes the chain of `a` and `b` zero liberties. Thus, both `a` and `b` are captured.

- *No Hidden Information.* Each player knows the same things, and all information is available from the board. This is also called a *perfect information* game.

Go has a very high number of possible configurations. A configuration specifies each intersection as unoccupied, occupied by a black stone, or occupied by a white stone (i.e., 3 possible scenarios at each position). The Go board has $19 \times 19 = 361$ intersections. Thus, there are $3^{361} \approx 1.74 \times 10^{172}$ configurations. Some of these configurations are invalid. For example, it is not possible to have only one white stone without any black stones because the black player starts first. The two players may reach the same configurations using different sequences of actions. Consider the four black stones in Figure 5.2 (a) (ignore white stones for now). There are $4! = 24$ different sequences to place these four black stones, and all of them reach the same configuration. Go is a difficult game due to the vast number of configurations, together with the many sequences for each configuration.

A stone's neighbors are the intersections along the horizontal or vertical lines (diagonals are not considered). A stone can have at most four neighbors; a stone at one of the four corners has only two neighbors. The black stone at (3, C) has four neighbors: (3, B), (3, D), (2, C), and (4, C). A stone's unoccupied neighbor is called a *liberty*. In Figure 5.1 (b), the black stone has 4 liberties, as does the white stone. For simplicity, we ignore white stones for now because the same rules for counting liberties are also applicable to white stones. When two or more stones of the same color reside at adjacent intersections, they form a *chain*, also called a *connection*. We can extend the definition of a chain to include only one stone. In Figure 5.1 (c), `a` and `b` form a chain; `c` and `d` form two other chains. The black stone of `c` has three liberties. The black stone of `d` at the corner has two liberties.

A connection can turn, as shown in Figure 5.2 (a). The black stones of `a` to `d` form a chain with eight liberties:

1. (1, D)
2. (2, C)
3. (2, E)
4. (3, B)
5. (3, E)
6. (4, B)
7. (4, D)
8. (5, C)

Now is the time to define the *capture rule* in Go. Figure 5.2 (b) shows a situation when the stone `a` has zero liberties because this black stone is surrounded by white stones. In this case, the black stone `a` is captured by the white player. Go does not allow "suicide": A player is not allowed to place a stone that immediately has zero liberties. In general, it is desirable to place a stone with higher liberties because a stone with few liberties is easier to capture. Thus, a corner and a side, such as `c` and `d` in Figure 5.1 (c), should not be used early in a game when many intersections are still unoccupied. If multiple stones form a chain, all stones in the chain share the same number of liberties. In Figure 5.2 (c), the chain `a` - `b` has one liberty. If the white player places `h` at (2, C), the chain `a` - `b` has zero liberties, and both are captured by the white player.

Go has different methods to decide the winner. These different methods often agree on the winner, but disagreements are also possible. For simplicity, this book uses a simple method: Count the number of stones on the board. The winner is the player with more stones.

---

## 5.2 Group Stones into Chains

When multiple stones of the same color form a chain, all stones have the same number of liberties. To calculate the number of liberties of each stone, we need to group the stones in each chain. Our method is illustrated in Figure 5.3. This figure considers only black stones; the method can also be applied to white stones. The method includes the following steps:

1. Each intersection is assigned a number starting from 0 at the upper left corner. This number is the index of the intersection.
2. The group identification (GID) of each intersection is initialized to $-1$.
3. The method visits each intersection to find a stone whose GID is still $-1$.

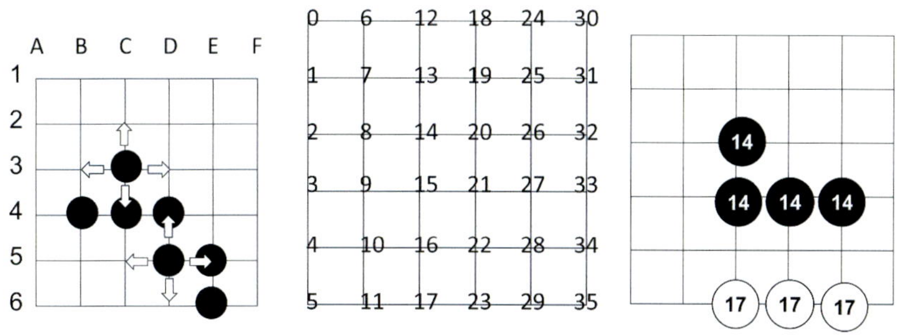


(a) (b) (c)

**FIGURE 5.3**: Group a chain of stones of the same color. (a) Find the neighbors occupied by stones of the same color. (b) Each intersection is assigned a number. (c) Each group is marked by the smallest number in the entire group. The black stones belong to group 14. The white stones belong to group 17.

4. Assign this stone's index as the stone's GID.
5. Assign the same GID to this stone's neighbors if they belong to the same chain.
6. Grow the group until no more stones can be added.

We are going to create a class called `GoGame` with the following attributes:

- `side`: How many intersections are on each side.
- `numposition`: The number of positions; it is `side` × `side`.
- `stones`: An array with `numposition` elements. Each element can be space (unoccupied), `B` (black stone), or `W` (white stone). The elements are initialized to space.
- `stoneLiberty`: An array with `numposition` elements, initialized to zero. Each element corresponds to the number of liberties of a chain of stones. Please remember that a single stone without any neighbors is also considered a chain.

```
options = [' ', 'B', 'W']
class GoGame:
    def __init__(self, side):
        self.side = side
        self.numposition = side * side
        self.stones = [' ' for index in range(self.numposition)]
        self.groups = [-1  for index in range(self.numposition)]
        self.stoneLiberty = [0  for index in
        ↪  range(self.numposition)]
```

```
15          self.blackLiberty = 0
16          self.whiteLiberty = 0
```

The `fill` function randomly assigns one of three possible options to each intersection (lines 54 - 55). The function finds the groups of stone chains (line 56). The function resets the values of liberties (line 58). Next, the function calls `countLiberty` to calculate the number of liberties of each group.

```
52      def fill(self):
53          # fill each intersection by ' ', 'B', or 'W'
54          for index in range(self.numposition):
55              self.stones[index] = random.choice(options)
56          self.group()
57          self.stoneLiberty = [0  for index in range(self.side * self.side)]
58          self.useLiberty = [False  for index in range(self.side * self.side)]
59          self.countLiberty()
```

The `group` function initializes `groups` of each position to `-1` (line 46). Next, the function checks each intersection. If an intersection is occupied (line 48) and it is not already a part of a group (line 49), this will be the first stone of a new group. The group's identification is this stone's index (line 50). Then, the program calls `growGroup` to find all the other stones in the same group.

```
44      def group(self):
45          side = self.side
46          self.groups = [-1  for index in range(self.numposition)] # reset
47          for index in range(self.numposition):
48              if (self.stones[index] != ' '): # black or white
49                  if (self.groups[index] == -1): # not in a group yet
50                      self.groups[index] = index
51                      self.growGroup(index, index, self.stones[index])
```

The `growGroup` function is recursive: it calls `findNeighbors` to find the neighbors. It grows the chain of stones by finding all neighbors of the same color not in any group yet (lines 41). Please notice the arguments of this function. The argument `index` is the position of the stone under consideration. The argument `label` is the label of this chain (the index of the first stone of this chain). The argument `color` is the color of this chain (black or white). This method checks whether a stone has a group value of $-1$. This value indicates that this stone is not in any group yet and should be added. This method of growing neighbors is recursive. The method finds this stone's neighbors, and their neighbors, until no more stones of the same color can be added to the group.

```
    def growGroup(self, index, label, color):
        neighbors = self.findNeighbors(index)
        for nei in (neighbors):
            if ((self.stones[nei] == color) and
            ↪  (self.groups[nei] == -1)):
                self.groups[nei] = label
                self.growGroup(nei, label, color)
```

The `findNeighbors` function returns a list of neighbors. The function calculates the four neighbors' indices. If the input `index` is already at the boundary of the Go board, this intersection does not have all four neighbors. In this function, `row` and `col` are the row and column of this stone's index, as shown in Figure 5.3 (a). Line 27 checks whether this stone is at the left edge of the Go board. Line 29 checks whether this stone is at the right edge of the Go board.

```
18      def findNeighbors(self, index):
19          upper  = index - 1
20          lower = index + 1
21          left = index - self.side
22          right = index + self.side
23          neighbors = []
24          col = int(index / self.side)
25          row = index % self.side
26          side = self.side
27          if ((left >= 0) and ((left % side) == row)): # same row
28              neighbors.append(left) # valid neighbor
29          if ((right < self.numposition) and ((right % side) ==
            ↪  row)):
30              # same row
31              neighbors.append(right)
32          if ((upper >= 0) and (int(upper / side) == col)): # same
            ↪  column
33              neighbors.append(upper)
34          if ((lower < self.numposition) and (int(lower / side) ==
            ↪  col)):
35              # same column
36              neighbors.append(lower)
37          return neighbors # a list
```

This algorithm is similar to the solution in Chapter 4 for finding exits in mazes. In Chapter 4, the paths from the starting point to the exits are restricted by bricks. In this chapter, finding groups of stones with the same colors is restricted by unoccupied intersections and the stones of the other color.

## 5.3 Calculate Liberties

This section explains how to calculate the number of liberties of each chain (group) by following these steps:

1. The group of each position is initialized to $-1$.
2. Find the groups' IDs using the methods described earlier in Figure 5.3
3. Liberties are the unoccupied intersections next to a stone. Thus, we need to find an unoccupied position.
4. Find all neighbors of this unoccupied position.
5. Add one to the group's liberties.

The method finds occupied positions first because we want to distinguish the different scenarios illustrated in Figure 5.4 (i.e., not finding a chain of stones first). In Figure 5.4 (a), this unoccupied position contributes to two chains of black stones and one single white stone. In Figure 5.4 (b), the neighbors belong to the same chain, and the number of liberties of the entire group increases by only one.

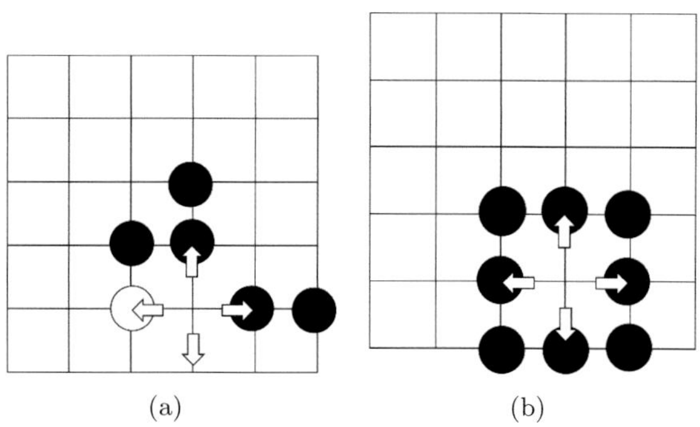


**FIGURE 5.4**: To calculate a chain's liberties, we find an unoccupied position and its neighbors.

This solution counts liberties for each group and starts by finding an unoccupied position (line 64). Next, the function finds the neighbors of this unoccupied position (line 65). The liberty count increments by only one for the entire chain. The function uses a set (line 66) so that stones of the same chain will count this unoccupied position only once (line 71). Only the stone that represents the entire chain has incremented the liberty count from this unoccupied position. It is important to note that an unoccupied position adds liberties to all stones of the same chain.

```
60      def countLiberty(self):
61          self.blackLiberty = 0
62          self.whiteLiberty = 0
63          for index in range(self.numposition):
64              if (self.stones[index] == ' '): # unoccupied
65                  neighbors = self.findNeighbors(index)
66                  neighborset = set()
67                  for nei in (neighbors):
68                      neighborset.add(self.groups[nei])
69                  for grp in (neighborset):
70                      if (grp != -1):
71                          self.stoneLiberty[grp] += 1
```

After finding the liberties of each chain, the next step assigns this value to every stone of this chain (line 78). Lines 79 - 80 add the liberties of every black chain. Lines 81 - 82 add the liberties of every white chain.

```
72          # fill the liberty values to all stones of the same group
73          for index in range(self.numposition):
74              if (self.stones[index] != ' '):
75                  group = self.groups[index]
76                  for index in range(self.numposition):
77                      if (self.groups[index] == group):
78                          self.stoneLiberty[index] = self.stoneLiberty[group]
79                          if (self.stones[index] == 'B'):
80                              self.blackLiberty += self.stoneLiberty[group]
81                          else:
82                              self.whiteLiberty += self.stoneLiberty[group]
```

After calculating the liberties of each chain, the program detects whether any stone has zero liberties. As explained earlier, having zero liberties is not allowed because a stone with zero liberties should be captured.

```
83          # detect any stone that has zero liberty
84          for index in range(self.numposition):
85              if ((self.stones[index] != ' ') and (self.stoneLiberty[index] == 0)):
86                  print(f'zero liberty of {self.groups[index]}')
87                  self.valid = False
88          self.valid = True
```

The program uses `matplotlib` to draw the board.

```
def drawGoBoard(board):
    size = board.side
    fig, ax = plt.subplots(figsize=(int(0.7 * size + 1), int(0.7* size + 1)))
    # Set limits to ensure points are at intersections
    ax.set_xlim(0, size)
    ax.set_ylim(0, size)
    ax.set_xticks(np.arange(0.5, size, 1))
    ax.set_yticks(np.arange(0.5, size, 1))
    ylabel = range(size, 0, -1) # decrement
    xlabel = [chr(ord('A') + num) for num in range(0, size)]
    ax.set_xticklabels(xlabel)
    ax.set_yticklabels(ylabel)
    ax.grid(True)
    stones = board.getStones()
    groups = board.getGroups()
    liberty = board.getLiberty()
    outlinecolor = 'black'
    for index in range(size * size):
        col = int(index / size)
        row = size - (index % size)
        pos = (col + 0.5, row - 0.5)
        if (stones[index] != ' '):
          group = groups[index]
          liberty = board.stoneLiberty[group]
          if (stones[index] == 'B'):
            textcolor = 'greenyellow'
            circle = plt.Circle(pos, 0.4, color= 'black', fill=True)
          elif (stones[index] == 'W'):
            textcolor = 'blue'
            circle = plt.Circle(pos, 0.4, color= 'lightgray', fill=True)
          ax.add_patch(circle)
          ax.text(pos[0], pos[1], f'{group}\n{liberty}', ha='center', va='center', fontsize=12, color=textcolor)
    plt.show()
drawGoBoard(gb)
```

Figure 5.5 shows two examples of board configurations. Each stone has two numbers. The top number is the group's ID; the bottom is the group's liberties.

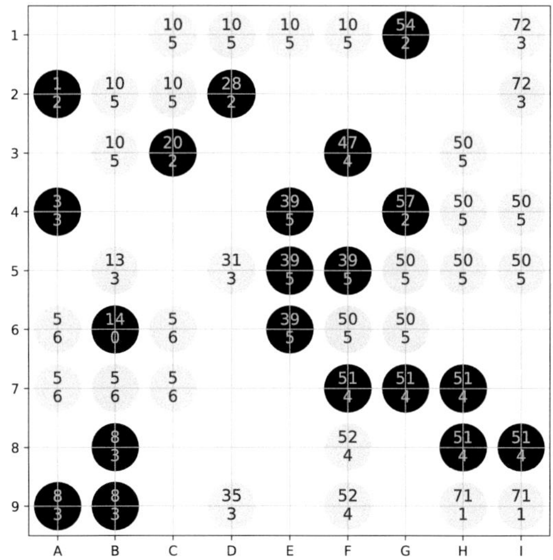


(a)

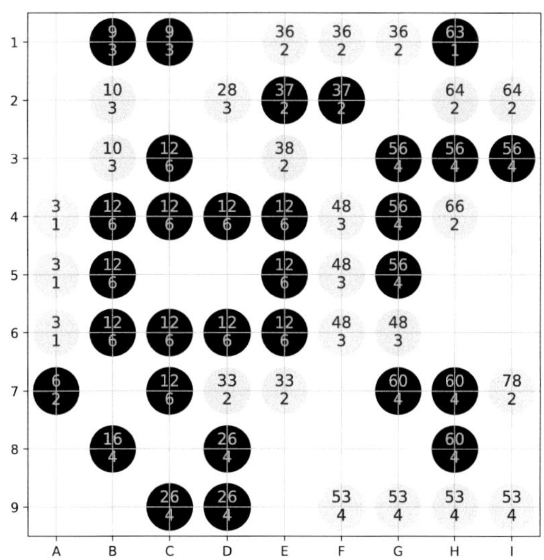


(b)

**FIGURE 5.5**: Two examples of groups and liberties. The top numbers are the group IDs. The bottom numbers are the liberties.

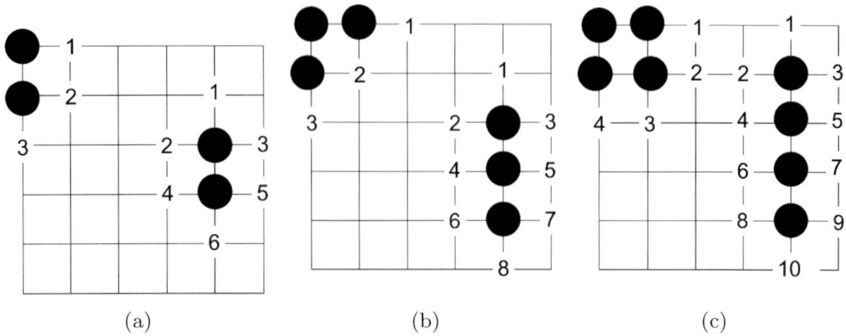


**FIGURE 5.6**: Smallest and largest liberties of groups of 2, 3, and 4 stones.

## 5.4 Problems

### 5.4.1 Maximize Liberties

Use the program given in this chapter. Write a computer program that can determine which position can increase a player's (either black or white) liberties the most.

### 5.4.2 Chain's ID

This book uses the smallest ID of a chain to represent the entire chain. Does it matter if the largest ID represents the entire chain?

### 5.4.3 Smallest and Largest Liberty

What is the largest possible number of liberties if a chain of stone contains 2, 3, or 4 stones of the same color?

**Answer:**

| Number of Stones | 2 | 3 | 4 |
|---|---|---|---|
| Smallest Liberties | 3 | 3 | 4 |
| Largest Liberties | 6 | 8 | 10 |

# Chapter 6

# Binary Trees

## 6.1 Terminology

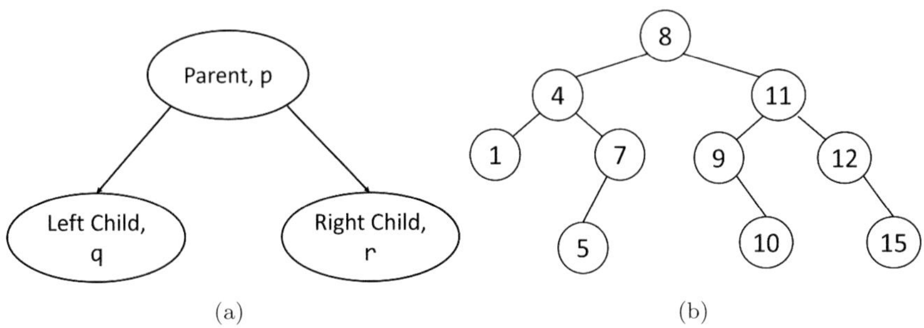


**FIGURE 6.1**: (a) A tree node can have two children called left and right. (b) Each node in a binary tree can store a number.

A *binary tree* is a data structure used to efficiently organize and manage information. A binary tree consists of *nodes* that are linked together. Every node can connect up to two child nodes, called the *left child* and *right child*, as illustrated in Figure 6.1 (a). Each node stores a piece of data. The following are some terms used for binary trees. Suppose `p`, `q`, and `r` are three binary tree nodes. If `q` is `p'`'s left child and `r` is `p`'s right child, we call `p` the *parent* of `q` and `r`. We also say that `q` and `r` are *siblings*. If a node has no child, then it is called a *leaf node*. All nodes on the left side of `p` are called `p`'s left *subtree*. All nodes on the right side of `p` are called `p`'s right subtree. A node's links go downward: each node can access its children. Usually, there are no upward links, so a node cannot directly access its parent. The top node is called the *root* node, and the root node can reach every other node in the tree. We can think of the root as the starting point of the tree. Suppose `x` and `y` are two nodes in a binary tree. Node `x` is an *ancestor* of `y` if one of two conditions is satisfied:

1. If `x` is `y`'s parent, `x` is `y`'s ancestor.

2. There is another node `z` such that `z` is `y`'s ancestor and `x` is `z`'s parent.

Please notice the definition is recursive: define ancestor by using ancestor itself. The first rule is the base case; the second rule is the recursive case. If `x` is `y`'s ancestor, then `y` is `x`'s *offspring*.

Figure 6.1 (b) shows an example of a binary tree storing numbers. The root stores the value 8. The value 4 is stored in the left child of the root. The nodes storing 1, 4, 5, and 7 are the left subtree of the root. The nodes storing 9, 10, 11, 12, and 15 are the right subtree of the root. The *distance* of a node from the root is the number of links between the root and the node. For example, the distance between node 7 and the root is 2. The *height* of a binary tree is one plus the longest distance in the tree. The height of the tree above is 4. In a *full* binary tree, each node has either two children or no children. The tree in Figure 6.1 (b) is not full because node 7 has only one child (also nodes 9 and 12). In a *complete* binary tree, each node, except the bottom level, is completely filled. Figure 6.1 (a) is complete. It is possible for a node in a complete binary tree to have only one child, and thus not be a full binary tree. It is also possible that a full binary tree is incomplete. Figure 6.2(a) is a full tree: each node has either two children or no children. Figure 6.2(b) is a complete tree: all nodes except the ones just above the leaf nodes have two children. Figure 6.2(a) is not a complete tree because some nodes above the bottom level (such as C's and D's children) are missing. Figure 6.2(b) is not a full tree because some nodes (such as H, K, N, and O) have only one child each.

If a binary tree is full and complete, it is a *perfect* binary tree. If a perfect tree's height is $n$ (i.e., the distance between a leaf node and the root is $n-1$), then the tree has precisely $2^n - 1$ nodes and $2^{n-1}$ leaf nodes. In a *balanced* binary tree, the difference between the height of the left subtree and the height of the right subtree is at most one.

We can create tree structures in which each node has three or more children. In a tertiary tree, each node may have up to three children. In a quaternary tree, each node may have up to four children. Some computer games take advantage of *octrees*: each node has up to eight children. Octrees can be used to partition three-dimensional space and are thus useful for indexing objects in three-dimensional worlds. This book focuses on binary trees because they are useful for a wide variety of problems.

A common question is why binary trees are so commonly used, but other types of trees (such as tertiary or quaternary) are not as common. The answer is that two, three, four, and eight have the same expressive capability. For any positive $n$, it is possible to find $k$ such that $2^k = n$. For example, if $n$ is 4, then $k$ is 2. If $n$ is 16, $k$ is 4. If $n$ is 0.25 (decimal), $k$ is $-2$. If $n$ is 7, $k$ is $\log_2(7)$ (this is an irrational number). Similarly, it is possible to find numbers $p$ and

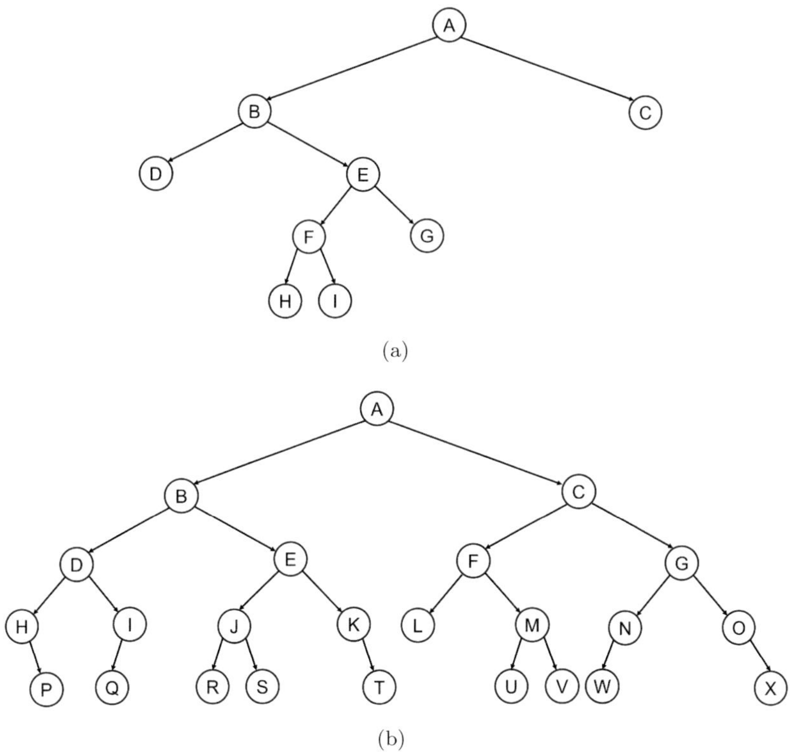


**FIGURE 6.2**: (a) A full tree. (b) A complete tree.

$q$ such that $3^p = n$ and $4^q = n$. In contrast, one does not have this expressive capability because the power of one is always one, i.e., $1^m = 1$ regardless of the value of $m$. Thus, two, three, and four have better expressive power than one.

---

## 6.2 Binary Search Tree

One type of binary tree is *binary search trees*; they can be used to process ordered data (such as integers, floating-point numbers, names, addresses, dates). A binary search tree has the following properties.

1. Each node stores a piece of data. The data can be a single value (e.g., an integer or a string) or a collection of information. If it is a single value, this value is used as a *key*. If it is a collection of information, one

part of the information is used as a key. For example, a node may store information about a person. The information may include the person's name, address, social security number, telephone, etc. The social security number may be used as this person's key.

2. The key must be distinct.
3. The keys must be *totally ordered.* If $a$ and $b$ are the keys in two different nodes, then either $a < b$ or $a > b$ must be true. Since the keys must be distinct, the case $a$ equal to $b$ does not exist. Transitivity must be satisfied (if $a < b$ and $b < c$, then $a < c$). For example, integers, characters, floating-point numbers, and strings all support total ordering. Complex numbers are not totally ordered.
4. For any node with key $p$, all keys in the entire left subtree must be smaller than $p$. All keys in the entire right subtree must be greater than $p$. Regardless of the information stored in each node, a binary search tree supports operations like insert, search, and delete.

Figure 6.1 (b) is an example of a binary search tree. Below is the class for a binary search tree. The information stored in each node (`val`) can be a single value of an object.

```
class BinaryTree:
    def __init__(self, val):
        self.value = val
        self.left = None
        self.right = None
```

### 6.2.1 Insert Data

Figure 6.3 shows a binary search tree storing integers. The figure illustrates how the tree grows as more integers are added. When the very first number (8) is added to a binary search tree, the number is stored at the root. This line creates a new binary search tree. The first argument `value` is the value for the root (line 96).

```
95 values = [8, 4, 11, 1, 9, 7, 10, 5, 12, 15]
96 tree = BinaryTree(values[0])
97 print(f'values = {values}, len = {len(values)}')
```

This is the program's output from line 97:

```
values = [8, 4, 11, 1, 9, 7, 10, 5, 12, 15], len = 10
```

After the root has been created, new information can be added by calling the `insert` function.

```
for i in range(1, len(values)):
    tree.insert(values[i])
```

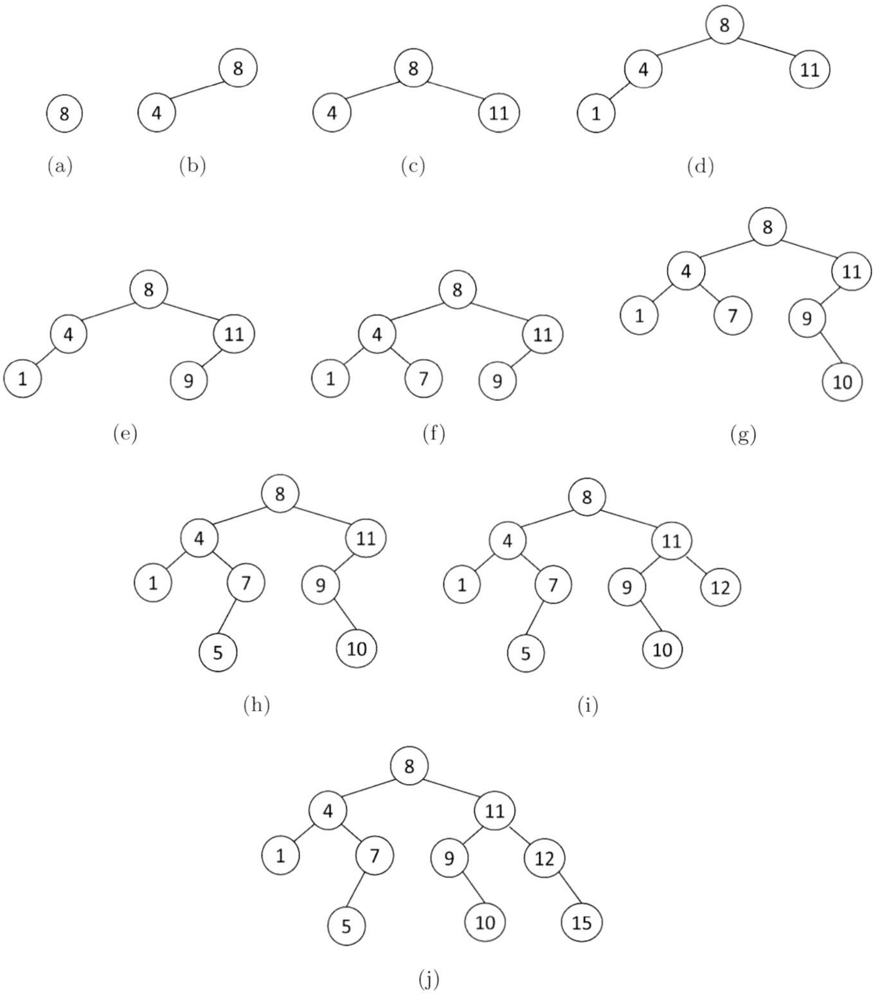


**FIGURE 6.3**: Insert values 8, 4, 11, 1, 9, 7, 10, 5, 12, 15.

The `insert` function first checks whether the value is already stored in the tree (line 32). If the value to be added matches the tree node's value, this value is not added again. This ensures that the values in the binary search tree are distinct. If the added value is smaller than the value currently stored in the node, the new value needs to be added to the left subtree (line 34). This can be further divided into two cases depending on whether the left subtree exists or not. If there is no left subtree now (line 35), this value is added as the left child (line 36). If the left subtree already exists, this value is added to the left subtree (line 39). Please notice that this is a recursive call. If the new value is neither equal to nor smaller than the node's value, it is inserted in the right subtree (lines 41 - 46). Please notice the recursive definition of the object: a child (left or right) is either `None` or a binary search tree.

```
31      def insert(self, val):
32        if (self.value == val): # do not insert the value again
33            return
34        if (val < self.value):
35            if (self.left == None):
36                self.left = BinaryTree(val)
37                return
38            else:
39                self.left.insert(val)
40                return
41        # val > self.value
42        if (self.right == None):
43              self.right = BinaryTree(val)
44              return
45        else:
46              self.right.insert(val)
```

### 6.2.2 Search

To find whether a given number is stored in a binary search tree, the `search` function compares the number with the value stored at the root. If the two values are the same, then we know that the value is stored in the tree.

```
    def search(self, val):
        if (self.value == val):
            return True
```

If the number is smaller than the value stored at the node, then the value is not on the right side of the tree. If the number is greater than the value stored at the root, then it is not on the left side of the tree. This property is applied recursively until either (1) there is nothing left to search or (2) the value is found. This is precisely why this structure is called a *binary search tree*: It is a tree that naturally supports searches. In each step, either the left subtree or the right subtree is discarded. It is most efficient when the left side and the right side of each node have the same number of nodes, so half of the nodes can be discarded after only one comparison. The following shows how to implement `search`.

```
        if (self.value > val):
            if (self.left != None):
                return self.left.search(val)
            else:
                return False
        if (self.right != None):
            return self.right.search(val)
        return False
```

Section 2.7 shows how to use binary search in a sorted array. Table 6.1 compares the two methods using an array and using a binary search tree. The preliminary advantage of a binary search tree is the ability to insert and delete information.

**TABLE 6.1**: Comparison of binary search using an array and a binary search tree.

| Comparison | Array | Tree |
|---|---|---|
| Simplicity | Easy to implement | More complex |
| Memory efficiency | Contiguous | Not Contiguous |
| Size | Fixed | Can change easily |
| Add or Delete | Difficult | Easy |
| Sorting | Need to sort first | Sort during insertion |
| Balance | Naturally balanced | Can be imbalanced |

As the name suggests, a binary search tree makes searching easy and fast due to its properties. Consider a full and complete binary search of height $n$. This tree has $2^n - 1$ nodes. By comparing with the root node only, it is possible to determine whether it is found (if it matches the data stored in the root) or discard one of the two subtrees. Binary search is extremely efficient. Please refer to Page 47 about the efficiency of binary search.

### 6.2.3 Print a Binary Tree

Visiting every node in a tree is also called *traversing* the tree. Traversing a tree has three steps:

1. Visit the node's left subtree,
2. Visit the node's right subtree,
3. Print the node's value.

There are $3! = 6$ ways to order these three steps. Visiting the left subtree usually precedes visiting the right subtree. Thus, the three ways to implement traversing are:

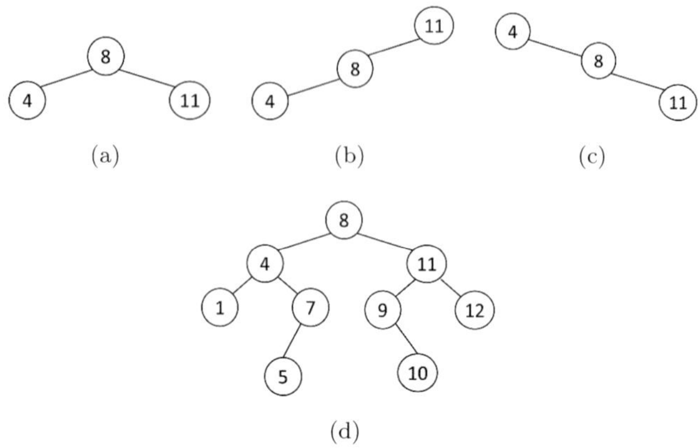


**FIGURE 6.4**: (a)-(c) Three binary search trees of different shapes. (d) A more complex binary search tree.

1. Pre-order traversal: The three steps are ordered as the node → left subtree → right subtree.
2. In-order traversal: The three steps are ordered as left subtree → the node → right subtree. For a binary search tree, in-order will print the values in the ascending order.
3. Post-order traversal: The three steps are ordered as left subtree → right subtree → the node.

**TABLE 6.2**: Traversing the three binary search trees in Figure 6.4 (a)-(c).

| | (a) | (b) | (c) |
|---|---|---|---|
| pre-order | 8 4 11 | 11 8 4 | 4 8 11 |
| in-order | 4 8 11 | 4 8 11 | 4 8 11 |
| post-order | 4 11 8 | 4 8 11 | 11 8 4 |

Consider the different shapes of binary search trees in Figure 6.4 (a)-(c). These three trees store the same values. They have different shapes due to the order of insertion. In (a), 8 is inserted first. In (b), 11 is inserted first. In (c), 4 is inserted first. Table 6.2 shows the outputs of the three traversal methods. In-order traversal outputs the values in the ascending order and has the same outputs for the three different trees. Thus, in-order traversal cannot distinguish between different shapes of trees.

Next, consider the more complex tree in Figure 6.4 (d). For pre-order, write the value of the root 8 first, followed by the outputs of the left subtree, and then the right subtree:

| 8 | pre-order of left subtree | pre-order of right subtree |
|---|---|---|

The pre-order traversal of the left subtree starts with 4. The pre-order traversal of 4's left subtree is 1, and the pre-order traversal of 4's right subtree is 7, then 5. The pre-order traversal of 8's right subtree starts with 11. The pre-order traversal of 11's left subtree is 9 and 10, and the pre-order traversal of 11's right subtree is 12. Thus, the output is

| 8 | 4 1 7 5 | 11 9 10 12 |
|---|---|---|

It is important to understand these three traversal methods because each one is useful in different circumstances. The next chapter explains how to use post-order in data compression. The code listing below shows how to print a tree using pre-order, in-order, and post-order traversals.

```
    def helper(self, retlist, order): # retlist: returned list
        if (order == 'pre'):
            retlist.append(self.value)
        if (self.left != None):
            self.left.helper(retlist, order)
        if (order == 'in'):
            retlist.append(self.value)
        if (self.right != None):
            self.right.helper(retlist, order)
        if (order == 'post'):
            retlist.append(self.value)
    def preorder(self):
        retlist = [] # returned list
        self.helper(retlist, 'pre')
        return retlist
    def postorder(self):
        retlist = []
        self.helper(retlist, 'post')
        return retlist
    def inorder(self):
        retlist = []
        self.helper(retlist, 'in')
        return retlist
```

```
preorder = tree.preorder()
postorder = tree.postorder()
```

```
inorder = tree.inorder()
print(f'preorder = {preorder}, len = {len(preorder)}')
print(f'postorder = {postorder}, len = {len(postorder)}')
print(f'inorder = {inorder}, len = {len(inorder)}')
```

This is the output of pre-order, post-order, and in-order of the tree in Figure 6.4 (d):

```
values = [8, 4, 11, 1, 9, 7, 10, 5, 12, 15], len = 10
preorder = [8, 4, 1, 7, 5, 11, 9, 10, 12, 15], len = 10
postorder = [1, 5, 7, 4, 10, 9, 15, 12, 11, 8], len = 10
inorder = [1, 4, 5, 7, 8, 9, 10, 11, 12, 15], len = 10
```

We can also write a `print` function that prints the tree turning 90 degrees counterclockwise (i.e., -90°).

```
    def print(self, level=0, prefix = "Root:"):
        # Print right subtree
        if (self.right != None):
            self.right.print(level + 1, "R--")
        # Print root value
        print(" " * 6 * level + prefix, self.value)
        # Print left subtree
        if (self.left != None):
            self.left.print(level + 1, "L--")
```

Figure 6.5 shows the trees depicted in Figure 6.3 and the rotated output by the `print` function. The prefix `L--` or `R--` indicates whether a node is the left child or the right child of this node's parent. Please notice that this function prints the right subtree first. If this function prints the left subtree first, then the output needs to be mirrored vertically after rotation.

### 6.2.4 Delete a Node

Deleting a node from a binary search tree is more complex than adding values because the latter adds only leaf nodes. Deleting a non-leaf node must maintain the tree's ordering property. When deleting a node, there are three different scenarios.

1. Delete a leaf node: Figure 6.6 (a) is the original binary search tree. Figure 6.6 (b) deletes node 5. The node is a leaf node (has no children). The left child of node 7 becomes `None`.
2. Delete a node that has only one child: Figure 6.6 (c) deletes node 14. This node has one child. The parent of node 11 (14) connects to the child of node 12 (14).
3. Delete a node that has two children: We want to delete 8 from Figure 6.6

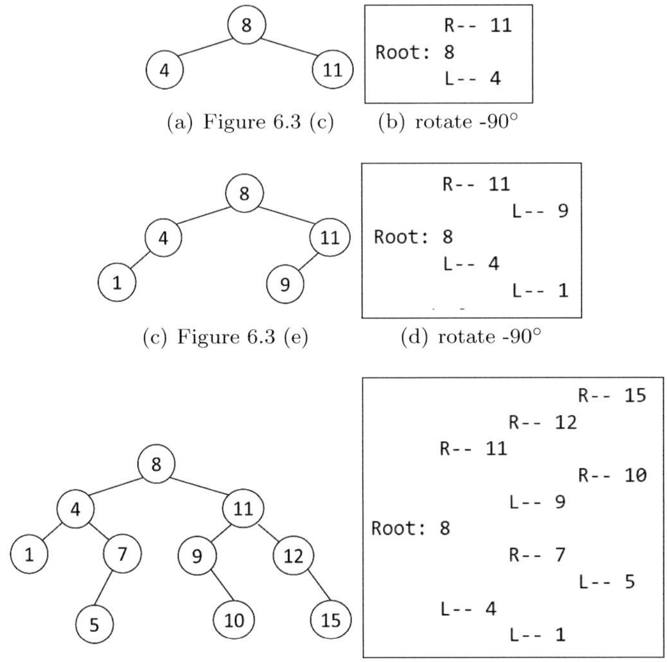


(a) Figure 6.3 (c) (b) rotate -90°

(c) Figure 6.3 (e) (d) rotate -90°

(e) Figure 6.3 (j) (f) rotate -90°

**FIGURE 6.5**: The `print` function rotates the trees in Figure 6.3 counterclockwise 90°.

(c), while maintaining the properties of a binary search tree. This node has two children. This is the procedure:

(a) We find the smallest value in the right subtree (node 9). This is referred to as node 8's *immediate successor*. The immediate successor is the node that appears immediately after node 8 in the in-order traversal. The immediate successor must be on the right side and must not have the left child (otherwise, the left child should be the immediate successor). The immediate successor may have the right child. It is also possible to use the immediate predecessor. This book uses the immediate successor.

(b) Swap these two values (8 and 9). As a result, 9 becomes the root of the tree. At this moment, the binary search tree is temporarily broken because 8 is on the right side of 9.

(c) Node 8 is deleted, and the tree becomes a binary search tree again. Since the immediate successor must not have the left child, after swapping the values, node 8 may have no child or a right child. Figure 6.6 (d) shows the result.

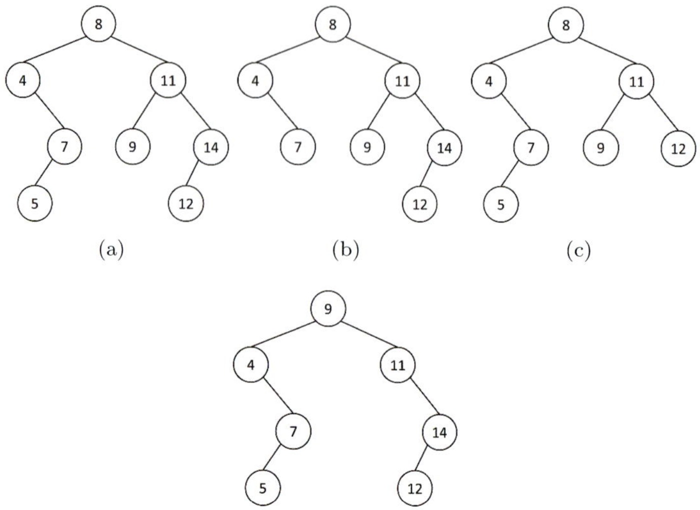

(a) (b) (c)

(d)

**FIGURE 6.6**: Delete a node in a binary search tree. (a) Original. (b) Delete 5. (c) Delete 14. (d) Delete 8.

Below is an implementation of the delete function. Lines 68 - 75 find the correct node to delete. Lines 77 - 79 handle the scenario when the deleted node has no children. Lines 81 - 84 handle the scenario when the deleted node has one child. If the program reaches line 85, the deleted node has both children. Lines 87 - 89 find the immediate successor. It is at the right side of `self`, and hence, `imsuc` starts with `self.right`. The immediate successor must be the leftmost node on `self`'s right side.

```
67      def delete(self, val):
68          if (val < self.value):  # look for value in left
            ↪ subtree
69              if (self.left != None):  # left child exists
70                  self.left = self.left.delete(val)
71              return self
72          if (val > self.value):
73              if (self.right != None):
74                  self.right = self.right.delete(val)
75              return self
76          # val equal to self.value, delete this node
77          if ((self.left == None) and (self.right == None)):
78              # this node has no child
79              return None
```

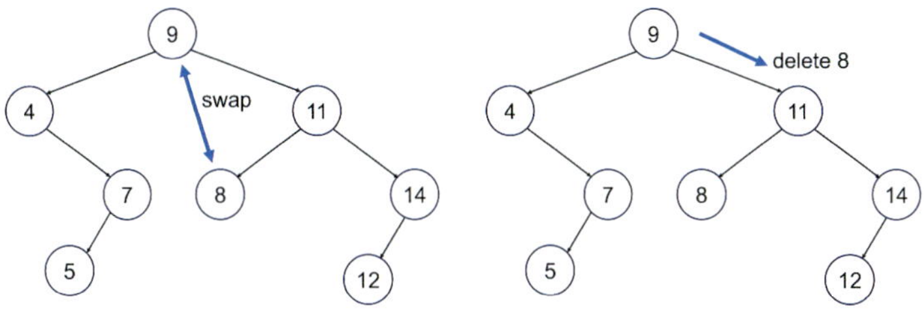


(a) (b)

**FIGURE 6.7**: Deleting 8 needs to swap 8 with the immediate successor (9). Then, delete 8 from the right side of 9.

```
80          # this node has at least one child
81          if (self.left == None):
82              return self.right
83          if (self.right == None):
84              return self.left
85          # this node has two children
86          # find immediate successor
87          imsuc = self.right
88          while (imsuc.left != None):
89              imsuc = imsuc.left
90          # swap the values
91          self.value = imsuc.value
92          imsuc.value = val
93          self.right = self.right.delete(val)
94          return self
```

Here are some common mistakes.

- Line 88 should use `imsuc.left != None`, not `imsuc != None`. The latter would result in `imsuc` being `None` when leaving the `while` loop. Line 91 would throw an error because `imsuc.value` would not exist if `imsuc` were `None`.
- Another common mistake occurs at line 93 by calling `self.delete(val)`. This is wrong because the node to be deleted (node 8) is now smaller than its immediate successor (node 9), but 8 is in the right subtree (of node 9). Using `self.delete(val)` causes the function to search for (and attempt to delete) 8 from the left side of 9, but node 8 cannot be found on the left side of 9.

## 6.3 Build a Binary Tree from In-Order and Post-Order

Section 6.2.3 explains three different ways to print a binary tree: pre-order, in-order, and post-order. Each of these three types of traversals alone cannot uniquely describe a binary tree. For example, three binary trees in Figure 6.4 (a)-(c) all have `4 8 11` as the in-order output. Thus, `4 8 11`, as in-order cannot describe a unique binary tree. Fortunately, it is possible to describe a unique binary tree when in-order and post-order are both given, and the values stored in the nodes are distinct.

Consider two arrays as the outputs of in-order and post-order:

- in-order: [440, 1425, 4746, 7985, 8168]
- post-order: [1425, 440, 8168, 7985, 4746].

From the last value in post-order, 4746 is the root, as shown in Figure 6.8 (a). After identifying the root, we can divide the in-order description into two parts:

1. Left subtree. (a) in-order: [440, 1425]; (b) post-order: [1425, 440].
2. Right subtree. (a) in-order: [7985, 8168]; (b) post-order: [8168, 7985].

This is illustrated in Figure 6.8 (c). From the post-order in 1, 440 must be the root of the left subtree. From the post-order in 2, 7985 must be the root of the right subtree. This is illustrated in Figure 6.8 (d). Continue this process. In the left subtree, 440 is the root, and 1425 appears after 440 in the in-order description. Thus, 1425 must be the right child. Similarly, for the right subtree, 7985 is the root, and 8168 appears after 7985 in the in-order description. Thus, 8186 must be the right child. Figure 6.8 (e) shows the constructed binary tree. This binary tree happens to be a binary search tree. In-order and post-order together can describe any binary tree, and it does not have to be a binary search tree, as long as the values are distinct. It is also possible to use in-order and pre-order to describe a unique binary tree. Pre-order and post-order together cannot describe a unique binary tree. Section 6.4.5 asks you to give an example.

The following shows how to implement this method of building a binary tree from in-order and post-order. The `buildTree` function takes two arguments: `inorder` and `postorder`.

```
def buildTree(inorder, postorder):
  if (len(inorder) != len(postorder)):
    print('inorder and postorder different lengths')
    return None
```

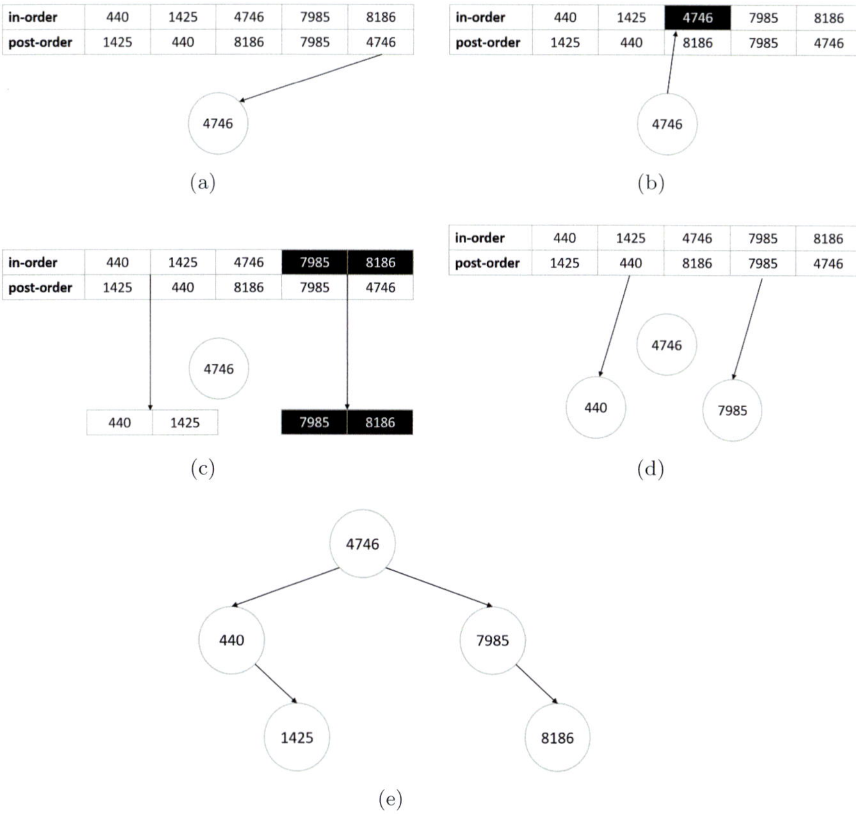


**FIGURE 6.8**: Build a binary tree from in-order and post-order descriptions.

```
  # are all elements distinct?
  if (len(set(inorder)) != len(inorder)):
    print('inorder has duplicate elements')
    return None
  # do the two arguments have the same elements?
  if (set(inorder) != set(postorder)):
    print('inorder and postorder have different elements')
    return None
  treesize = len(inorder)
  indexes = [0, treesize - 1, treesize - 1]
  # indexes[0]: starting index of the array for a subtree
  # indexes[1]: ending index of the array for a subtree
  # indexes[2]: index for the element used for root
  root = buildHelper(inorder, postorder, indexes)
  return root
```

Before building the tree, the program checks whether the in-order and post-order descriptions have the same length (line 75). The function also checks whether all elements are distinct (line 79) and the two arguments contain the same values (line 83). The `set` function creates a set in which the order of elements is ignored. Two indices are used to specify the range of the array as the in-order and post-order descriptions. Another index refers to the last element of this range and is used to find the root of the tree.

The `buildHelper` function takes the in-order and post-order descriptions, together with the range of the array and the index of the root, as the arguments. The function first takes the last element in the post-order description (line 60) and builds a node as the root (line 61). One node has already been used by the root. Thus, the last index should decrease by one (line 62). If the starting index equals the ending index, only one node needs to be built, and this function returns the newly constructed node (lines 63 - 64). Otherwise, this node has at least one child. Line 66 finds the index of the root in the in-order description. From here, the in-order and post-order descriptions are divided into the left subtree and the right subtree. The function builds the right subtree first because `indices[2]` keeps track of the last node to be used for the root of the right subtree. For the right subtree, the first element's index is the root's index + 1 (line 68). Line 69 builds the right subtree. After building the right subtree, the function builds the left subtree (lines 70 - 72).

```
54 def buildHelper(inorder, postorder, indexes):
55     startindex = indexes[0]
56     endindex   = indexes[1]
57     postindex  = indexes[2]
58     if (startindex > endindex):
59         return None  # empty list
60     val = postorder[postindex]
61     tn = BinaryTree(val)
62     indexes[2] = indexes[2] - 1
63     if (startindex == endindex):
64         return tn # no child
65     # build the subtrees
66     rootindex = inorder.index(val)
67     # the root index decrements correctly
68     indexes[0] = rootindex + 1  # index after root
69     tn.right = buildHelper(inorder, postorder, indexes)
70     indexes[0] = startindex     # restore the value
71     indexes[1] = rootindex - 1  # index before root
72     tn.left = buildHelper(inorder, postorder, indexes)
73     return tn
```

## 6.4 Problems

### 6.4.1 Count the Nodes

Write a function that counts the number of nodes in a binary tree.

### 6.4.2 Tree Height

Write a function that reports the height of a binary tree.

### 6.4.3 Check a Binary Search Tree

Write a function that reports whether a binary tree is a binary search tree.

### 6.4.4 Ancestor-Offspring

Write a function that takes two nodes and determines whether one is an ancestor of the other.

### 6.4.5 Pre-Order and Post-Order

Give an example when pre-order and post-order together cannot describe a unique binary tree.

**Answer:**

There is an infinite number of possibilities. Here is one simple example. Suppose the pre-order output is `A B`. We know that `A` is the root and `B` is a child. Thus, the post-order output must be `B A`. However, we do not know whether `B` is the left child or the right child. Thus, this pair of pre-order and post-order together cannot describe a unique binary tree.

### 6.4.6 Number of Nodes in a Complete Binary Tree

If a complete binary tree has height $n$, how many nodes does this tree have?

**Answer:**

Please see Figure 6.9. The top level (root) has one node. The second level (root's children) has two nodes. The $(n-1)^{th}$ level has $2^{n-2}$ nodes. The bottom level has at least one node and at most $2^{n-1}$ nodes. Thus, the number of nodes is between $1 + \sum_{k=1}^{n-1} 2^{k-1} = 2^{n-1}$ and $\sum_{k=1}^{n} 2^{k-1} = 2^n - 1$.

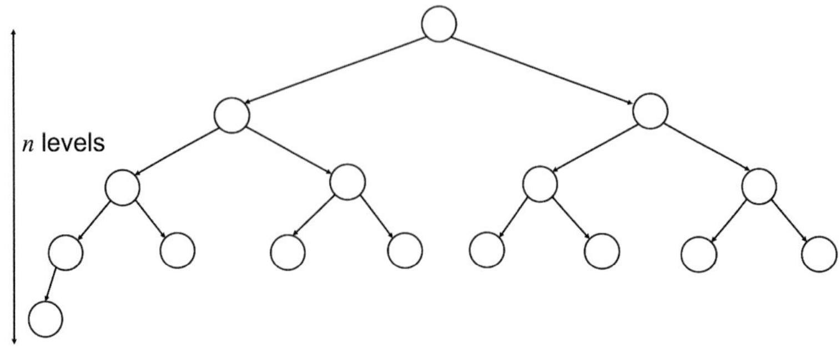


(a)

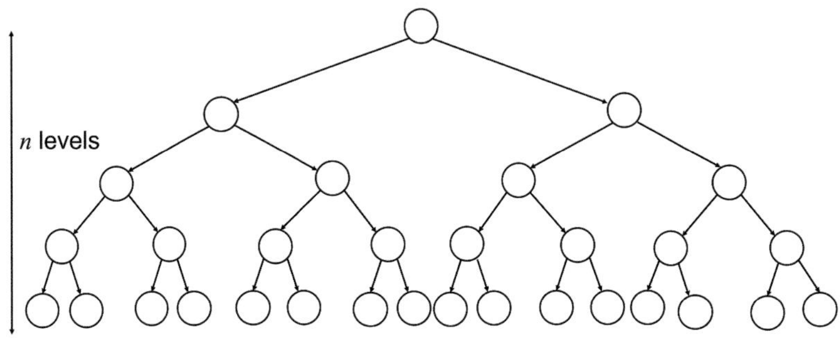


(b)

**FIGURE 6.9**: (a) A complete tree of $n$ levels with $2^{n-1}$ nodes. (b) A complete tree of $n$ levels with $2^n - 1$ nodes.

### 6.4.7 Number of Nodes in a Full Binary Tree

If a full binary tree has height $n$, how many nodes does this tree have?

**Answer:**

Please see Figure 6.10. In a full binary tree, each node has zero or two children. The top level (root) has one node and two children. One of the root's children has two children; the other child has no children. Thus, the second level has only two nodes. Similarly, each of the other levels has only two nodes. The number of nodes is between $1 + 2 \times (n - 1) = 2n - 1$ and $\sum_{k=1}^{n} 2^{k-1} = 2^n - 1$.

### 6.4.8 Count the Shapes

How many unique shapes can a binary tree with $n$ nodes possibly have? First, we need to define shapes. Two binary trees have the same shape if each node has the same number of nodes in the left subtree and the same number of nodes in the right subtree. This rule is applied recursively until reaching leaf

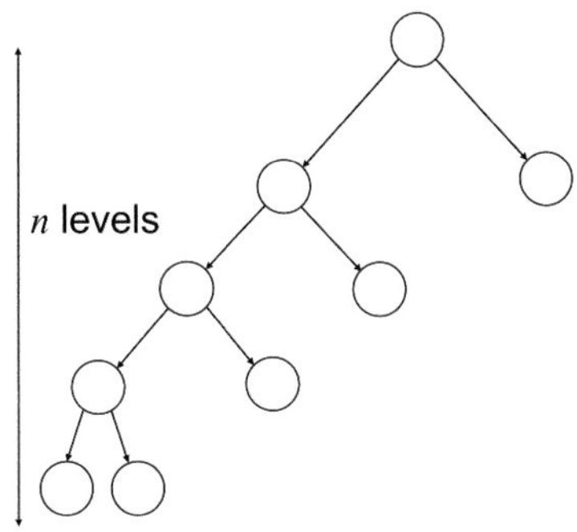


**FIGURE 6.10**: A full tree of $n$ levels with $2n-1$ nodes.

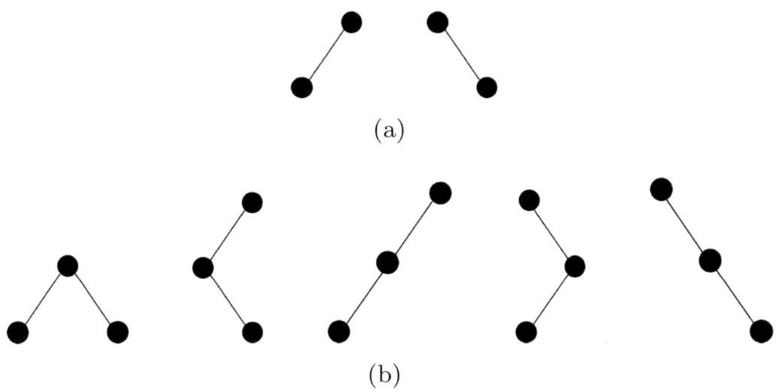

**FIGURE 6.11**: (a) There are two uniquely shaped binary trees with 2 nodes. (b) There are five uniquely shaped binary trees with 3 nodes.

nodes. Figure 6.11 shows the different shapes of trees with two or three nodes. Table 6.3 gives the number of uniquely shaped binary trees with 1 through 10 nodes.

**Answer:**

Table 6.3 gives the number of uniquely shaped binary trees with 1 through 10 nodes.

**TABLE 6.3**: The number of shapes for binary trees of different sizes.

| n | 1 | 2 | 3 | 4 | 5 | 6 | 7 | 8 | 9 | 10 |
|---|---|---|---|---|---|---|---|---|---|---|
| number of shapes | 1 | 2 | 5 | 14 | 42 | 132 | 429 | 1430 | 4862 | 16796 |

How can we obtain the values in the table? Suppose there are $f(n)$ shapes for a binary tree with $n$ nodes. By observation, we can tell that $f(1) = 1$ and $f(2) = 2$. We can use them as base cases for a recursive function. If there are

$k$ nodes on the left side of the root node, then there must be $n - k - 1$ nodes on the right side of the root node (we need to exclude one node for the root). By definition, the left subtree has $f(k)$ possible shapes, and the right side has $f(n - k - 1)$ possible shapes. The shapes on the two sides are independent of each other. This means that for every possible shape in the left subtree, we count every shape in the right subtree. Thus, the number of shapes is: $f(k) \times f(n - k - 1)$. The value of $k$ is between 0 and $n - 1$ nodes. The total number of shapes is the sum of all the different possible values of $k$.

$$f(n) = \sum_{k=0}^{n-1} f(k) \times f(n - k - 1) \tag{6.1}$$

The values of $f(n)$ are called the *Catalan numbers.*

# Chapter 7

# Huffman Compression

Do you send emails, download files from the Internet, post photos on social networks, or watch movies online? Has the network ever been too slow? Do you exceed the limit of the data plan of your mobile phone? When you have too much data and want to save space or reduce transmission time, you should *compress* the data.

## 7.1 Compression

Compression reduces the size of data. Compression can be classified as *lossless compression* and *lossy compression.* Lossless compression means the original data can be fully recovered, and it is commonly used to compress documents, such as bank statements. If data is compressed by a lossy method, the original data cannot be fully recovered. Lossy compression may achieve a higher *compression ratio* than lossless compression, and is useful when full recovery of the original data is unnecessary. Lossy compression is commonly used to compress images, videos, and sound. JPEG is an example of lossy compression for images; MP3 is an example of lossy compression for audio. The compression ratio is defined as:

$$\frac{\text{size of uncompressed file}}{\text{size of compressed file}}. \tag{7.1}$$

This chapter considers only text files and only lossless compression. English texts are usually encoded using ASCII (American Standard Code for Information Interchange). English has 26 letters A to Z. If we distinguish upper cases (A to Z) from lower cases (a to z), there are 52 letters. Adding symbols (e.g., &, %, $, #), numeric (0 to 9), as well as control symbols (e.g., newline `'\n'`), the total is fewer than 128 and can fit in one byte (8 bits). One byte can accommodate 256 values (0 to 255). This book discusses how to use as few bits as possible to store the data. The chapter uses "encode" and "compress" interchangeably. Similarly, "decode" and "decompress" are used interchangeably. Also, "letter" and "character" are used interchangeably. This chapter uses ASCII for English as examples. The same concept can be applied to other languages that use Unicode (such as Chinese, Korean, Japanese, Russian, Greek, Arabic, Hebrew, Thai, or Hindi).

### 7.1.1 Variable-Length Coding

ASCII uses *fixed-length coding*: Each English letter, symbol, or numeral is represented by exactly one byte (8 bits). One commonly adopted strategy for compression uses *variable-length coding* based on the following principle: *Optimize for the common cases.*

In many articles, some English letters (such as e and s) appear more frequently than others (such as q and z). If the frequent letters use few bits and the rare letters use more bits, the entire data can use fewer bits on average. This book uses the *Huffman Compression* method, also called *Huffman Coding* [3]. The method is widely used for compression. This chapter explains the concepts and how to implement the algorithm using Python. Huffman compression uses the following principles:

- Each letter in the text is expressed by a code. If a letter does not appear in the data, no code is created for this letter.
- Suppose $x$ and $y$ are two letters; $c_x$ and $c_y$ are the codes for $x$ and $y$. If $x$ occurs more often than $y$, then $|c_x| \leq |c_y|$, meaning that the length of $c_x$ is no greater than the length of $c_y$. Please notice that their codes may have the same length, i.e., $|c_x| = |c_y|$. However, $|c_x| = |c_y|$ does not imply that the two letters have the same occurrences. Moreover, $|c_x| < |c_y|$ does not imply that $x$ occurs more often than $y$ (they may have the same occurrences).
- No code is a *prefix* of another code. This is the definition of a prefix: Suppose $c_1 = a_1 a_2 ... a_m$ and $c_2 = b_1 b_2 ... b_n$ are two codes. If $c_1$ is a prefix of $c_2$, then $m \leq n$ and $a_1 = b_1$, $a_2 = b_2$, ... $a_m = b_m$. For example, $c_1 = 001$ is a prefix of $c_2 = 00101$. In Huffman compression, one letter's code must not be a prefix of another letter's code; otherwise, ambiguity occurs. To be more precise, if $c_1$ and $c_2$ are the codes of two different letters, it is not possible that $c_1$ is a prefix of $c_2$.

Let's consider two documents. Both documents use only eight letters: a, b, c, d, e, f, g, and h. To encode these letters, only 3 bits are sufficient because $2^3 = 8$. That means that each character can be assigned to a unique 3-bit sequence. Next, consider the situation when the letters' occurrences are quite different, as shown in Table 7.1. The table also shows the codes (bit sequences) for the characters. The method to generate the codes will be explained soon. The average number of bits per letter is

**TABLE 7.1**: Example 1. The average number of bits per letter is 2.8125.

| Letter | Count | Probability | Code | Length |
|---|---|---|---|---|
| a | 54 | 22.50% | 01 | 2 |
| b | 21 | 8.75% | 1111 | 4 |
| c | 18 | 7.50% | 1101 | 4 |
| d | 24 | 10.00% | 000 | 3 |
| e | 63 | 26.25% | 10 | 2 |
| f | 12 | 5.00% | 1100 | 4 |
| g | 27 | 11.25% | 001 | 3 |
| h | 21 | 8.75% | 1110 | 4 |
| **Average** | | | | 2.8125 |

**TABLE 7.2**: Example 2. The average number of bits per letter is 2.37.

| Letter | Count | Probability | Code | Length |
|---|---|---|---|---|
| a | 116 | 29.0% | 10 | 2 |
| b | 12 | 3.0% | 11000 | 5 |
| c | 20 | 5.0% | 11101 | 5 |
| d | 16 | 4.0% | 11100 | 5 |
| e | 160 | 40.0% | 0 | 1 |
| f | 36 | 9.0% | 1111 | 4 |
| g | 12 | 3.0% | 11001 | 5 |
| h | 28 | 7.0% | 1101 | 4 |
| **Average** | | | | 2.37 |

$2 \times 22.50\% + 4 \times 8.75\% + 4 \times 7.50\% + 3 \times 10.00\% + 2 \times 26.25\% + 4 \times 5.00\% + 3 \times 11.25\% + 4 \times 8.75\% = 2.8125.$

This is a $1 - \frac{2.8125}{3} = 6.25\%$ reduction in the length over using 3-bit codes. This saving is quite modest because the occurrences are not dramatically different.

Next, consider the example in Table 7.2. Letter e accounts for 40% of the occurrences, and letter a accounts for 29% of the occurrences. The average number of bits is

$2 \times 29.0\% + 5 \times 3.0\% + 5 \times 5.0\% + 5 \times 4.0\% + 1 \times 40.0\% + 4 \times 9.0\% + 5 \times 3.0\% + 4 \times 7.0\% = 2.37.$

The reduction is $1 - \frac{2.37}{3} = 21\%$. The reduction is more noticeable.

These two examples show that Huffman compression is more advantageous when the occurrences are imbalanced (i.e., some letters are much more likely than the others), like the second example. If the letters' occurrences are similar (the first example), the benefit of Huffman compression is not as effective.

### 7.1.2 Encode

Huffman compression has two steps:

1. *Encoding*: Take the original text file $\mathbb{T}$ and compress it so that the new file $\mathbb{C}$ is shorter. This is also called compression. The file $\mathbb{C}$ is "binary", i.e., not readable by humans using a text editor. In most cases, the size of $\mathbb{T}$ is longer than the size of $\mathbb{C}$, i.e., $|\mathbb{T}| > |\mathbb{C}|$. However, it is possible that $|\mathbb{T}| < |\mathbb{C}|$ when the original file $\mathbb{T}$ is already very small.
2. *Decoding*: Reverse the compression process. Take the compressed binary file $\mathbb{C}$ and restore the original text file $\mathbb{T}$. Huffman compression is lossless; thus, the restored file should be identical to the original text file.

To encode a file, the following seven steps are needed:

1. Count the occurrences of the characters.
2. Sort the characters by occurrences in ascending order.
3. Build a binary tree based on the occurrences.
4. Save the tree at the top of the compressed file. This is necessary because the tree contains only the letters in the original file. Different input files may produce different trees. A newline character `'\n'` is added as a separator.
5. Convert the binary tree to the code book.
6. Save the length of the original file to the compressed file. A newline character `'\n'` is added as a separator.
7. Use the code book to compress the file.

Let's consider how to create the codes in Table 7.1. This process corresponds to steps 1 to 3 above. Figure 7.1 illustrates the process to create the Huffman compression tree.

1. The letters are sorted by the occurrences in ascending order. If two letters have the same number of occurrences, it does not matter which letter is the first. The order will affect the codes but will not change the average number of bits per letter. The occurrence of each letter is marked above the letter, as shown in Figure 7.1 (a). Each box is actually a binary tree node.
2. Create a binary tree node as the parent of the first two letters. This parent node's occurrence is the sum of the occurrences of the two children, as shown in Figure 7.1 (b). This parent node does not store any letter.
3. Insert the newly created binary tree back and maintain the ascending order, as illustrated in Figure 7.1 (c).
4. Figure 7.1 (d) repeats the second step by creating a binary tree node as the parent of the first two nodes.

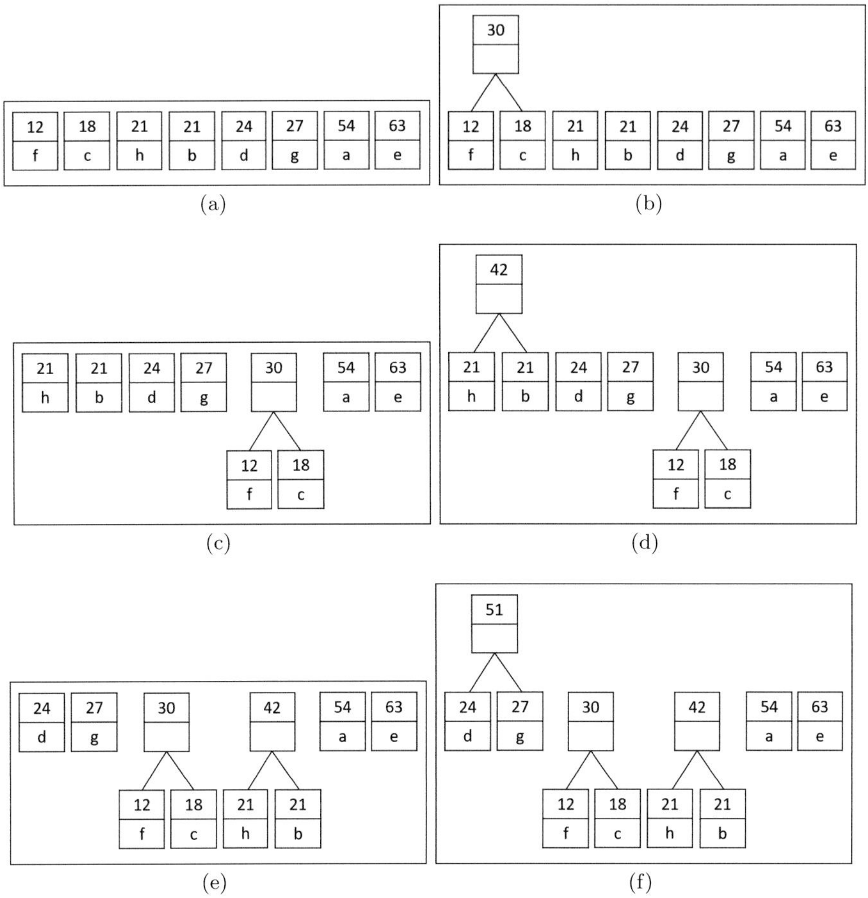


**FIGURE 7.1**: Process to create the Huffman compression tree.

5. Figure 7.1 (e) repeats the third step by inserting the newly created parent node back and maintaining the ascending order.
6. Figure 7.1 (f) repeats the second step by creating a binary tree node as the parent of the first two nodes. This newly created tree node is inserted while maintaining the ascending order.

The final result of Table 7.1 is the tree shown in Figure 7.2 (a). The letters are the leaf nodes (i.e. no node below). Figure 7.2 (b) is the tree for Table 7.2.

Figure 7.3 illustrates the method to assign codes to the letters. Starting from the tree's root (i.e., nothing above), moving left adds 0 to the code and moving right adds 1 to the code. The code for e is 10 because from the root, the path moves right first (adding 1)

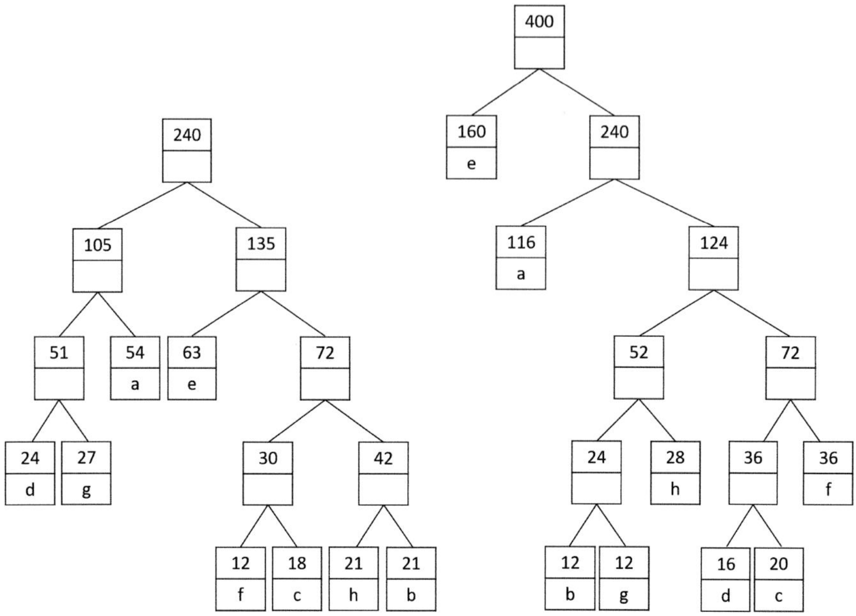


(a) (b)

**FIGURE 7.2**: The process stops when all letters belong to the same tree. (a) for Table 7.1. (b) for Table 7.2.

and then moves left (adding 0). The code for g is 001 because the path from the root moves left twice (adding 00) and then moves right once (adding 1). Please verify the codes in the tree are the same codes in Table 7.1. This tree has the following properties, matching the rules on Page 142.

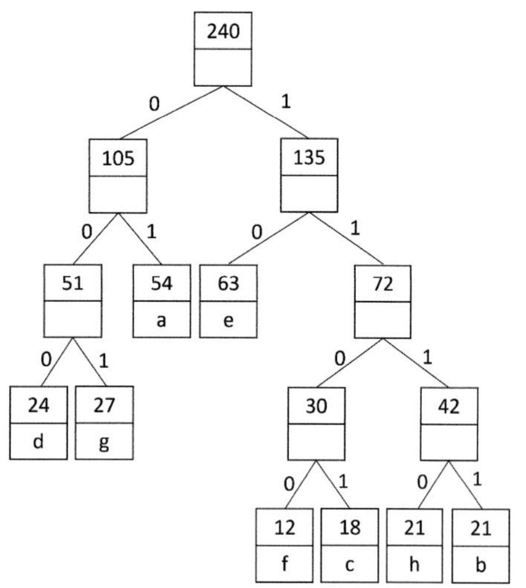


**FIGURE 7.3**: From the root, moving left adds 0 to the code; moving right adds 1 to the code.

1. The tree's leaf nodes store the eight letters.
2. If a letter (such as g) occurs more often than another letter (such as c), the code for the former (length 3) is no longer than the code for the latter (length 4).
3. Only the leaf nodes store the letters. If a node is not a

leaf node, it does not store
any letter. From the root, a parent node is the prefix of its child nodes.

The tree is built by selecting two nodes as the siblings of a new node. Thus, any node in the tree must have zero or two children. It is not possible to have a node that has only one child.

### 7.1.3 Count the Letters' Occurrences

Page 144 lists the steps to implement Huffman compression. The first step reads the letters and counts their occurrences. This can be done by the `countOccur` function shown below. This function uses a dictionary (line 155), and the keys are the letters in the file.

```
150 class Compressor:
151     def __init__(self, infile, text_outfile, binary_outfile):
152         self.infile = infile
153         self.text_outfile = text_outfile
154         self.binary_outfile = binary_outfile
155         self.count = dict()
156         self.length = 0
157         self.tree = None
158         self.code = None
159         self.book = None
160     def countOccur(self):
161         fhd = open(self.infile, 'r')
162         # key: letter; value: count
163         self.content = fhd.read()  # read the entire file
164         for i in range(0, len(self.content)):
165             ascii = self.content[i]  # get the ASCII value
166             if (ascii in self.count):  # already seen
167                 self.count[ascii] = self.count[ascii] + 1
168             else:
169                 self.count[ascii] = 1  # first time
170         fhd.close()
171         self.length = len(self.content)
172         print(f'length = {self.length}')
```

### 7.1.4 List of Trees

The second step on Page 144 sorts the characters by the occurrences. Figure 7.4 illustrates the method to build the trees in Figure 7.2. We will use two data structures: lists and trees.

This is the `Tree` class. A `Tree` object has these attributes:

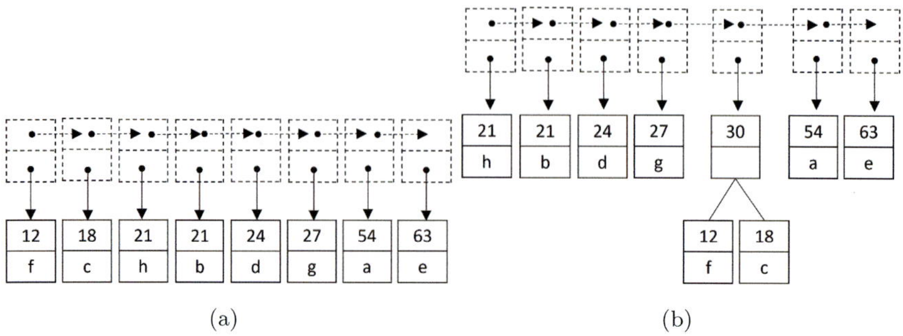


**FIGURE 7.4**: (a) Tree nodes (solid lines) are connected by list nodes (dash lines). The nodes are sorted in the ascending order. (b) The first two nodes become siblings and the occurrences are added. The newly created node is inserted back in the ascending order.

1. `ascii`: This attribute stores the letter.
2. `occur`: This attribute stores the number of occurrences.
3. `left` and `right`: The left and right children. They are initialized to `None`

```
42 class Tree:
43     def __init__(self, ascii, occur):
44         self.ascii = ascii
45         self.occur = occur
46         self.left = None
47         self.right = None
```

We will create a `List` class. Each object has two attributes: `tree` and `next`. The `tree` attribute refers to the downward arrow in Figure 7.4. The `next` attribute refers to the right arrow.

```
112 class List:
113     def __init__(self):
114         self.tree = None
115         self.next = None
```

After obtaining the occurrences of the letters, these letters are added to the list by calling `addASCIIoccur`; line 117 creates a `Tree` object and adds the `Tree` object into the list in the ascending order. Line 120 creates a `List` object; line 121 assigns the argument of the `Tree` object to the `tree` attribute of the newly created `List` object. If the list has nothing yet (line 122), the newly created `List` node is the first node. This `addTree` function is used for both compression and decompression. For compression, the nodes are sorted. Thus, `tosort` is `True`. Later, when we use the same `addTree` function for decompression, `tosort` will be `False`. If the list already has one or more nodes, the function checks whether the newly added `List` object should be the first node because the letter's occurrence is smaller (line 130). If the newly created `List` object is not the first, then the function finds where it should be inserted. Line 137 finds the right place. This `while` condition stops when either the list reaches the end and `q` is `None`, or a node's occurrence is larger.

```
116     def addASCIIoccur(self, ascii, occur):
117         t = Tree(ascii, occur)
118         self.addTree(t, True)
119     def addTree(self, tree, tosort = True):
120         ln = List()
121         ln.tree = tree
122         if (self.next == None): # first node
123             self.next = ln
124             return
125         if (tosort == False): # add at the beginning
126             ln.next = self.next
127             self.next = ln
128             return
129         occur = tree.occur
130         if (occur < ((self.next).tree).occur):
131             ln.next = self.next # ln becomes the first
132             self.next = ln
133             return
134         # find where to insert ln
135         p = self.next
136         q = p.next
137         while ((q != None) and ((q.tree.occur) < occur)):
138             p = p.next
139             q = q.next
140         # It is possible that q is None, but that does not
         ↪  matter
141         p.next = ln
142         ln.next = q
```

### 7.1.5 Build the Huffman Code Tree

The third step on Page 144 builds a binary tree by making the first two `Tree` nodes siblings and then inserting the parent node back to the list in the ascending order. This is accomplished by the `buildTree` function. The function adds all letters (lines 175 - 176) into the list. After this step, the data is organized in the format shown in Figure 7.4 (a); the list has eight `List` nodes. Line 177 checks whether there are at least two `List` nodes. Lines 179 - 180 take the `Tree` nodes from the first two `List` nodes. Line 181 creates a new `Tree` node. The letter is `-`; it can be any letter because we will not use this letter. The new `Tree` node's occurrence is the sum of the two `Tree` nodes. The `merge` function makes `t1` and `t2` the left and right children of `tp`. Lines 185 - 186 delete the first two `List` nodes. Line 188 inserts the newly created `Tree` node back to the list. Comparing Figure 7.4 (a) with (b), we can discover that each iteration removes two `List` nodes and adds one back. Thus, the number of `List` nodes decreases by one. Eventually, only one `List` node remains, and the entire tree has been built.

```
173     def buildTree(self):
174         ln = List()
175         for ascii in self.count:
176             ln.addASCIIoccur(ascii, self.count[ascii])
177         while ((ln.next).next != None):
178             # get the first two Tree nodes
179             t1 = ln.next.tree
180             t2 = ln.next.next.tree
181             tp = Tree('-', t1.occur + t2.occur) # parent
182             # make them siblings
183             tp.merge(t1, t2)
184             # remove the first two from the list
185             ln.delete()
186             ln.delete()
187             # insert back in the ascending order
188             ln.addTree(tp, True)
189         self.tree = ln.next.tree
```

This is the `merge` function:

```
    def merge(self, left, right):
        # make this the parent of two tree nodes
        self.left = left
        self.right = right
```

This is the `delete` function

```
    def delete(self): # delete the first node
        self.next = (self.next).next
```

### 7.1.6 Convert the Tree to the Code Book

The next step converts the binary tree to the code book. Figure 7.5 shows an example. The tree's height is 5 and the length of the longest code is 4. The longest code is the longest distance from the root to a leaf node. If a tree's height is $n$, then the length of the longest code is $n - 1$. This is because the root does not need any code. The `buildCodeBook` function visits the tree and builds the code book. Line 201 finds the height of the tree. Line 202 creates an array of this length; the elements are initialized to space. Even though the

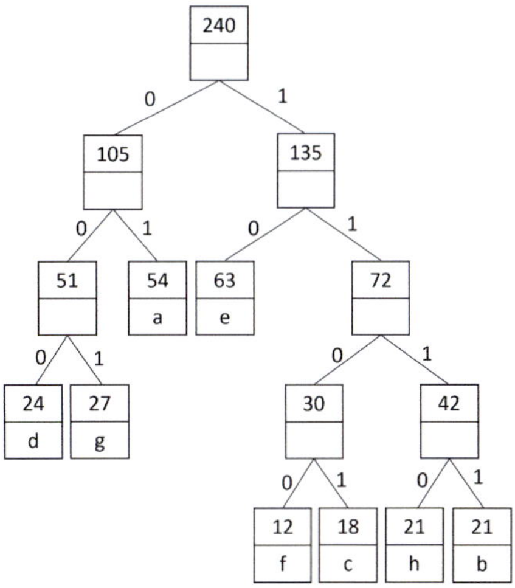


(a)

| | Column | | | | |
|---|---|---|---|---|---|
| **Key** | 0 | 1 | 2 | 3 | 4 |
| d | 0 | 0 | 0 | | |
| g | 0 | 0 | 1 | | |
| a | 0 | 1 | | | |
| e | 1 | 0 | | | |
| f | 1 | 1 | 0 | 0 | |
| c | 1 | 1 | 0 | 1 | |
| h | 1 | 1 | 1 | 0 | |
| b | 1 | 1 | 1 | 1 | |

3 rows (d, g, a); 5 rows (e, f, c, h, b)

(b)

**FIGURE 7.5**: Convert the binary tree in (a) to the code book in (b). The first column has 3 rows of zeros because the root's left subtree has 3 leaf nodes. The first column has 5 rows of ones because the root's right subtree has 5 leaf nodes.

longest code has a length of 4, we create an array of one additional element. Huffman coding uses variable-length codes (using either 0 or 1). Thus, we need a way to indicate the end of a code. In this program, space is used to indicate the end, as illustrated in Figure 7.5 (b). The code book is a dictionary (line 203). The keys are the letters and the values are the codes. Line 204 calls the `codeHelper`.

```
200     def buildCodeBook(self):
201       h = self.tree.getHeight()
202       self.code = [' ' for i in range(0, h)]
203       self.book = dict()
204       self.codeHelper(self.tree, 0)
205       print(f'codebook = {self.book}')
```

The `getHeight` function finds a tree's height. It finds the height of the left subtree and the height of the right subtree. Then, the function returns the higher one of the two subtrees. The function needs to add one to include the root itself. This is another recursive function.

```
    def getHeight(self):
        if (self == None):
            return 0
```

```
        if (self.left == None):
            leftheight = 0
        else:
            leftheight = self.left.getHeight()
        if (self.right == None):
            rightheight = 0
        else:
            rightheight = self.right.getHeight()
        if (leftheight > rightheight):
            return (leftheight + 1) # add one to include the root
        return (rightheight + 1)
```

The `codeHelper` function is recursive. This function's stop condition is when reaching a leaf node (lines 191 - 193). We need to check only the left child because each node has either no child or two children. If a node has no left child, this node must have no right child, either. If the stop condition is not met, the function visits the left subtree (lines 195 - 196). As shown in Figure 7.5 (a), 0 is added when visiting the left subtree. Next, the function visits the right subtree (lines 198 - 199). One is added to the code when visiting the right subtree.

```
190    def codeHelper(self, tree, ind):
191      if (tree.left == None): # leaf node
192        self.book[tree.ascii] = self.code[0:ind]
193        return
194      # left subtree
195      self.code[ind] = '0'
196      self.codeHelper(tree.left, ind + 1)
197      # right subtree
198      self.code[ind] = '1'
199      self.codeHelper(tree.right, ind + 1)
```

### 7.1.7 Express the Huffman Tree

The Huffman trees in Figure 7.2 depend on the inputs. Different inputs have different trees because some letters may not appear in a particular input. Also, different authors have their own styles and preferred words. Thus, it is necessary to provide the tree in the compressed file. Section 6.3 explains that it is possible to uniquely specify a binary tree by providing in-order and post-order traversals. This section describes another method to uniquely specify a binary tree using post-order only, with some additional information.

Consider the post-order output of Figure 7.2:

```
dg-a-efc-hb----
```

Here - indicates a node that is not a leaf node. We will add some more information to the description by taking advantage of properties of Huffman compression trees:

1. Only the leaf nodes store the letters.
2. A node has no child or both children. No node has only one child.

If a leaf node is encountered, the node is printed using two letters: 1 followed by the letter stored in this node. If a non-leaf node is encountered, print 0 (to replace - above). If a tree has $n$ leaf nodes, there should be $n - 1$ non-leaf nodes. A final 0 is added after the root to indicate that the tree's description has ended. There should be the same number of 1s and 0s. From the post-order description above, `d` becomes `1d`; `g` becomes `1g`. The parent of `d` and `g` is shown as `-`, and it is converted to `0`. The entire binary tree is expressed as follows:

```
1d1g01a01e1f1c01h1b00000
```

This is the function to print the post-order description of the tree. So far, we explain the compression process using text output. Section 7.3 will explain how to use bits for binary output. This function can handle both text and binary. If the output is text, `text` is `True`; if the output is binary, `text` is `False`. For now, focus on the parts when `text` is `True`.

```
    def postOrder(self, fhd, text = True, bitobj = None):
        if ((text == False) and (bitobj == None)):
            # if text is False, bitobj cannot None
            return
        if (self == None): # should not occur
            return
        if (self.left == None): # leaf node
            if (text == True):
              fhd.write('1')
              fhd.write(self.ascii)
            else: # binary
              bitobj.bit = 1;
              bitobj.writeBit(fhd)
              bitobj.writeByte(self.ascii, fhd)
            return
        self.left.postOrder(fhd, text, bitobj)
        self.right.postOrder(fhd, text, bitobj)
        if (text == True):
          fhd.write('0')  # non-leaf node
        else:
```

```
            bitobj.bit = 0;
            bitobj.writeBit(fhd)
```

The function takes an argument `fhd` as the file handler because the tree's description is one part of the compressed file. The file contains other pieces of information.

The `save` function saves the tree's post-order description. After the tree is written, an ending `0` is used to ensure there are the same number of `1` (or leaf nodes) and `0` for non-leaf nodes. Then, a newline character `'\n'` is added as a separator.

```
    def save(self, filename, text = True):
        if (text == True):
            bitobj = None
            fhd = open(filename, 'w')
            self.postOrder(fhd, text, bitobj)
            fhd.write('0') # end the tree
            fhd.write('\n') # separator
```

### 7.1.8 Save the Length and Compress Text

The `compress` function follows the steps explained on Page 144. Line 207 is the first step: count the occurrences of letters. Line 208 combines the second and the third steps and builds the tree. Line 210 saves the tree using post-order; this is the fourth step. Line 212 is the fifth step building the code tree. Line 216 is the sixth step saving the input file's length to the output file. Line 217 adds the newline separator.

```
206     def compress(self):
207       self.countOccur()
208       self.buildTree()
209       self.tree.print()
210       self.tree.save(self.text_outfile, True)
211       self.tree.save(self.binary_outfile, False)
212       self.buildCodeBook()
213       # write the original file's length
214       # text output
215       text_fhd = open(self.text_outfile, 'a') # 'a': append
216       text_fhd.write(str(len(self.content)))
217       text_fhd.write('\n')
```

The seventh step reads the input characters, converts to code, and saves the code to the output. This step is implemented below:

```
        for i in range(0, len(self.content)):
            code = self.book[self.content[i]]
            for j in range(0, len(code)):
                text_fhd.write(code[j])
```

### 7.1.9 Examples

This section provides several examples of the original files and the compressed files.

This is the first input:

```
##########$$$$$$$$$$$$$$$
```

This input has 10 `#` followed by 15 `$`. Figure 7.6 (a) is the tree. The code for `#` is 0; the code for `$` is 1. This is the post-order of the tree:

```
1#1$00
```

The file's length is 25.

```
25
```

This is the codes of the letters:

```
0000000000111111111111111
```

This is the output by the `print` function of `Tree` class:

```
      R-- $ 15
Root: - 25
      L-- # 10
```

Consider another example:

```
aDDbffffbccccDDDDDDfffffffffff
```

Figure 7.6 (b) shows the tree. Figure 7.6 (c) shows the code book. Let's consider the first few letters `aDDbffffb` from the input and understand how they are converted to code.

1. The code for `a` is 0000.
2. The code for `D` is 01. So far, we have 0000 01. The space here is added for clarity; space does not actually exist in the compressed file. The third letter is also `D`. Thus, we have 0000 01 01.
3. The fourth letter is `b`, and its code is 0001. Adding this we obtain 0000 01 01 0001.
4. The next four letters are `f`, and its code is 1. Thus, we add four 1's and obtain 0000 01 01 0001 1 1 1 1.
5. The next letter is `b` again. We add 0001 to the output and obtain
   ```
   0000 01 01 0001 1 1 1 1 0001
   ```

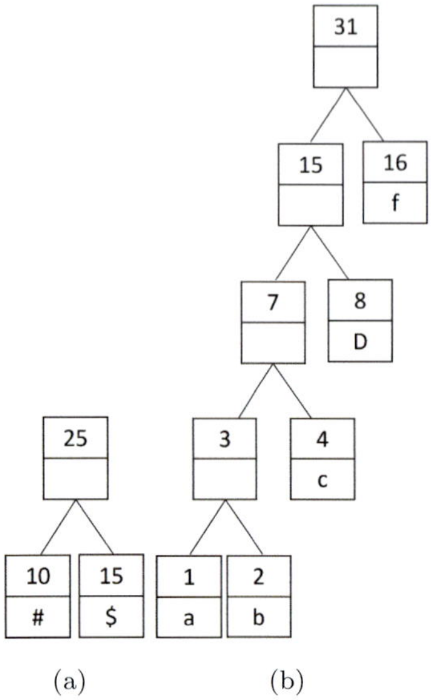


| key | Code | | | |
|---|---|---|---|---|
| a | 0 | 0 | 0 | 0 |
| b | 0 | 0 | 0 | 1 |
| c | 0 | 0 | 1 | |
| D | 0 | 1 | | |
| f | 1 | | | |

(c)

**FIGURE 7.6**: (a) Tree for 10 `#` followed by 15 `$`. (b) Tree for an input with one `a`, two `b`, four `c`, eight `D`, and sixteen `f`. (c) Code book for the input.

## 7.2 Decompression

The decoding program follows these steps:

1. Read the tree's post-order description.
2. Read the file's length.
3. Start from the root.
4. Read one digit from the encoded file. It can be zero or one,
5. If the digit is 0, move to the left child. If the digit is 1, move to the right child.
6. Keep reading digits until a leaf node is encountered; print the letter stored at this node.
7. Move back to the root and repeat steps 4 - 7 until enough letters are printed (based on the length of the original file).

The `Decompressor` class takes compressed files in both the text format and the binary format. For now, we focus on the text format. Compression and decompression in the binary format will be described in Section 7.3. The input takes both the text format and the binary format.

```
class Decompressor:
    def __init__(self, text_infile, binary_infile, outfile):
```

```
        self.text_infile = text_infile
        self.binary_infile = binary_infile
        self.outfile = outfile
        self.text_tree = None
        self.binary_tree = None
```

A compressed file has three parts:

1. Description of the tree using post-order: 1 is added in front of a letter (stored in a leaf node), and 0 indicates a non-leaf node. An additional 0 indicates the end of the tree. A newline is added after the description as a separator.
2. Length of the original file. A newline is added after the length.
3. The original file is expressed using the codes of 0 or 1.

The decoding program does not need to count the occurrences of letters. Instead, it can read the encoded tree directly. The encoded tree is described by the post-order rule. Consider this description of the tree (the same tree seen on Page 154)

`1d1g01a01e1f1c01h1b00000`

Let's rebuild the tree from this description.

1. After reading `1d1g`, two tree nodes are added, and they are connected by two list nodes, as shown in Figure 7.7 (a). The most recently added nodes are at the beginning of the linked list. Thus, the direction of the links is the opposite of Figure 7.4.
2. Next, `0` is read, and the two tree nodes share the same parent. At this moment, there is only one list node. Reading `1a` adds another tree node, as shown in Figure 7.7 (b).
3. The next `0` makes the two most recently added tree nodes siblings, as shown in Figure 7.7 (c).
4. After reading `1e1f1c`, the list nodes and tree nodes are shown in Figure 7.7 (d).
5. The next `0` creates a tree node and makes the most recent two tree nodes siblings, shown in Figure 7.7 (e).
6. Figure 7.7 (f) shows the tree after reading `1h1b0`. The remaining `0` will build the tree like Figure 7.2 (a).

After reading the tree, the decoding program reads the newline separator and an integer as the length of the original file. The `buildTree` function closely reflects the procedure described in Figure 7.7. The function reads one letter from the file and checks whether it is '1' or '0'. If it is '1', the function reads another letter and adds a tree node. If it is '0', the function takes the most recently added two tree nodes and makes them siblings. After the same number

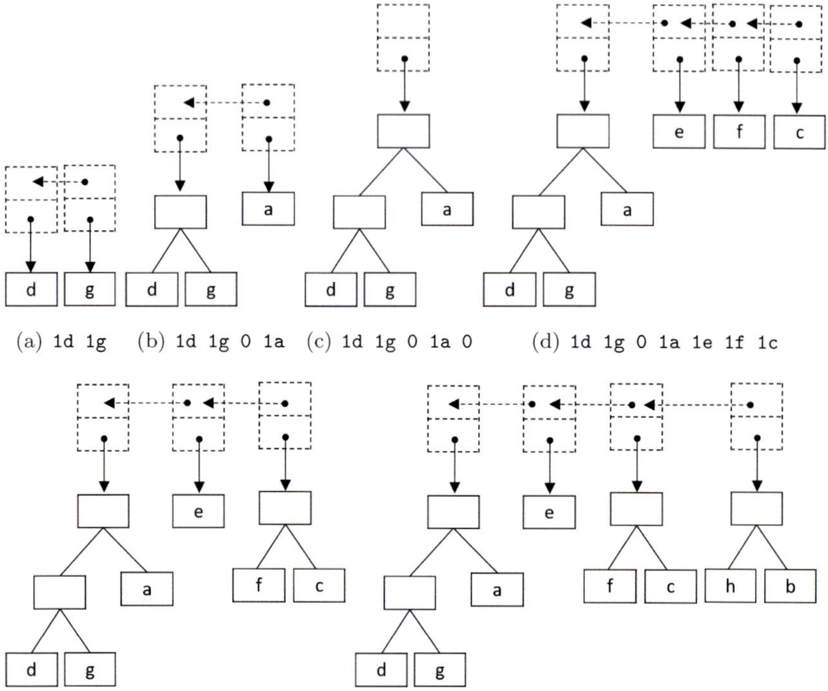

(a) `1d 1g` (b) `1d 1g 0 1a` (c) `1d 1g 0 1a 0` (d) `1d 1g 0 1a 1e 1f 1c`

(e) `1d 1g 0 1a 1e 1f 1c 0` (f) `1d 1g 0 1a 1e 1f 1c 0 1h 1b 0`

**FIGURE 7.7**: Process to create the encoded tree from post-order description. Spaces are inserted to improve readability.

of '1' and '0', the tree is completed. The function reads one more letter, and it should be '\n'.

```
    def buildTextTree(self, text_fhd):
        ln = List()
        finishedtree = False
        numOne  = 0
        numZero = 0
        while (finishedtree == False):
            ctrl = text_fhd.read(1)
            if (ctrl == '1'):
                numOne = numOne + 1
                ascii = text_fhd.read(1) # read the letter
                tn = Tree(ascii, -1) # do not care about occur,
                ↪  use -1
                ln.addTree(tn, False) # False = do not sort
            if (ctrl == '0'):
```

```
                numZero += 1
                # get the latest two trees
                tr1 = (ln.next).tree
                if (ln.next.next != None):
                    tr2 = ((ln.next).next).tree
                    tp = Tree('-', -1)
                    # do not care about the letter or occur of a
                    ↪  non-leaf node
                    tp.merge(tr2, tr1) # careful about the
                    ↪  order
                    ln.delete()
                    ln.delete()
                    ln.addTree(tp, False) # False = do not sort
            if (numZero == numOne):
                finishedtree = True
        text_fhd.read(1) # remove '\n'
        self.text_tree = ln.next.tree
```

The decompress function needs to perform tasks:

1. Build the tree (line 300),
2. Read the length with a newline ending (line 302),
3. Keep reading the input. Read one byte (line 306),
4. Decrease the length by one (line 313),
5. Restart from the root of the tree (line 314).

After reading one byte (step 3), if it is '0', the function moves to the left child (line 307). If it is '1', the function moves to the right child (line 309). When a leaf node is reached (line 311), the letter stored in the leaf node is appended to the output (line 312).

```
297     def decompress(self):
298         # decompress the text format
299         text_fhd = open(self.text_infile, 'r')
300         self.buildTextTree(text_fhd)
301         text_output=[]
302         text_length = int(text_fhd.readline())
303         print(f'text_length = {text_length}')
304         tn = self.text_tree
305         while (text_length > 0):
306           code = text_fhd.read(1) # read one byte
307           if (code == '0'):
308               tn = tn.left
309           if (code == '1'):
310               tn = tn.right
```

```
            if (tn.left == None): # leaf node
                text_output.append(tn.ascii)
                text_length -= 1
                tn = self.text_tree
        text_fhd.close()
```

## 7.3 Bit Representations

The method explained so far does not actually compress the input. In fact, the size of the output is larger than the size of the input. In the last example on Page 156, the letter `a` is replaced by four letters `0000`. The size of the original input is 31 bytes. The "compressed" file is 75 bytes, more than twice as large. This section explains how to use bits for these 0's and 1's to actually compress the file.

**TABLE 7.3**: One byte has 8 bits. Each bit can represent either 0 or 1. It is conventional to add space between every four bits to improve readability.

| One Byte |
|---|
| 0 1 1 0    0 0 1 1 |

To compress a file, the codes in Table 7.1 and Table 7.2 are actually bits. In other words, letter e in Table 7.2 is replaced by a single bit. In the original file, letter e is expressed by one byte. Thus, this compression can reduce the data size by $1 - \frac{1}{8} = 87.5\%$. This is a significant reduction. Even for d and u, the reduction is 50% (from one byte to four bits).

### 7.3.1 Control Bits and Data Bytes

Let's consider the example of Figure 7.5 again. This is the post-order description of the tree:

`1d1g01a01e1f1c01h1b00000`

This representation contains two types of information:

1. *Control Bit*: It can be 1 or 0 to indicate whether a tree node is a leaf node or not.
2. *Data Byte*: Each letter (such as `a` or `b`) uses one byte (8 bits) from the ASCII table.

| | | | | | | | | | | | | | | | | | | | | | | |
|---|---|---|---|---|---|---|---|---|---|---|---|---|---|---|---|---|---|---|---|---|---|---|
| 1 | d | 1 | g | 0 | 1 | a | 0 | 1 | e | 1 | f | 1 | c | 0 | 1 | h | 1 | b | 0 | 0 | 0 | 0 |
| C | D | C | D | C | C | D | C | C | D | C | D | C | D | C | C | D | C | D | C | C | C | C |

**FIGURE 7.8**: Mark the tree description as control (C) or data (D).

<table>
<tr><td>description</td><td>1</td><td>d</td><td>1</td><td>g</td><td>0</td><td>1</td><td>a</td><td>0</td></tr>
<tr><td>bits</td><td>1</td><td>0110 0100</td><td>1</td><td>0100 0111</td><td>0</td><td>1</td><td>0110 0001</td><td>0</td></tr>
<tr><td>remove boundary</td><td colspan="8">1 0110 0100 1 0100 0111 0 1 0110 0001 0</td></tr>
<tr><td>arrange as bytes</td><td colspan="8">1 0110 010 | 0 1 0100 01 | 11 0 1 0110 | 0001 0</td></tr>
</table>

**FIGURE 7.9**: Use bits to describe the tree. The last row uses thicker lines to highlight byte boundaries.

**TABLE 7.4**: ASCII values for `d`, `g`, and `a`.

| Letter | Decimal | Hexadecimal | Binary |
|---|---|---|---|
| d | 100 | 64 | 0110 0100 |
| g | 103 | 67 | 0110 0111 |
| a | 97 | 61 | 0110 0001 |

Figure 7.8 marks the tree description as control bits (C) or data bytes (D). Figure 7.9 shows how to handle the bits.

1. The first row shows the beginning of the tree using the post-order description. Control bits 1 and 0 are added.
2. The second row replaces each letter with its ASCII value. Table 7.4 shows the binary values of letters `d`, `g`, and `a`.
3. The third row removes the boundaries of control bits and data bytes.
4. The fourth row inserts boundaries | between bytes.

The first bit of the first byte is used for a control bit. As a result, only seven bits are available for storing the data byte of `d`. The last bit of `d` has to move to the first bit of the second byte; here | separates the first seven bits of `d` from the last bit of `d`. The next bit is a control bit. Two bits in the second byte have been used, and only six bits are available for the letter `g`. The last two bits of `g` use the first two bits of the third byte. The next two bits are both control bits. Only four bits are available for `a`. Thus, the last four bits of `a` have to move to the fourth byte. This example shows that the locations of the control bits change, and it is necessary to keep track of the locations as well as the starting bit of a data byte.

**TABLE 7.5**: ASCII values for # and /.

| Letter | Decimal | Hexadecimal | Binary |
|---|---|---|---|
| # | 35 | 23 | 0010 0011 |
| / | 47 | 2F | 0010 1111 |

Consider another example, a file composed of 10 # and 15 /. The original file is

```
##########$$$$$$$$$$$$$$$
```

The compression file in the text format is

```
1#1$00
25
0000000000111111111111111
```

To convert this text format into the binary format, first consider the tree description. Table 7.5 shows the ASCII values of # and /. Figure 7.10 shows the compression tree in bits.

| | | | | | | | |
|---|---|---|---|---|---|---|---|
| description | 1 | # | 1 | / | 0 | 0 | padding |
| bits | 1 | 0010 0011 | 1 | 0010 1111 | 0 | 0 | 0000 |
| remove boundary | 1 0010 0011 1 0010 1111 0 0 | | | | | | 0000 |
| arrange as bytes | 1 0010 001 \| 1 1 001011 \| 11 00 0000 | | | | | | |

**FIGURE 7.10**: Use bits to describe the tree of a file composed of 10 # followed by 15 /. The unused bits of the last byte are filled by zero (called *padding*).

The first seven bits of # are 0010 001. Adding the leading control bit 1, the first byte is 1001 0001. The last bit of # is 1, and it becomes the first bit of the second byte. The second control bit is 1, and it becomes the second bit of the second byte. The first six bits of / are 0010 11. Together with the earlier two bits, the second byte is 1100 1011. The remaining two bits from / become the first two bits of the third byte. The next two control bits are both zeros. Only four bits of the third byte are used. If the last byte is not fully used, zero bits are added to complete the last byte (called zero *padding*). In this case, four bits are padded at the end. Thus, the third byte is 1100 0000.

### 7.3.2 Byte Ordering: Little or Big Endian

Different computers organize bytes in different ways. Two popular methods are *little endian*, used in Intel processors, and *big endian*, used in IBM processors.

| Address | Little Endian | Big Endian |
|---|---|---|
| | Value | Value |
| A+24 | 0X12 | 0X78 |
| A+16 | 0X34 | 0X56 |
| A+8 | 0X56 | 0X34 |
| A | 0X78 | 0X12 |

(a)

| Address | A | A+8 | A+16 | A+24 |
|---|---|---|---|---|
| Little Endian | 0X78 | 0X56 | 0X34 | 0X12 |
| Big Endian | 0X12 | 0X34 | 0X56 | 0X78 |

(b)

**FIGURE 7.11**: Big endian and little endian are different formats to store data.

ARM processors can support both and are usually configured for little endian. These two data formats are illustrated in Figure 7.11. Consider a larger number `0X12345678` (the leading `0X` means hexadecimal). If it is stored in the little endian format, the four bytes are ordered as `0X78`, `0X56`, `0X34`, `0X12`. If it is stored in the big endian format, the four bytes are ordered as `0X12`, `0X34`, `0X56`, `0X78`. Figure 7.11 (a) shows the addresses vertically in the descending order from bottom to top. In little endian, `0X12` (the leftmost byte) appears on the top and `0X78` (the rightmost byte) appears at the bottom. Figure 7.11 (b) rearranges the addresses horizontally, and the rightmost byte `0X78` appears first in little endian. Figures 7.9 and 7.10 are little endian because the first byte appears as the leftmost byte. Big endian treats four bytes as a group. In contrast, little endian treats each byte individually.

### 7.3.3 File Length and Codes

After the binary tree, the compressed file's next byte is the newline character '`\n`' as a separator; its ASCII value is 10 (decimal) or 0000 1010 (binary). The next four bytes (32 bits) are the length of the original file. This is sufficient for an article of more than 4 billion letters because $2^{32} = 4,294,967,296$. If a novel has 1,000 pages and 2,000 letters per page (including spaces and symbols), the novel has approximately 2,000,000 letters (2 million). This is much smaller than 4 billion. Thus, a 4-byte integer is more than sufficient to encode a novel of 1,000 pages. Another newline character '`\n`' (`0000 1010`) is added as the separator.

The earlier example

```
#########$$$$$$$$$$$$$
```

has 25 letters. This value expressed in hexadecimal is `0X0001 1001`. Three other bytes are all zeros. In little endian, the four bytes are `0X0001 1001 0000 0000 0000 0000 0000 0000`. These four bytes are followed by a newline character (`0000 1010`).

The code for `#` is 0; the code for `/` is 1. Thus, the code in the compressed file has 10 bits of 0 followed by 15 bits of 1, 25 bits total. These bits need four bytes (32 bits). The last 7 bits are unused and are filled by 0 (paddings).

| | | | | | | | |
|---|---|---|---|---|---|---|---|
| tree description | 1 | # | 1 | / | 0 | 0 | padding |
| bits | 1 | 0010 0011 | 1 | 0010 1111 | 0 | 0 | 0000 |
| remove boundary | 1 0010 0011 1 0010 1111 0 0 0000 | | | | | | |
| **arrange as bytes** | 10010001 | 11001011 | 11000000 | | | | |
| separator | \n | | | | | | |
| **byte** | 00001010 | | | | | | |
| length | 25 | 0 | 0 | 0 | | | |
| **bytes** | 00011001 | 00000000 | 00000000 | 00000000 | | | |
| separator | \n | | | | | | |
| **byte** | 00001010 | | | | | | |
| data | 10 times of 0, 15 times of 1 | | | padding | | | |
| remove boundary | 0000 0000 00 1111 1111 1111 111 | | | 0000000 | | | |
| **arrange as bytes** | 00000000 | 0011111 | 11111111 | 10000000 | | | |

**FIGURE 7.12**: Compressed file of 10 `#` followed by 15 `/`. The black ground indicates the bytes in the compressed file.

Figure 7.12 puts everything together:

1. The first three bytes describe the tree (including 4 bits of padding).
2. The next byte is a separator.
3. Four bytes describe the length of the original file. This example uses little endian.
4. The next byte is another separator.
5. The next four bytes describe the data (including 7 bits of padding).

The entire compressed file has $3 + 1 + 4 + 1 + 4 = 13$ bytes. This is half of the original 25 bytes. The compression ratio is $\frac{25}{13} = 1.92$. The compressed file is a *binary file* and cannot be read by a text editor because the binary file contains many unprintable symbols (for example, any byte starts with 1).

### 7.3.4 Bit Operations

Python does not have a way to store only one bit (most programming languages have no data types for bits). Instead, the smallest unit is one byte. Python has a set of operators to manipulate bits using bytes. Table 7.6 shows several operators for bit values.

The bit-wise AND operation is used between two numbers. If the bits from both numbers are 1, the resultant bit is 1. If one or both bits are zero, then the resultant bit is zero. Table 7.7 (a) shows that the output bit is 1 only if both input bits are 1. Sometimes, a program wants to keep some bits while discarding the other bits. For example, if the program wants to keep only the lower (right) four bits of a byte, then the program uses bit-wise AND with 0X0F ($0000\ 1111_b$). Here 0X means a hexadecimal number (base 16), and the subscript $_b$ means a binary number (base 2). Table 7.7 (b) shows this example. It does not matter whether - is 0 or 1, the first (higher, left) four bits of the result will always be 0. The other four bits (a, b, c, and d) do not change. The value 0X0F is an example of a *mask*. A mask blocks some bits and allows the other bits to pass through. If a program wants to check whether the leftmost bit of `n` is 1 or 0, the program can use a mask whose binary representation is $1000\ 0000_b$ (0x80 in hexadecimal). If (`n & 0X80 != 0`) is true, then the leftmost bit of `n` must be 1. Please be aware that `!= 0` and `== 1` are different. If `n`'s leftmost bit is 1, then `n & 0X80` is actually `0X80` not 1.

| operation | operator |
|---|---|
| bit-wise AND | `&` |
| bit-wise OR | `\|` |
| shift left | `<<` |
| shift right | `>>` |

**TABLE 7.6**: Operators for bits.

The second bit-wise operator, OR (`|`), is also used between two numbers. If the bit from either number is 1, the resultant bit is 1. If both are 0, then the resultant bit is 0. This is shown in Table 7.8 (a). The bit-wise OR operator `|` is useful for setting some bits to 1, regardless of the original bits. Table 7.8 (b) shows that if the number `n` has bit-wise OR with 0XF0, then the left four bits will always be 1. The right four bits depend on the bits in a, b, c, and d.

**TABLE 7.7**: (a) The output of AND (`&`) is 1 only if both bits are 1. (b) Use AND to block or pass bits.

| | | |
|---|---|---|
| **input 1** | 0 1 1 0 1 0 0 1 | - - - - a b c d |
| **input 2** | & 1 1 0 1 0 0 1 1 | & 0 0 0 0 1 1 1 1 |
| **output** | 0 1 0 0 0 0 0 1 | 0 0 0 0 a b c d |
| | (a) | (b) |

**TABLE 7.8**: (a) The output of OR (|) is 0 only if both bits are 0. (b) Use OR to set some bits to 1.

<table>
<tr><td>input 1</td><td>0 1 1 0 1 0 0 1</td><td>- - - - a b c d</td></tr>
<tr><td>input 2</td><td>| 1 1 0 1 0 0 0 0</td><td>| 1 1 1 1 0 0 0 0</td></tr>
<tr><td>output</td><td>1 1 1 1 1 0 0 1</td><td>1 1 1 1 a b c d</td></tr>
<tr><td></td><td>(a)</td><td>(b)</td></tr>
</table>

The third operator is the bit-wise shift left operation <<. It moves bits to the left and adds zeros to the right. Table 7.9 (a) shows left-shifting by two. Row (1) is the original number. Shifting left by two first discards the leftmost two bits (marked as -), shown in row (2). Then, the number is shifted left by adding two zeros to the right, shown in row (3). Shifting left by two is equivalent to multiplication by four (discard any value above 256). The bit-wise shift right operation (>>) moves bits to the right and adds zeros to the left. Table 7.9 (b) shows an example of shifting right by two. Row (2) shows that the rightmost two bits are discarded (marked as -). Row (3) adds two zeros to the left. Shifting right by two is equivalent to division by four.

**TABLE 7.9**: (a) Shift left <<. (b) Shift right >>.

| | | |
|---|---|---|
| (1) | 0 1 1 0 1 0 0 1 << 2 | 0 1 1 0 1 0 0 1 >> 2 |
| (2) | - - 1 0 1 0 0 1 | 0 1 1 0 1 0 - - |
| (3) | 1 0 1 0 0 1 0 0 | 0 0 0 1 1 0 1 0 |
| | (a) | (b) |

For the compression program, many parts can be used without any change. A new class called `Bit` is created. It has three attributes called `bit`, `whichbit`, and `byte`.

```
3  class Bit:
4      def __init__(self):
5          self.bit = 0
6          self.whichbit = 0 # which bit in the byte?
7          self.byte = 0     # keep other bits in the byte
```

The `writeBit` function stores one bit at a time. When `whichbit` is zero, `self.byte` is reset to zero (lines 9 - 10). Otherwise, the partially used byte is stored in `self.byte` (lines 11 - 12). This function writes one byte to the file only when an entire byte is used (lines 13 - 14). Every time a bit is written, `self.whichbit` increases by one (line 15).

```
8      def writeBit(self, fhd):
9          if (self.whichbit == 0): # start a new byte
```

**TABLE 7.10**: Operations of `writeBit`. *A byte 0XB7 ($1011\ 0111_b$) is written to the file. Boldface shows which bit in `byte` is changed by `t`.

| line | 9 | 10 | 11 | 12 | 15 |
|---|---|---|---|---|---|
| attribute | `whichbit` | `byte` | `t` | `byte` | `whichbit` |
| initial | 0 | 0 | - | - | - |
| 1 | 0 | 0 | $1000\ 0000_b$ | $\mathbf{1}000\ 0000_b$ | 1 |
| 0 | 1 | $1000\ 0000_b$ | 0 | $1\mathbf{0}00\ 0000_b$ | 2 |
| 1 | 2 | $1000\ 0000_b$ | $0010\ 0000_b$ | $10\mathbf{1}0\ 0000_b$ | 3 |
| 1 | 3 | $1010\ 0000_b$ | $0001\ 0000_b$ | $101\mathbf{1}\ 0000_b$ | 4 |
| bit 0 | 4 | $1011\ 0000_b$ | 0 | $1011\ \mathbf{0}000_b$ | 5 |
| 1 | 5 | $1011\ 0000_b$ | $0000\ 0100_b$ | $1011\ 0\mathbf{1}00_b$ | 6 |
| 1 | 6 | $1011\ 0100_b$ | $0000\ 0010_b$ | $1011\ 01\mathbf{1}0_b$ | 7 |
| 1 | 7* | $1011\ 0110_b$ | $0000\ 0001_b$ | $1011\ 011\mathbf{1}_b$ | 0 |
| 1 | 0 | 0 | $1000\ 0000_b$ | $\mathbf{1}000\ 0000_b$ | 1 |

```
10                self.byte = 0
11            t = self.bit << (7 - self.whichbit)
12            self.byte |= t
13            if (self.whichbit == 7): # use up all bit
14                fhd.write(struct.pack('B', self.byte)) # one byte
15            self.whichbit = (self.whichbit + 1) % 8
```

Table 7.10 explains how information is stored in a `Bit` object after calling the `writeBit` function 9 times with inputs 1 0 1 1 0 1 1 1 1.

There are two situations when an entire byte needs to be written to the file:

1. the letters and
2. newline '\n' to separate the tree, the length, and the codes.

The `writeByte` function first converts the letter to an integer by using the `ord` function and then writes one bit (the leftmost bit) at a time by calling `writeBit` 8 times. After one bit is written, the byte shifts left by one (line 21).

```
16        def writeByte(self, onebyte, fhd):
17            onebyte = ord(onebyte) # convert a letter to its ASCII
          ↪   value
18            for i in range(0, 8):
19                self.bit = int((0X80 & onebyte) != 0)
20                self.writeBit(fhd)
21                onebyte <<= 1
```

The `padZero` function adds zero to a partially used byte until the byte is completely filled (`whichbit` becomes zero).

```
35        def padZero(self, fhd): # add zero bits to remaining bits
```

```
36          while (self.whichbit != 0):
37              self.bit = 0
38              self.writeBit(fhd)
```

To save the compression tree, the compress function creates a Bit object (line 220) to keep track of which bit is being used.

```
220       bitobj = Bit()
```

The postOrder function writes bit 1 (lines 71 - 72) before writing a letter (line 73) if the node is a leaf node. If a node is not a leaf node, the function writes bit 0 (lines 80 - 81).

```
66          if (self.left == None): # leaf node
67              if (text == True):
68                fhd.write('1')
69                fhd.write(self.ascii)
70              else: # binary
71                bitobj.bit = 1;
72                bitobj.writeBit(fhd)
73                bitobj.writeByte(self.ascii, fhd)
74              return
75          self.left.postOrder(fhd, text, bitobj)
76          self.right.postOrder(fhd, text, bitobj)
77          if (text == True):
78            fhd.write('0')  # non-leaf node
79          else:
80            bitobj.bit = 0;
81            bitobj.writeBit(fhd)
```

After writing the tree, one more zero is added to end the tree (lines 93 - 94). More zeros are added if necessary by calling padZero (line 95). Then a newline '\n' is written (line 96).

```
93              bitobj.bit = 0
94              bitobj.writeBit(fhd)
95              bitobj.padZero(fhd)
96              bitobj.writeByte('\n', fhd)
```

The compress function needs to make a few changes from the text output to the binary output by using bits. Line 221 writes the length to the file; here the format struct.pack('i' means a 4-byte integer. Line 222 writes '\n' to separate the length and the codes. The codes are written one bit at a time (lines 228 - 229). After writing all codes, if the last byte has any unused bits, zero padding is added (line 230).

```
221       binary_fhd.write(struct.pack('i', len(self.content))) #
          ↪  4-byte int
222       bitobj.writeByte('\n', binary_fhd)
```

```
# write the content
for i in range(0, len(self.content)):
  code = self.book[self.content[i]]
  for j in range(0, len(code)):
    text_fhd.write(code[j])
    bitobj.bit = int(code[j])
    bitobj.writeBit(binary_fhd)
bitobj.padZero(binary_fhd)
```

The `decompression` function for a binary file is very similar to the process of decompressing a text file. The main difference is that only one bit is used each time (in a text file, one byte is used each time). Line 330 reads one bit from the input file. If this bit is zero, the program moves to the left child (line 332 - 333). If this bit is one, the program moves to the right child (line 334 - 335). When a leaf node is encountered, the program adds the letter to the output (lines 336 - 337) and returns to the root of the tree (line 338).

```
325 while (binary_length > 0):
326   if (self.binary_tree.left == None):
327    binary_output.append(tn.ascii)
328    binary_length -= 1
329   else:
330    bitobj.readBit(binary_fhd)
331    code = bitobj.bit
332    if (code == 0):
333      tn = tn.left
334    if (code == 1):
335      tn = tn.right
336    if (tn.left == None): # leaf node
337      binary_output.append(tn.ascii)
338      tn = self.binary_tree
339      binary_length -= 1
340 binary_fhd.close()
```

How efficient is this compression method? Let's consider the LaTeX source for Chapter 1 (this book is written using LaTeX, a text formatting program). The original LaTeX file has 47,964 bytes. The compressed file has 29,573 bytes. The compression ratio is $\frac{47964}{29573} = 1.62$.

### 7.3.5 Analyze Binary Files

The compressed files are binary files and cannot be read or modified by using a typical text editor (such as `vim` or `emacs` or `vscode`). In Linux, `xxd` is a tool that can read binary files. Consider the example (10 `#` and 15 `/`). This is the

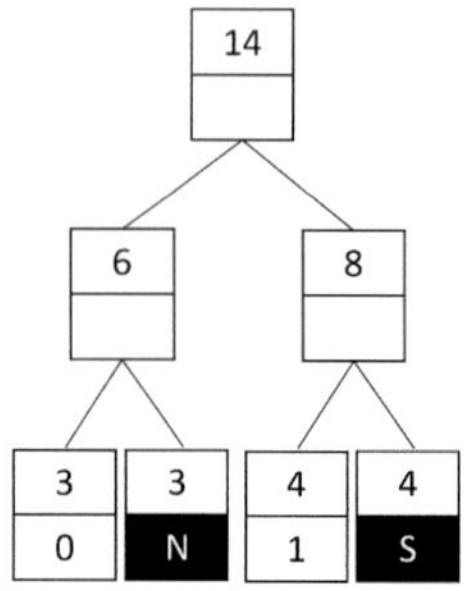


**FIGURE 7.13**: The tree includes unprintable symbols. N means newline, i.e., '\n'; S means space.

output of running `xxd -b`. Here, `-b` means using binary output (otherwise, the output is hexadecimal).

```
00000000: 10010001 11001011 11000000 00001010 00011001 00000000  ......
00000006: 00000000 00000000 00001010 00000000 00111111 11111111  ......
0000000c: 10000000                                               .
```

Each row in the output has six bytes. The second row contains the $6^{th}$ to the $11^{th}$ bytes. The third row is the $12^{th}$ byte; 12 in decimal is C in hexadecimal. If the binary numbers do not correspond to printable letters, dots are printed on the right side. The output of `xxd` matches Figure 7.12.

Consider another input

```
0 1
0 1
0  1
1
```

The input has 14 letters:

- 0 appears 3 times
- newline appears 3 times (the last line has no newline)
- space appears 4 times (twice in the third line)
- 1 appears 4 times.

The compression tree is shown in Figure 7.13. The input has four types of letters. Table 7.11 shows their ASCII values. The post-order expression of the tree is shown in Table 7.12.

After rearranging the bits into bytes, the tree is

```
1001 1000 0100 0010 1001 0011 0001 1001 0000 0000
```

The file's length is 14 bytes; written in bits, it is

```
0000 1110 0000 0000 0000 0000 0000 0000
```

Putting everything together, this is the output of running `xxd -b`.

```
00000000: 10011000 01000010 10010011 00011001 00000000 00001010  .B....
00000006: 00001110 00000000 00000000 00000000 00001010 00111001  .....9
0000000c: 00111001 00111110 01100000
```

---

## 7.4 Summary

This chapter explains Huffman compression. It uses variable-length coding to reduce the size of text files. The method uses fewer bits for letters that occur frequently, and more bits for letters that occur rarely. The implementation uses binary trees and lists. Recursion is used for building the tree and expressing the tree using post-order.

---

## 7.5 Problems

### 7.5.1 Encode 1 or 0

Can this method encode 1 or 0?

**Answer:**

Yes, as shown in Figure 7.13.

### 7.5.2 Encode Output

This is the input

```
101010001
```

**TABLE 7.11**: ASCII values for 0, 1, space, and newline.

| Letter | Decimal | Hexadecimal | Binary | Code |
|---|---|---|---|---|
| 0 | 48 | 30 | 0011 0000 | 00 |
| 1 | 49 | 31 | 0011 0001 | 10 |
| space | 32 | 20 | 0010 0000 | 11 |
| newline | 10 | 0A | 0000 1010 | 01 |

**TABLE 7.12**: Mark the tree description as control (C) or data (D). The third row replaces the letters with their ASCII values.

| | | | | | | | | | | | |
|---|---|---|---|---|---|---|---|---|---|---|---|
| 1 | 0 | 1 | N | 0 | 1 | 1 | 1 | S | 0 | 0 | 0 |
| C | D | C | D | C | C | D | C | D | C | C | C |
| 1 | 0011 0000 | 1 | 0000 1010 | 0 | 1 | 0011 0001 | 1 | 0010 0000 | 0 | 0 | 0 |

What is the compressed output in the text format?

**Answer:**

```
111000
9
010101110
```

Figure 7.14 shows the tree. The code for `1` is 0 and the code for `0` is 1.

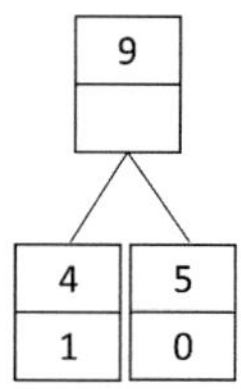


**FIGURE 7.14**: Tree for input `101010001`.

### 7.5.3 Encode Unprintable Symbols

Can this method encode unprintable symbols, such as space or newline?

**Answer:**

Yes. Space's ASCII code is 32. Newline's ASCII code is 10. Figure 7.13 shows how to encode space and newline.

### 7.5.4 Encode a File with `a`, `b`, and `c`

This is the input

`aaaaaaaaabbbbbbbbbbbbbbbbbbccccccccccccccc`

what is the output in the text format?

**TABLE 7.13**: Replace the letters by their codes

| | | | | | | | | | | | | | | |
|---|---|---|---|---|---|---|---|---|---|---|---|---|---|---|
| **letter** | 0 | S | 1 | N | 0 | S | 1 | N | 0 | S | S | 1 | N | 1 |
| **code** | 00 | 11 | 10 | 01 | 00 | 11 | 10 | 01 | 00 | 11 | 11 | 10 | 01 | 10 |

| Letter | Probability | Code |
|---|---|---|
| a | 55% | 1 |
| b | 30% | 01 |
| c | 15% | 10 |

**TABLE 7.14**: Calculate the average number of bits.

**Answer:**

The input has 10 `a`, 20 `b`, and 15 `c`.

The codes are

- `a`: 10
- `b`: 0
- `c`: 11

```
1b1a1c000
45
1010101010101010101000000000000000000000111111111111111111111111111111
```

### 7.5.5 Decompress

If the compressed file (in the text format) is

```
1#1/00
26
00000000000111111111111111
```

what is the original file?

**Answer:**

`###########///////////////`

11 `#` followed by 15 `/`.

### 7.5.6 Average Number of Bits

Consider a text file using three letters: a, b, and c. Their probabilities and code are shown in Table 7.14. What is the average number of bits per letter?

**Answer:**

$1 \times 55\% + 2 \times 30\% + 2 \times 15\% + = 1.45$.

### 7.5.7 Code Book

Consider a text file using four letters: a, b, c, and d. Their probabilities and code are shown in Table 7.15. What are the codes for these letters?

| Letter | Probability |
|---|---|
| a | 42% |
| b | 28% |
| c | 18% |
| d | 12% |

**TABLE 7.15**: Determine the codes of these letters.

**Answer:**

- a: 0
- b: 10
- c: 111
- d: 110

### 7.5.8 Compression Tree

A file has 20 `a` followed by 20 `b`. Write down the post-order description of the compression tree in the text format.

**Answer:**

```
1a1b00
```

### 7.5.9 Compressed File

Continue the previous problem. Write down the entire compressed file (including the tree, the length, the codes) in the text format.

**Answer:**

```
1a1b00
40
0000000000000000000011111111111111111111
```

### 7.5.10 Compressed File

Continue the previous problem. What is the output of `xxd -b` when the input is the binary format of the compressed file?

**Answer:**

```
00000000: 10110000 11011000 10000000 00001010 00101000 00000000  ....(.
00000006: 00000000 00000000 00001010 00000000 00000000 00001111  ......
0000000c: 11111111 11111111
```

### 7.5.11 One-Letter Input

If the input file has only one letter $ and it repeats 100 times, what is the compressed file in the text format?

**Answer:**

```
1$0
100
```

### 7.5.12 Binary Format of One-Letter Input

If the input file has only one letter $ and it repeats 100 times. What is compressed file in the binary format? Write down the output of `xxd -b`.

**Answer:**

```
00000000: 10010010 00000000 00001010 01100100 00000000 00000000  ...d..
00000006: 00000000 00001010
```

### 7.5.13 Compression Ratio

If an input file has 100 letter $'s (i.e., $ repeats 100 times), what is the compression ratio using the binary format?

If an input file has 10,000 letter X's followed by 10,000 letter Y's, what is the compression ratio using the binary format?

**Answer:**

For 100 $, the compressed file needs two bytes to store the tree, one byte to store '`\n`', four bytes to store the length 100, and one more byte to store '`\n`'. In total, eight bytes are used. Please notice that this letter does not need any code. The compression ratio is $\frac{100}{8} = 12.5$.

For 10,000 X's followed by 10,000 Y's, X's code is 0 and Y's code is 1. The output file needs

- 3 bytes for the tree
- 1 byte for '`\n`'
- 4 bytes for the length
- 1 byte for '`\n`'
- 1250 bytes (10,000 bits) are needed for X
- 1250 bytes (10,000 bits) are needed for Y.

Totally, $3 + 1 + 4 + 1 + 1250 + 1250 = 2509$ bytes are needed. The original file is 20,000 bytes. Thus, the compression ratio is $\frac{20{,}000}{2509} = 7.97$.

# Chapter 8

## Conclusion

This book uses many examples showing how recursion can be used for solving real problems such as Sudoku, Go, and Huffman compression. The authors hope readers have a solid understanding about the concepts and the programming methods using Python. The book integrates Python programming with mathematics and provides different views of the problems and solutions.

# Appendix A

## Stack Memory

Recursive functions are called multiple times. How does a computer keep track of these multiple calls? The answer is *stack memory*. The knowledge about stack memory can help readers understand and design recursive programs. Stack memory may store four types of information: (1) *Return location*, (2) *Arguments*, (3) *Local variables*, (4) *Value destination*.

## A.1 Stack Memory

In a computer, programs and data must be kept in *memory*. Computer memory is organized into three types: (1) stack memory, (2) heap memory, (3) program memory. The first two store data, and the last stores computer programs.

Before talking about stack memory, we must first introduce the concept of a *stack*, such as a stack of books. Adding a book means placing it on the top of the stack. Removing a book takes the one from the top. Thus, the first book to be removed will be the last book placed on the stack. This arrangement is called "last in, first out" (or "first in, last out"). Placing an item on the top is called *push*; removing an item from the top is called *pop*. The stack concept is used in everyday life. To wear both socks and shoes, the socks must be put on before the shoes—push the socks, push the shoes. Then, to remove both the socks and the shoes, the shoes come off before the socks—pop the shoes, pop the socks. The order is reversed, and this is an example of "last in, first out".

Figure A.1 illustrates these two operations of stack memory. In Figure A.1, originally the top of the stack stores the number 720. The number 653 is pushed onto the top of the stack. Later, the data is retrieved (popped) from the stack. Pushes and pops can only occur at the top of the stack. Although this figure illustrates the idea with integers, a stack is a general concept and can manage any type of data.

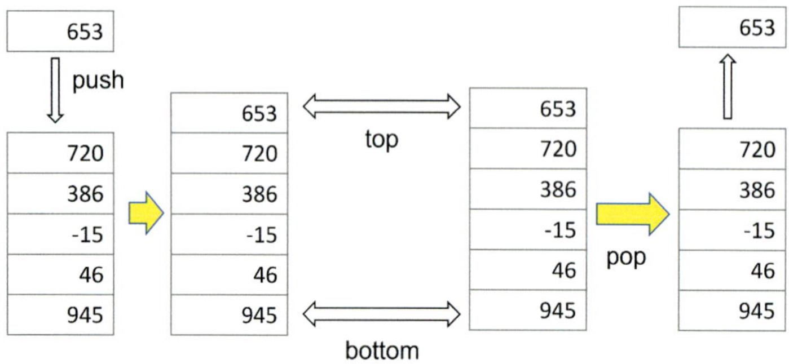


**FIGURE A.1**: Pushing and popping data on a stack.

### A.1.1 Return Location

Stack memory stores a function call's return location. Consider the following code snippet:

```
1 def f1():
2     # does some work here
3 def f2():
4     # does some work here
5     f1();
6     # return location for f1
7     # does more work
```

The function `f2` calls `f1` at line 5. After `f1` finishes its work, the program continues running `f2` from line 6. Imagine that a mark called *return location* is inserted right below the place where `f1` is called. This mark tells the program where it should continue after `f1` finishes.

Next, consider another example:

```
1 def f1():
2     # does some work here
3 def f2():
4     # does some work here
5     f1();
6     # return location for the first call
7     # does more work
8     f1();
9     # return location for the second call
```

Function `f2` calls `f1` twice, at line 5 and line 8. Each call has a corresponding return location, at line 6 and line 9 respectively. The return location specifies where the program should continue. When `f1` is called the first time and

**TABLE A.1**: Progression of the program. R.L. means return location. R.L. B is pushed first; then R. L. A is pushed.

| program at | line 9 | line 4 | line 2 | line 6 | line 10 |
|---|---|---|---|---|---|
| stack | - → | R.L. B → | R.L. A<br>R.L. B → | R.L. B → | - |

returns, the program should continue from line 6. When `f1` is called the second time, the program should continue from line 9.

The next example has three functions:

```
1  def f1():
2      # does some work here
3  def f2():
4      # does some work here
5      f1();
6      # return location, called it A
7  def f3():
8      # does some work here
9      f2();
10     # return location, called it B
```

This example has three functions: `f1`, `f2`, and `f3`; `f2` calls `f1` and `f3` calls `f2`. Table A.1 illustrates the progression of the program's execution and the stack memory. There are two corresponding return locations called A (line 6) and B (line 10). Suppose the program starts at function `f3`. When `f3` calls `f2`, the return location B is pushed to the stack memory. When `f2` calls `f1`, the return location A is pushed to the stack memory. In other words, B is pushed to the stack memory first; then A is pushed to the stack memory. Please remember that push adds a new item on the top. When `f1` finishes, the program continues from line 6. This is return location A. When `f2` finishes, the program continues from line 10. This is return location B. When function `f1` finishes, the program continues from the top of the stack memory (return location A). This return location is popped, and the stack contains the return location of B only. This is the behavior of the stack memory. The *last in, first out* property of stack memory is important. The stack memory stores the *reverse order* of function calls: function `f3` starts first, then `f2`, then `f1`. When `f1` finishes, the program continues from `f2`, not `f3`. Every program has stack memory to control the flow of execution of the functions. Almost all computer programming languages use this scheme. This book uses line numbers as the return locations in a simplified conceptual model and does not reflect any specific processor hardware. This conceptual model is sufficient for this book.

### A.1.2 Function Arguments

The stack memory stores more than the return locations. Consider this example:

```
1 def f1(a):
2     # does some work here
3     print(a)
4 def f2():
5     # does some work here
6     f1(5);
7     # return location for f1
8     # does more work
```

Function `f2` calls `f1` with an argument, and the value is 5. Inside `f1` this argument is called `a`, and it stores the value of 5. This argument is also stored in the stack memory. The argument exists only when function `f1` is running. When `f1` finishes and the program continues from line 7, this argument `a` no longer exists.

### A.1.3 Local Variable

Let's add a local variable called `a` in `f2`:

```
def f1(a):
    # does some work here
    print(a)
def f2():
    # does some work here
    a = 8
    f1(5);
    # return location for f1
    # a is still 8
    # does more work
```

This local variable `a` in `f2` is independent of the argument `a` in `f1`. They happen to have the same name, but they are not related to each other. One way to understand why they are unrelated is to rename the argument in `f1` and call it `x`. This new name of the argument does not change the program in any way.

Next, let's add a local variable inside `f1`:

```
def f1(x):
    # does some work here
    a = x # a is a local variable, its value is 5 (same as x)
    print(x)
```

```
5  def f2():
6      # does some work here
7      a = 8
8      f1(5);
9      # return location for f1
10     # a is still 8
11     # does more work
```

Inside `f1`, the argument `x` is 5 (because 5 is used at line 8). Line 3 assigns `x` to `a`; thus, `a` is also 5. When `f1` finishes and the program resumes from line 9, the value of `a` inside `f2` is still 8. This is because the two local variables are unrelated, even though both are called `a`. Renaming either of the local variables does not change the program.

### A.1.4 Value Destination

If a function returns a value, the stack memory also stores where that value will be assigned. Consider this example:

```
def f1(x, y):
    a = x
    return (x + y)
def f2():
    a = 8
    b = 3
    b = f1(5, 12);
    # a is still 8
    # b is 5 + 12 = 17
```

Function `f2` has two local variables, `a` and `b`. Function `f2` calls `f1` with two arguments of values 5 and 12. Function `f1` returns the sum of the values. The value 17 needs to be written to `b` in `f2`, not `a`. In this case, `b` is called the *value destination*.

### A.1.5 Stack Frame

To summarize, the stack memory stores four types of information when a function is called:

1. return location,
2. arguments,
3. local variables,
4. value destination.

The four pieces of information are a *frame* of the function call. Table A.2 shows the information stored in the frame when calling `f1`. The first item (return location) is always pushed to the stack memory when a function is called. The other three depend on whether the function has arguments, local variables, or a returned value. When a function finishes, the top frame is popped, and all information in the frame is deleted. What happens when a function calls itself (i.e., the function is recursive)? Consider the following example:

**TABLE A.2**: A frame is pushed to the stack memory when a function is called.

| Frame | Information |
|---|---|
| `f1` | return location: line 8<br>argument: `x` = 5<br>argument: `y` = 12<br>local variable: `a` = 5<br>value destination: `b` in `f2` |

```
1  def f1(n):
2      if (n <= 1):
3          return 1
4      a = f1(n - 1)
5      # return location A
6      b = n + a
7      return b
8  def f2():
9      x = 5
10     y = 3
11     y = f1(2);
12     # return location B
```

When function `f2` calls `f1`, the return location (line 12), argument (2), local variable (`a`), and value destination (`y` in `f2`) are stored in a frame in the stack memory, as shown in Table A.3. The value of `a` is unknown now because it needs to call a function. Line 4 is a function call; a new frame is pushed to the top of the stack memory. Table A.3 shows the stack memory. Function `f1` has been called twice. Hence, the stack memory has two frames. The two frames are different.

**TABLE A.3**: Two frames in the stack.

| Frame | Information |
|---|---|
| `f1` called by `f1` | return location: line 5<br>argument: `n` = 1<br>local variable: `a` = ?<br>value destination: `a` in `f1` by `f2` |
| `f1` called by `f2` | return location: line 12<br>argument: `n` = 2<br>local variable: `a` = ?<br>value destination: `y` in `f2` |

To distinguish these frames, the frames are marked as (1) `f1` called by `f2` and (2) `f1` called by `f1` to indicate the first and the second time when `f1` is called. These two frames are different in several ways: First, the return locations are different. When `f1` is called the first time by `f2`, the return location is line 12 inside `f2`. When `f1` is called by `f1`, the return location is line 5 inside `f1`. Second, the value destinations are different. When `f1` is called the first time, the value destination is `y` inside `f2`. When `f1` is called the second time, the value destination is `a` inside the first frame of `f1`. Third, the argument `n` has different values. Understanding the stack memory is helpful when writing recursive programs. Table A.4 summarizes the four types of information that may be stored in a frame.

---

## A.2 Call by Value vs. Reference

Python has two ways of passing arguments to functions. Suppose we want to swap the values of two integers.

```
# Appendix A.2:swap1.py
def swap1(a, b):
    print(f"in swap1: line 3: {a, b}")
    a, b = b, a
    print(f"in swap1: line 5: {a, b}")
if __name__ == "__main__":
    x = 2
    y = 19
    print(f"line 9: {x, y}")
    x, y = y, x
    print(f"line 11: {x, y}")
    swap1(x, y)
```

**TABLE A.4**: Four types of information may be pushed to the stack memory.

| Information | Meaning |
|---|---|
| Return location | The place where the program will continue when the currently running function ends (i.e., returns). |
| Argument(s) | The value(s) from the caller to the called function. |
| Local variable(s) | The variable(s) that exist only when a function is currently running. |
| Value destination | The destination to store the value returned from the called function. |

```
13     print(f"line 13: {x, y}")
```

This is the program's output:

```
line 9: (2, 19)
line 11: (19, 2)
in swap1: line 3: (19, 2)
in swap1: line 5: (2, 19)
line 13: (19, 2)
```

Lines 7 and 8 assign 2 to `x` and 19 to `y`. Line 9 prints their values. Line 10 swaps their values. Line 11 shows that `x`'s value is 19 and `y`'s value is 2. Their values have been swapped. Next, the program calls the `swap1` function. The value of `a` is 19, and the value of `b` is 2. Line 4 swaps their values, and line 5 prints the swapped values. As expected, the values of `a` and `b` have swapped: `a`'s value is 2 and `b`'s value is 19. The program's last output, however, shows that `x`'s and `y`'s values are unchanged by the `swap1` function. The value of `x` at line 13 is 19, the same as the value at line 11. The value of `y` at line 13 is 2, the same as the value at line 11.

What does this mean? When `x` and `y` are used for calling `swap1`, their values (i.e., 19 and 2) are sent to the function `swap1`. As a result, `a` and `b` copy the values. In the frame of `swap1`, `a` and `b` are additional copies of the values. Changing `a` and `b` in `swap1` does not affect the values of `x` and `y`. This method of using arguments is *call by value*: only the value is passed to the function.

Next, consider a similar program that uses a class called `Pair`.

```
# Appendix A.2::swap2.py
class Pair:
    def __init__(self, a, b):
        self.x = a
        self.y = b
    def print(self, arg=""):
        print(f"{arg} Pair.print: {self.x, self.y}")
def swap2(p):
    p.print("in swap2 line 9")
    p.x, p.y = p.y, p.x
    p.print("in swap2 line 11")
if __name__ == "__main__":
    p = Pair(2, -9)
    p.print("line 14")
    p.x, p.y = p.y, p.x
    p.print("line 16")
    swap2(p)
    p.print("line 18")
```

This is the program's output:

```
line 14 Pair.print: (2, -9)
line 16 Pair.print: (-9, 2)
in swap2 line 9 Pair.print: (-9, 2)
in swap2 line 11 Pair.print: (2, -9)
line 18 Pair.print: (2, -9)
```

Each `Pair` object has two attributes called `x` and `y`. A `Pair` object is created at line 13; `x` and `y` are 2 and $-9$ respectively. Line 14 prints the values. Line 15 swaps the values, and line 16 shows `x` is $-9$. This object is used as an argument for the `swap2` function. The `swap2` function prints object `p` twice. The first time (line 9) shows that `p.x` is $-9$; the second time (line 11) shows that `p.x` is 2. After `swap2` finishes, the value of `x` is still 2 (line 18). In other words, the changes inside `swap2` are kept outside the function. This is different from `swap1` because the argument for `swap2` is an object. In Python, when an argument is an object, it is *call by reference*. The object inside `swap2` is the same object outside `swap2`. Thus, if this object is changed in `swap2`, the change persists outside `swap2`.

These two `swap` functions show the two methods of passing arguments to functions. In `swap1`, the arguments are integers. They are *primitive types*, and the functions' arguments use call by value. In `swap2`, the argument is an object, and the function uses call by reference.

# Appendix B

## Tail Recursion

Tail recursion occurs when a recursive call is the last part of a function. In other words, the function returns the result of the recursive call directly, without performing any additional computation after the call. Tail recursion is pretty common and can often be modified to non-recursive function calls.

Consider the factorial function shown below.

```
1  # Appendix B: tail_recursion.py
2  def factorial1(n):
3    if (n == 1):
4      return 1
5    return n * factorial1(n - 1)
```

This is not tail recursion because the last line of the function requires multiplication after the recursive call. This function can be rewritten into tail recursion by using two arguments. This new function performs the computation `n * acc` inside the call of line 9. As a result, this is tail recursion. The function uses recursion to reduce the first argument `n` while accumulating the value of the second argument toward the final value. This function uses the base condition (line 7) as the default value of the second argument (line 8) and moves the multiplication in line 5 to the operation inside the tail recursion call in line 9.

```
6  def factorial2(n, acc = 1):
7    if (n == 1):
8      return acc
9    return factorial2(n - 1, n * acc)
```

Tail recursion can be easily converted to `while` without recursion, as shown below.

```
10 def factorial3(n):
11   product = 1
12   while (n > 0):
13     product *= n;
14     n -= 1
15   return product
```

Next is another example: It calculates GCD (greatest common divisor). This is already tail recursion.

```
16 def gcd1(a, b):
17     if (b == 0):
18         return a
19     return gcd1(b, a % b)
```

Next, we can convert the tail recursion to `while`:

```
20 def gcd2(a, b):
21     while (b != 0):
22         a, b = b, a % b
23     return a
```

The third example is the *Fibonacci numbers*. This is the original recursive implementation. It is not tail recursion because the last line of this function needs addition.

```
24 def fib1(n):
25     if (n <= 2):
26         return 1
27     return fib1(n - 1) + fib2(n-2)
```

We can convert the recursive function above to tail recursion. The original function (line 24) has only one argument. When we convert it to tail recursion, we need three arguments (line 28). Please notice that the default values of `a` and `b` correspond to the base case (line 26). As `n` decreases, the arguments accumulate. The arguments of the recursive call (line 31) reflect the changes of `a` and `b`. This is tail recursion.

```
28 def fib2(n, a = 1, b = 1):
29     if (n <= 1):
30         return a
31     return fib2(n - 1, b, a + b)
```

From tail recursion, we can convert it to a `for` loop:

```
32 def fib3(n):
33     a, b = 1, 1
34     for _ in range(1, n):
35         a, b = b, a + b
36     return a
```

Why do we need to understand tail recursion? What is the advantage of converting tail recursion to `while`? Appendix A explains function calls and the stack memory. Recursive calls push new frames to the stack memory. Adding frames requires many steps: keeping track of return locations, value addresses, and arguments. Thus, tail recursion is usually slower than `while` (i.e., `factorial2` is slower than `factorial3`; `fib2` is slower than `fib3`).

Section 2.10.2 explains that the recursive implementation of Fibonacci numbers is inefficient because it has a significant amount of redundant computation. Optimizing tail recursion can eliminate redundant computation and can be faster. From these examples, we can summarize the following steps to convert recursion to tail recursion and from tail recursion to no recursion:

1. Identify the computation needed after recursive calls: For factorials, it is a multiplication. For Fibonacci numbers, it is an addition.
2. Rewrite the recursion so that the computation is performed through the arguments.
3. Convert recursive calls to `while` or `for`.

Some compilers may eliminate tail recursion automatically. Unfortunately, Python does not eliminate tail recursion.

# Appendix C

# Google Colab

*Google Colaboratory*, commonly known as *Colab*, is a free, cloud-based platform that allows users to write and execute Python code through a web browser. Colab is integrated with Google Drive for storage and sharing. Colab provides a Jupyter notebook environment without the need for any setup.

## C.1 Advantages of Colab

Colab has many advantages, including:

- Colab notebooks use the Jupyter Notebook format (i.e., `.ipynb`). A notebook is organized by *cells*. It is possible to execute the code of each cell individually.
- Colab provides a common computing platform. Any user can access Colab through a web browser, regardless of their operating system. It is unnecessary to install any software on their machines.
- Google drive allows easy sharing. Users can share the programs in the same Google Drive in several ways: (1) allow specific people to view or edit, (2) allow everyone with a link to view or edit.
- Users can visualize the program's output using graphics libraries such as `matplotlib`. This book uses `matplotlib` to draw Sudoku, maze, and Go game figures.
- Colab also provides fast computer hardware, including GPU (Graphics Processing Unit) and TPU (Tensor Processing Unit) for free.
- Many Python packages are available in Colab. The Python command `import` can be used. If a Python package is not already available, the package can be installed using
  `!pip install`
  For example, the following command installs the `nbconvert` package.
  `!pip install nbconvert`
  This package can convert a notebook file `.ipynb` to a Python file `.py`.

**FIGURE C.1**: Colab supports mathematical equations using LaTeX.

Please notice the starting exclamation mark before the shell commands (such as `pip` or `ls`).

- Programs in Colab can be managed by version control, such as `git`.
- Colab allows a flexible mixture of code and explanation. It is possible to add a Code cell or a Text cell. The text cell can use Markdown or LaTeXequations. Figure C.1 shows a text cell and a code cell. The left side of the text cell uses LaTeXto write an equation; the right side shows the rendering of the equation.
- Colab has assistance with generative artificial intelligence. It is possible to ask the generative artificial intelligence to produce code. When this book was written, the generated code was not always correct. Users must carefully inspect the generated code before accepting it.
- The Command Palette offers many commands to edit the notebook and to control execution. For example, `Run cells before the current` can run a program up to the current location. This is very helpful in development and debugging.

## C.2 Debug

Colab supports interactive debugging. Insert `pdb.set_trace()` at a place as a *breakpoint*. When the program reaches a breakpoint, it stops and waits for the software developer to inspect the program.

```
1 # Appendix C.2 debug
2 import pdb
3 def f(x):
4   pdb.set_trace()
5   if (x <= 0):
6     return x
7   else:
8     y = f(x -1)
9     return (x * y)
10 a = f(5)
```

After clicking `Run all`, the program stops at line 4, right after `pdb.set_trace()`. A user can enter commands after the `ipdb>` prompt. Entering `help` will print the valid commands:

```
> /tmp/ipython-input-3282820433.py(4)f()
      2 def f(x):
      3   pdb.set_trace()
----> 4   if (x <= 0):
      5     return x
      6   else:

ipdb> help

Documented commands (type help <topic>):
========================================
EOF    commands   enable    ll        pp       s                until
a      condition  exit      longlist  psource  skip_hidden      up
alias  cont       h         n         q        skip_predicates  w
args   context    help      next      quit     source           whatis
b      continue   ignore    p         r        step             where
break  d          interact  pdef      restart  tbreak
bt     debug      j         pdoc      return   u
c      disable    jump      pfile     retval   unalias
cl     display    l         pinfo     run      undisplay
clear  down       list      pinfo2    rv       unt

Miscellaneous help topics:
```

```
===========================
exec  pdb

ipdb>
```

Typing `x` after the `ipdb` prompt prints `x`'s value:

```
ipdb> x
5
```

It is possible to set a *breakpoint* at function `f` by typing

```
ipdb> b f
Breakpoint 1 at /tmp/ipython-input-3282820433.py:2
```

Suppose we continue the program and reach the condition when `x` is 3. The `bt` command shows the stack memory:

```
ipdb> x
3

ipdb> bt

  /tmp/ipython-input-3282820433.py(9)<cell line: 0>()
      5     return x
      6   else:
      7     y = f(x -1)
      8     return (x * y)
----> 9 a = f(5)

  /tmp/ipython-input-3282820433.py(7)f()
      5     return x
      6   else:
----> 7     y = f(x -1)
      8     return (x * y)
      9 a = f(5)

  /tmp/ipython-input-3282820433.py(7)f()
      5     return x
      6   else:
----> 7     y = f(x -1)
      8     return (x * y)
      9 a = f(5)

> /tmp/ipython-input-3282820433.py(7)f()
      5     return x
```

```
      6   else:
----> 7     y = f(x -1)
      8     return (x * y)
      9 a = f(5)


```

---

## C.3 Graphics

Colab supports `matplotlib` for graphics. The following program produced this book's cover:

```
# Appendix C.3: create the pattern for the book's cover
import matplotlib.pyplot as plt
import numpy as np
def draw_rotating_squares(num_shapes=8, scale=400.0,
↪   rotation_increment=5):
    fig, ax = plt.subplots(figsize=(6, 6))
    ax.set_facecolor('black')
    ax.set_aspect('equal')
    ax.axis('off')
    # Define base square
    base_square = np.array([
        [1, 1],
        [1, -1],
        [-1, -1],
        [-1, 1]
    ]) * scale
    # Use a colormap for varying colors
    cmap = plt.colormaps.get_cmap('viridis')
    colors = cmap(np.linspace(0, 1, num_shapes))
    colors = ['b', 'g', 'r', 'c', 'm', 'y', 'k']
    for i in range(num_shapes):
        # Adjust scaling so squares stay within the largest
        ↪   square and are more visible
        current_scale = scale * (1 - i / (num_shapes * 1.2)) #
        ↪   Adjusted scaling factor
        scaled_square = base_square * current_scale / scale #
        ↪   Apply scaling
        angle = np.radians(i * rotation_increment)  # Rotation
        ↪   increment
```

```
            rotation_matrix = np.array([
                [np.cos(angle), -np.sin(angle)],
                [np.sin(angle),  np.cos(angle)]
            ])
            rotated_square = scaled_square @ rotation_matrix.T
            ax.plot(*np.append(rotated_square,
            ↪   [rotated_square[0,:]], axis=0).T, color= colors[i %
            ↪   len(colors)]) # Close the square with varying color
        plt.show()
draw_rotating_squares()
```

Figure C.2 is generated by the program.

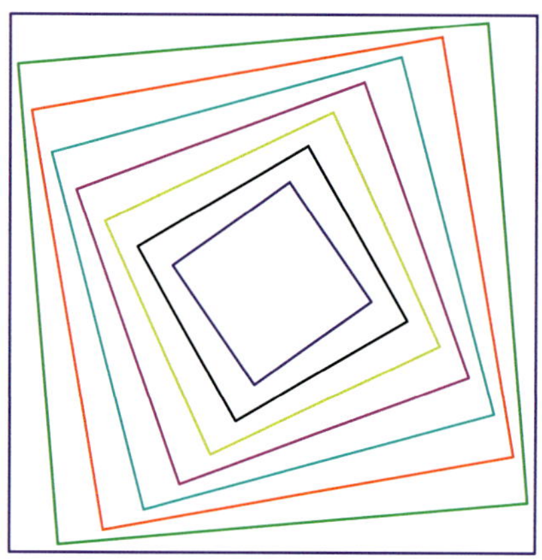

**FIGURE C.2**: The pattern on this book's cover. This program is suggested by the AI tools in Google Colab.

## C.4 Using Google Drive

It is possible to read from or write to files in Google Drive. Before using Google Drive, a Python program in Colab must `import drive` (line 1 below). The second step uses `drive.mount` (line 2). After mounting the drive, the path starts with `'/content/drive/My Drive/'` (line 3).

```
from google.colab import drive
drive.mount('/content/drive')
path = '/content/drive/My Drive/'
```

# Appendix D

## Test Python Programs

This chapter explains how to test Python programs using the `unittest` framework.

### D.1 Separate Production Code from Testing Code

Software has been used in controlling safety-critical systems, including military equipment, airplanes, and self-driving vehicles. Software failures can lead to substantial amounts of financial damage and even loss of life. Searching "cost of software error" on the Internet will bring up dozens of examples where software errors cost millions of dollars. It is important to detect software errors (also called *bugs*) early in development. Correcting bugs is much more expensive after the software has been shipped to customers. Testing is a critical part of software development. Testing can help discover problems before the software is shipped to customers.

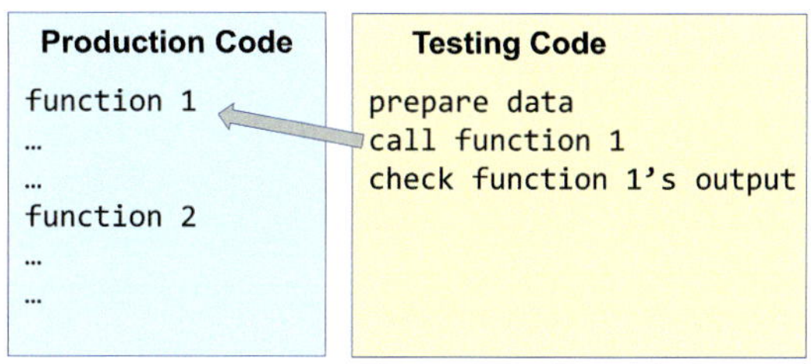


**FIGURE D.1**: Separate production code from testing code.

Figure D.1 illustrates an important principle of writing tests: separate *production code* from *testing code*. Production code is the code used in actual products, such as the control software of a vehicle. Customers use this software directly. Testing code is used by software developers and is not intended to be used (or seen) by customers. Production code and testing code should be separated. Mixing them can lead to many undesirable situations including:

- **Confusing customers**. Testing code may reveal internal operations and details that are not intended for customers, such as debugging messages. This information may surprise and confuse customers.
- **Disclosing trade secrets**. The revealed operations and details may include trade secrets, such as algorithms. Such information may become available to competitors.
- **Degrading performance**. Running testing code in products may slow down execution and reduce customer satisfaction.
- **Complicating future tests**. When a product has new functions, the tests need to be updated as well. If testing code is mixed with production code, it is difficult to add new tests for the new functions.

---

## D.2 Test Levels

Software testing can be classified into three levels: (1) unit tests, (2) integration tests, and (3) system tests. Each level serves a specific purpose in assuring software quality.

Unit testing focuses on the smallest testable parts of software, usually the correctness of individual functions, methods, or classes. The goal is to verify that each unit performs as expected in isolation. Unit tests are designed to detect bugs before they propagate into other parts of the software. Unit tests should be fast (short execution time) and checked frequently. Unit tests are usually independent of the other parts of the software.

Integration testing checks whether different units can work together. Software usually relies on many components, such as different classes, files as inputs and outputs, user interactions, network connections, etc. Integration tests evaluate whether these interactions are correct and that combined modules produce expected outcomes. Integration tests may discover that one component (such as a library) may produce data in a format incompatible with another component (such as network connections).

System testing evaluates all components as a complete functional product, often in real deployments or environments sufficiently similar to real deployments. The programs in this book are very small and do not belong to any specific systems (such as flight control, e-commerce). Thus, the tests written for this book are unit tests.

## D.3 Python `unittest` for Unit Test

Python provides a testing framework called `unittest` as a part of the standard library. Let's start by writing a simple program using `unittest`. We will test the following three functions (i.e., the production code).

```
1 # Appendix D.3: testarithmetic.py
2 def myadd(a, b):
3     return (a + b)
4 def mysub(a, b):
5     return (a - b)
6 def mymul(a, b):
7     return (a - b)
```

Next, we write a testing program:

```
8 import unittest
9 class TestFunc(unittest.TestCase):
10     def test_myadd(self):
11         self.assertEqual(myadd(3, 5), 8)
12     def test_mysub(self):
13         self.assertEqual(mysub(13, 5), 8)
14 if __name__ == "__main__":
15     unittest.main(argv=['first-arg-is-ignored'], exit=False)
```

In this example, the ninth line creates a new class called `TestFunc`, and it is derived from Python's `unittest.TestCase`. This `TestFunc` class can have one or several functions whose names start with `test`. This example includes two `test` functions: `test_myadd` and `test_mysub`. The first one tests the `myadd` function by giving arguments 3 and 5. The expected value is 8. Different `test` functions should be independent of each other. In other words, we should not assume that `test_myadd` runs first and `test_mysub` runs later. The tests use `assertEqual` to check whether `myadd(3, 5)` returns 8 and whether `mysub(13, 5)` returns 8. Python's `unittest` has many options, such as `assertEqual`, `assertNotEqual`, `assertTrue`, `assertFalse`, `assertGreater`, `assertLess`. Both tests pass, and this is the program's output:

```
----------------------------------------------------------------------
Ran 2 tests in 0.004s

OK
```

The unittest.main's arguments are argv=['first-arg-is-ignored'], exit=False because we test the program inside Colab (explained in Chapter C). Without argv=['first-arg-is-ignored'], exit=False, running the test will cause a runtime error in Colab.

Next, consider the test for mymul. The function mymul should multiply its arguments, but instead, it subtracts them. The following test should reveal this bug.

```
# Appendix D.3: testarithmetic2.py
class TestFunc(unittest.TestCase):
    def test_mymul(self):
        self.assertEqual(mymul(3, 5), 15)
if __name__ == "__main__":
    unittest.main(argv=['first-arg-is-ignored'], exit=False)
```

The output shows a test failed because mymul returned −2 but the expected value was 15.

```
F
======================================================================
FAIL: test_mymul (__main__.TestFunc.test_mymul)
----------------------------------------------------------------------
Traceback (most recent call last):
  File "/tmp/ipython-input-4085791109.py", line 3, in test_mymul
    self.assertEqual(mymul(3, 5), 15)
AssertionError: -2 != 15

----------------------------------------------------------------------
Ran 1 test in 0.002s

FAILED (failures=1)
```

Since the test failed, we know mymul is not implemented correctly.

---

## D.4 Test with Known Results

When writing tests, one challenge is to create meaningful test cases. The test cases shown above are very simple (addition, subtraction, and multiplication). If a problem is difficult and complex, finding a correct solution can be challenging. Without a correct solution, we cannot create a valid test case. Without a valid test case, we cannot test whether our software is correct. To find a correct solution, we may need correct software. This creates a "chicken-egg" situation illustrated in Figure D.2.

We can break this cyclic dependence by using existing Python functions as our trusted software. Consider the `quickSort` function on Page 51. The program has a function `checkOrder` to check whether the array's elements are increasing. This function, however, is insufficient because the `checkOrder` function does not guarantee that the original elements are still in the array `arr`. Consider this example: Suppose the original array is

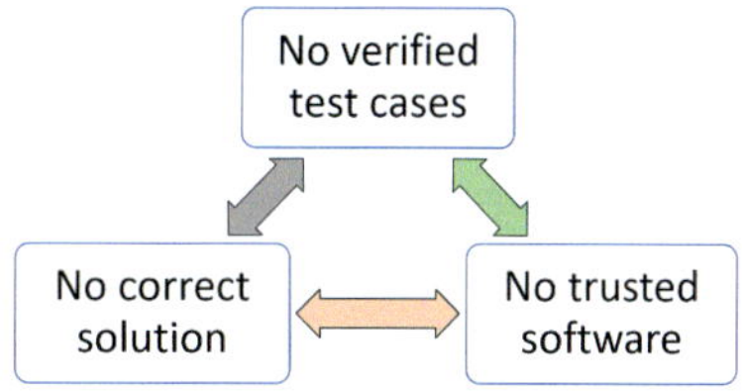


**FIGURE D.2**: A cyclic problem when creating test cases.

```
5, 6, 8, 1, 4, 3
```

If `quickSort` returns

```
1, 2, 3, 4, 5, 6
```

this array can pass the `checkOrder` function, even though the second array has added a new element (2) and removed an original element (8).

A better approach is to utilize Python's built-in `sorted` function for tests. In this example, the function `test_sort` calls `quickSort` 10 times (line 18). Each time an array of random elements is created (lines 19 and 20), it is possible that same value may appear multiple times in the test data. This array is copied (line 21). We need to use `deepcopy` to ensure that the two arrays use different memory space. We need to have two different arrays because we want to sort them using different methods (`data1` is sorted by our `quickSort`; `data2` is sorted by Python's `sorted` method) and compare the results. If we do not use `deepcopy`, i.e., if we use

```
data2 = data1
```

then changing `data1` also changes `data2`. As a result, these two arrays are always equal, even if the `quickSort` function is wrong. Line 22 uses our `quickSort` function to sort the input array `data1`. Line 23 uses Python's `sorted` function to sort the input array `data2`. The two sorted arrays are compared using `assertEqual` (line 24).

```
13 import unittest
14 import random
15 import copy
16 class TestFunc(unittest.TestCase):
17   def test_sort(self):
18     for numtest in range(10):
19       size = random.randint(1000, 100000)
```

```
        data1 = [random.randint(-10000, 100000) for _ in range(size)]
        data2 = copy.deepcopy(data1)
        result1 = quickSort(data1)
        result2 = sorted(data2)
        self.assertEqual(result1, result2)
```

---

## D.5 Match Programs and Mathematics

Another way to create test cases is to match a program's outputs with analysis from mathematics. Page 12 explains that there are $2^{n-1}$ ways to partition a positive integer $n$. The next test compares the number of partitions with the mathematics equation. Page 14 explains that number 1 is used $(n+2)2^{n-3}$ times when partitioning number $n$ ($n \geq 3$). The following test uses Python's `count` function to calculate whether the `partition` indeed returns the expected number of partitions.

```
from partition import partition
import unittest
import random
import copy
class TestFunc(unittest.TestCase):
  def test_sort(self):
    for numtest in range(3, 10):
      n = random.randint(5, 20)
      result = partition(n)
      sum = 0
      for i in range (len (result)):
        sum += result[i].count(1)
      self.assertEqual(sum, (n + 2) * (2 ** (n-3)))
      self.assertEqual(len(result), 2 ** (n-1))
```

This section gives two examples matching programs' outputs with the results from mathematical analysis. When it is difficult to create test cases, mathematical analysis can be helpful to match the sizes of the programs' outputs.

# *Bibliography*

[1] Ronald L. Graham, Donald E. Knuth, and Oren Patashnik. *Concrete Mathematics: A Foundation for Computer Science.* Addison-Wesley, Reading, MA, 1989.

[2] Kappa Books. *Sudoku Collection, Volume 124.* Kappa Books, Blue Bell, PA, 2019.

[3] Ralph P. Grimaldi. *Discrete and Combinatorial Mathematics: An Applied Introduction.* Pearson, 5 edition, 2003. Fifth edition.

# Index

For Product Safety Concerns and Information please contact our EU representative GPSR@taylorandfrancis.com Taylor & Francis Verlag GmbH, Kaufingerstraße 24, 80331 München, Germany

Batch number: 10777146

Printed by Printforce, the Netherlands